Economic Geography of Higher Education

Today's economy is best characterised as a knowledge-based economy where knowledge is the most important resource and learning the most important process. Higher education institutions (HEIs) play a crucial role in providing knowledge and learning opportunities.

This exhaustive study from an experienced and respected set of editors and authors looks at the impact that universities have on their surroundings, with particular reference to regional development. Providing a fresh critique of HEIs this book is a starting point for discussion about their role and importance in the twenty-first century.

With contributions from such leading scholars as Peter Maskell and Gunnar Törnqvist, this book will be of great interest to students and academics involved in regional economics, economic geography and innovation studies.

Roel Rutten is Assistant Professor at Tilburg University, the Netherlands.

Frans Boekema is Professor of Economic Geography at Nijmegen University and Associate Professor of Regional Economics at Tilburg University.

Elsa Kuijpers is a consultant for ERAC (European Regional Affairs Consultants).

Routledge Studies in Business Organizations and Networks

Economic Geography of Higher Education

Knowledge infrastructure and
learning regions

**Edited by Roel Rutten, Frans Boekema
and Elsa Kuijpers**

Routledge
Taylor & Francis Group

LONDON AND NEW YORK

First published 2003 by Routledge
11 New Fetter Lane, London EC4P 4EE

Simultaneously published in the USA and Canada
by Routledge
29 West 35th Street, New York, NY 10001

Routledge is an imprint of the Taylor & Francis Group

Typeset in Goudy by LaserScript Ltd, Mitcham, Surrey
Printed and bound in Great Britain by MPG Books Ltd, Bodmin

British Library Cataloguing in Publication Data
A catalogue record of this book is available from the British Library

Library of Congress Cataloging in Publication Data
Economic geography of higher education: knowledge, infrastructure, and learning
regions / [edited by] Roel Rutten, Frans Boekema, and Elsa Kuijpers.
    p. cm. – (Routledge studies in business organizations and networks; 23)
      Includes bibliographical references and index.
      1. Education, Higher–Economic aspects–Europe. 2. Regionalism–Economic
aspects–Europe. I. Rutten, Roel, 1971– II. Boekema, Frans. III. Kuijpers, Elsa. IV.
Routledge studies in business organization and networks; 23.

    LC67.68.E85 E26 2003
    378.4′3378′094–dc21
                                                     2002190838

ISBN 0–415–26772–2

Contents

List of figures

List of tables

Notes on contributors

Jacqueline Bax is Policy Coordinator in the Department of Science, Policy, and International Cooperation of the Dutch Ministry of Education, Culture and Sciences, Zoetermeer, the Netherlands.

Frans Boekema graduated in Regional Economics in 1977 at Tilburg University in the Netherlands. That same year he started his career as Assistant Professor of Regional Economics and Economic Geography at the same university. In 1986, he completed his dissertation on local initiatives and regional development. In 1990, he was appointed Associate Professor in Regional Economics and Economic Geography. In 1995, he became a part-time professor in Economic Geography at the Faculty of Management Sciences at Nijmegen University in the Netherlands. He also works as Head and Senior Researcher at the Regional Economics Department of the Economic Institute Tilburg, a research and consultancy institute. His main fields of research are local and regional growth and development, innovation and technological development and regions, border-crossing activities, learning regions and knowledge infrastructure, regional innovation policy and the network economy. He was co-editor of *Knowledge, Innovation and Economic Growth: The Theory and Practice of Learning Regions* (Boekema *et al.* 2000).

Paul Chatterton is Senior Researcher at CURDS (Centre for Urban and Regional Development Studies) of the University of Newcastle-upon-Tyne in the United Kingdom.

Tony Eastham is Professor at the Hong Kong University of Science and Technology.

Huib Ernste is Professor of Human Geography in the Department of Human Geography at the Faculty of Management Sciences at the University of Nijmegen, the Netherlands.

Michael Gibbons is Professor of Science and Technology Policy at the Association of Commonwealth Universities in London.

John Goddard is Professor of Regional Economics at CURDS (Centre for Urban and Regional Development Studies) at the University of Newcastle-upon-Tyne in the United Kingdom.

Jerald Hage is Associate Professor at the Center for Innovation, the University of Maryland, Washington, DC, USA.

Aimée Hoeve works as a researcher at STOAS Research, a research institute in Wageningen, the Netherlands.

Paul Huijts was Vice-Director of Technology Policy at the Dutch Ministry of Economic Affairs and now works at the Ministry of General Affairs in the Netherlands.

Elsa Kuijpers graduated in Public Management in 2002 at Tilburg University, the Netherlands. She now works as a junior consultant for ERAC (European Regional Affairs Consultants). In 2000, she was the Research Assistant of Regional Economics and helped organise an international seminar on learning regions.

Arnoud Lagendijk is Assistant Professor of the Faculty of Management Sciences at the University of Nijmegen in the Netherlands.

Peter Maskell is Professor at the Business School of Copenhagen in Denmark.

Marius Meeus is Professor in the Department of Innovation Studies, the Faculty of Geographical Sciences, the University of Utrecht, the Netherlands.

Loek Nieuwenhuis is Director of STOAS Research in Wageningen, the Netherlands.

Leon Oerlemans is Associate Professor in the Department of Innovation Studies at the Faculty of Geographical Sciences, the University of Utrecht, the Netherlands.

Jerry Patchell is working as a researcher in the Division of Social Sciences of the Hong Kong University of Science and Technology.

Roel Rutten graduated in Policy and Organisation Studies at Tilburg University, the Netherlands. From 1994 till 2001, he worked as a consultant for ERAC (European Regional Affairs Consultants). His activities for ERAC centred on regional innovation policy. From 1996 till 2001, he also worked as a PhD student at the Department of Policy and Organisation Sciences at Tilburg University. In 2002, he completed his dissertation on inter-firm collaboration on innovation. Roel Rutten has co-organised three international seminars on learning regions and has co-edited a book on this subject (*Knowledge, Innovation and Economic Growth: The Theory and Practice of Learning Regions*, Boekema *et al.* 2000). Since 2002, he has been working as Assistant Professor, again in the Department of Policy and Organisation

Studies at Tilburg University. His current research focuses on learning regions and inter-firm collaboration on innovation.

Gunnar Törnqvist is Head of the Department of Social and Economic Geography at Lund University, Sweden.

Yvonne van Rooy is Chairperson of the Board of Directors at Tilburg University, the Netherlands.

Peter Vaessen is a freelance researcher at the University of Nijmegen in the Netherlands.

Martin van der Velde is Assistant Professor at the Faculty of Management Sciences at the University of Nijmegen, the Netherlands.

Kees Verhaar is Senior Researcher/Consultant at STOAS Consultancy and Training in Wageningen, the Netherlands.

Marc Vermeulen is Senior Researcher at IVA Tilburg, an institute specialising in applied policy research. He is also Director of Studies at the TIAS Business School in the Netherlands.

Foreword

Tilburg University was proud to host the international seminar on 'Universities, Knowledge Infrastructure, and the Learning Region' on 13 April 1999. The learning region is a very interesting and relatively new paradigm in science, the importance of which was discussed in a previous seminar in 1998.[1] However, the relevance of the learning region paradigm stretches beyond the mere scientific. Regions throughout Europe are making efforts to become 'learning regions'. But their attempts can only be successful if all socio-economic actors are committed to concerted action to further the region's 'knowledge production system'. A well-functioning regional knowledge production system that is based on knowledge and, therefore, more durable will help a region gain a competitive advantage over other regions. There must be a network of learning and cooperation relations between businesses, education institutes, other knowledge and research organisations, consultancy agencies, and the government to support this knowledge production system. Only intensive cooperation and knowledge exchange between these regional partners can ensure a region's economic development in the knowledge-based economy of the twenty-first century.

This message is not lost on the Executive Board of Tilburg University. After all, universities are potential key players in the development of the regional knowledge production systems described above. Universities – with their main tasks of scientific education and research – could be the driving institutions behind the realisation of learning regions. The word 'could' in the previous sentence is used for a reason: if the learning region were a reality, there would be no need for a seminar or a book to discuss the issue. And if universities, in this case Tilburg University, had assumed a leading role in developing learning regions, discussing the role of universities in learning regions would also have been superfluous. However, this is not the case. Without pointing a finger at any of the regional players, Tilburg University, in the past, has not been able to play a networking role and has not been embedded in the region as much as it has wanted to. This raises three important questions:

- Why is this the case?
- How do other universities cope with similar problems concerning regional embeddedness?

- How can Tilburg University change its policies in such a way that the university and the regional economy can benefit from each other to a greater extent than is currently the case?

These and other questions are addressed in this volume. From the experiences of Tilburg University, it follows that easy answers to these questions will not be found. For example, it is not a matter of Tilburg University not doing enough to become an important regional actor. Tilburg University has expressed its views on the regional knowledge production system and the role it wants to play in this system in the report *Regionale Verankering* (Regional Anchoring). Moreover, Tilburg University has a well-functioning Science Shop. In 2000, for example, the Science Shop carried out eighty-five projects on a variety of issues, such as the multi-cultural society and labour conditions, mostly for regional organisations. In addition, serious efforts have been made to put regionalisation, knowledge transfer, and socio-economic justification on the policy agenda. The problem, it seems, is not so much a matter of not wanting to be a key regional actor but, rather, a matter of not being able to set up the structures through which this can be done with a substantial degree of success.

In this context, it may be helpful to refer to the implications for universities of the globalisation versus localisation paradox. Learning region theory says that universities have to make an effort to become global players embedded in a regional environment. But practice is more complicated. Take Tilburg University, for example. Like most other Dutch and, indeed, European universities, Tilburg University wishes to play in the top league. This means that it has to establish an increasingly internationally oriented outlook, emphasising international research, personnel, and education. The CentER institute at the Faculty of Economics is a typical example of this process. Such institutes are invaluable to Tilburg University and enable it to gain a place on the world map of science in terms of scientific quality standards and reputation. The problem, however, is that this international approach is of a fundamental, abstract, and theoretical nature where regional embeddedness is often better served with a more down-to-earth approach. After all, the more abstract the socio-economic research, the more difficult it will be to overcome the gap between research and practice and to translate the academic research results into input for society. It is a matter of finding a balance because, no matter how highly valued a university's international position is, it can never underestimate its position in, and its obligations to, society at large.

These are the tensions that Tilburg University, and many other universities, face every day. The 1999 seminar hosted by Tilburg University and this book, which results from it, are a search for answers. Answers that will help us find new guidelines for regionalisation policy and new ideas for knowledge production and distribution in cooperation with our regional partners.

Finally, I would like to thank a number of people who have made the seminar and this book possible. The help of Silvia Bakkers was indispensable in the organisation of the seminar. She also made an important contribution to this book. Roos Pijpers and Paul Heuts also deserve credit for their work on this book. I am also grateful for the financial support that the Foundation Knowledge on the Move (Stichting Kennis in Beweging) offered this project.

Yvonne van Rooy
Tilburg University
President of the Executive Board

Note

1 The results of the 1998 seminar on learning regions were published in, F. Boekema *et al.* (2000) *Knowledge, Innovation and Economic Growth: The Theory and Practice of Learning Regions*, Cheltenham: Edward Elgar.

Reference

Tilburg University (1999), Strategisch Instellingsplan, Tilburg: Tilburg University.

1 Economic geography of higher education

Setting the stage

Roel Rutten, Frans Boekema and Elsa Kuijpers

Adam Smith – the founding father of economic science – was probably the first to recognise the value of knowledge for economic development when he wrote: 'A man educated at the expense of much labour and time to any of those employments which require extraordinary dexterity and skill, may be compared to one of those expensive machines' (Smith 1776, book I: 118).

From this cautious beginning, knowledge has progressed to the centre of economic theory, particularly in the last decade (see, for example, Cooke and Morgan 1998, and Maskell *et al.* 1998 for a discussion). In the earliest discussions on the role of knowledge in the economy, the importance of scientific, academic knowledge was stressed.

Following a linear model of dissemination, higher education institutions (HEIs) were largely responsible for developing new knowledge which was then transferred to the business community, who applied the knowledge in the creation of new products and services. This linear model, of course, is obsolete and other institutions besides HEIs have a significant role to play in the production of knowledge (Gibbons *et al.* 1994). However, this does not make HEIs unimportant. On the contrary, they still are the most important source of scientific knowledge and they feature prominently in the regional innovation strategies of many regions in the European Union (Cobbenhagen 1998). The same, of course, can be said about the role of HEIs in the United States, Japan, and elsewhere. On the other hand, the role of HEIs in regional development should not be overestimated.[1] If all regions had companies like Microsoft in their borders, few people would worry about HEIs (Rees 2001). Moreover, HEIs are currently going through a transition phase. In the European Union, for example, HEIs are obliged to adopt the Bachelor–Master system. This should encourage students to change their university more readily and, therefore, introduce more competition between European HEIs. In addition, the funding of HEIs has changed considerably. Once government-funded, disciplinary-structured institutions operating at arm's length from the business community, HEIs are now trying to access new sources of funding, such as contract research. More often than not, this requires them to develop more intimate relations with the business community and other (regional) actors and to work across disciplinary boundaries. This, of course, poses substantial challenges to HEIs, ranging from different organisational structures and implementing cultural changes to new reward structures and incentives for their scientific staff (Kitigawa 2001; Rees 2001). In short, as the economy becomes knowledge-based, the role of the actors in the economy also changes (Etzkowitz and Leydesdorff 1996).

This book sets out to explore the changes taking place within and around one particular actor: HEIs. We believe that the changes that are taking place must be properly understood in order for HEIs to be able to respond to them. HEIs in the twenty-first century will differ from HEIs in the twentieth century, but to what extent remains unclear. What is clear, however, is that HEIs and regional communities can engage in a mutually beneficial relationship that will provide HEIs with new students and new sources of funding and will provide the regional community with a powerful source of economic development for the knowledge-based economy of the twenty-first century.

Introduction

HEIs went through a revolutionary transition in the late nineteenth century. Instead of being mere centres for academic teaching, they increasingly assumed social functions in both research and teaching. This differentiation of functions can be understood in terms of changes in the knowledge infrastructure. HEIs offered a specific setting for the integration and differentiation of functions in the knowledge infrastructure, such as scholarly learning, on the one hand, and theorising and experimental practices, on the other. This extension of the higher education sector was accomplished under the patronage of nation-states and produced highly country-specific academic traditions and practices. In the second half of the twentieth century, the situation changed again due to increased international competition. In addition, the emergence of new modes of knowledge-based economic development (see, for example, Best 1990; Cooke and Morgan 1998) have called the traditional role of HEIs – often referred to as the ivory tower – into question. As late as the 1970s, laboratories of large private companies provided a largely self-sufficient technological support system for product development. From the 1980s onward, however, increased international competition, a quicker pace of technological development, and the downsizing of firms to their core competencies have made companies more aware of and receptive to external sources of knowledge and innovation. Furthermore, an 'innovation gap' has since emerged due to the shortening of product and technology life cycles, on the one hand, and the increased technological inputs required in order to accomplish innovations, on the other. In other words, the short-term needs for product development and innovation are competing with the need for long-term research commitments in order to achieve research results. Long-term research commitments are widely regarded as the responsibility of HEIs. Not being able to choose between long-term commitments and short-term results, company research has looked for ways to do both – while trying to avoid the costs associated with this. The solution that companies found was to outsource many of their research activities and to engage in collaboration efforts with other (private and public) research centres. This, in effect, makes the unit of analysis with regard to knowledge creation increasingly that of technological systems or knowledge-creating networks. Private research centres are probably the best advocates of the Mode 2 production of knowledge to date (see Gibbons *et al.* 1994).

These kind of developments in the economy induce change in other parts of the knowledge infrastructure as well.[2] Under previous conditions, HEI–industry collaboration was often informal in nature, involving, for example, consultancy relations between companies and individual professors in exchange for fellowship and departmental research funds. Today, however, HEI–industry collaboration is often much more formalised. Partly as a result of their more formal role in knowledge production, the perception of HEIs as mere institutions of higher learning is giving way to the view that they are important drivers of economic growth and development. In other words, HEIs are looked upon as actors in a web of knowledge producers. This view has two important consequences. First, HEIs have been ousted from their dominant position in the landscape of knowledge producers. They are, instead, only one actor among many, such as private research centres, R&D performing companies, and consultancy agencies. Second, and as a result of the former, HEIs have to adapt to their 'new' position – they have to become team players. Although some are more reluctant than others, HEIs are increasingly adopting a more outgoing, market-led commercial attitude, plugging into and supporting economic development. According to some (Smilor *et al.* 1993), this has led to the emerging paradigm of the 'entrepreneurial university', which encompasses a more direct involvement in the commercialisation of research activities, and a more proactive approach to the role of academic research in the market place. The paradigm of the entrepreneurial university stresses that the environmental forces in today's globalised competitive environment are forcing a reassessment of internal and external forces, resulting in support systems and linking mechanisms which are altering the research, teaching, and service missions of HEIs. HEIs now pay increasing attention to the value of more applied research and innovative and relevant teaching and services to the local, regional, national and global public, and private sectors (Smilor *et al.* 1993). The paradigm shift to become more entrepreneurial appears to be real, particularly with regard to mechanisms for increasing technology transfer between HEIs and industry. Common mechanisms in this respect are the introduction or expansion of university offices involved in licensing and patenting, small business development, research and technology centres, incubators, and investment/endowment offices (Dill 1995).

An important feature of the development of HEI entrepreneurship has been the foundation of science parks in an attempt to develop stronger links with industry. Science parks were envisioned as locations with a critical mass of scientifically sophisticated individuals generating new technologies and innovative ideas, often produced in universities and channelled and diffused by universities. Whether or not science parks have contributed significantly to economic development remains unclear, however. Science parks are increasingly accused of being essentially real estate developments. Although they are usually presented as key elements in technology transfer policy, the quality of the buildings and the environment rather than the input of HEI research are primarily responsible for selling the space. Furthermore, the direct economic benefits have not always been impressive – which seemed to have had little effect on the view of these knowledge centres as important cornerstones of urban and regional development strategies. It is also important to bear in mind that institutional differences between countries make it impossible to develop a generic model of science parks. A more general approach to understanding the role of HEIs in relation to knowledge transfer is thus required. A final issue that needs to be mentioned here is the fact that start-up firms need more than merely technological support. Other services they need to acquire are in the fields of marketing, finance, human resources, and business planning. Although HEIs can provide such services, science parks are probably not the best transfer mechanisms in this respect. Firms seem to prefer tailor-made solutions from individual consultants or scientists. The problem for HEIs here is that, in general, firms are at a large psychological distance from HEIs and do not see HEIs as 'natural' partners when it comes to knowledge transfer (Technopolis 2001).

This brings the discussion back to an observation made earlier – that HEIs are no longer the sole providers of knowledge. Companies draw knowledge from a variety of sources and – in order to understand the process of knowledge transfer, and the contributions that HEIs make to regional development through knowledge transfer – it is important to look at HEIs and knowledge transfer in a regional context. Keane and Allison (2000) observe that HEIs consider it important to establish close and long-term links with their home regions, as this enables them to draw more funding (through contract research) and attract students. At a time when government funding for HEIs is continuing to decrease, this is a welcome opportunity for these institutions. Regions also benefit from the presence of HEIs, and they do so in three ways. First, there are socio-economic benefits as HEIs generate employment which, in turn, leads to more spending and increased housing demand. Moreover, HEIs tend to stimulate cultural life in their home regions. Second, HEIs generate information and knowledge and are involved in teaching and other forms of knowledge transfer. This benefits the growth of the knowledge-based economy. Third, HEIs are part of the associations needed to offer flexible and innovative regional response to rapidly changing economies. In other words, HEIs are an important element in a region's knowledge infrastructure and the knowledge infrastructure, to a large extent, decides the success of a region in today's knowledge-based economy (Keane and Allison 2000: 896). It is clear, then, that HEIs can make a substantial contribution to regional development. The question is how best to approach this contribution from a conceptual point of view. Keane and Allison propose taking the literature on learning regions as a point of departure – a view which the present book wholeheartedly subscribes to. According to Keane and Allison: 'A learning region conceptualizes the knowledge economy within the local/regional context and the concept can be translated into a workable framework for analysis' (2000: 900). They argue that '[the] key characteristic of the learning region is the way in which knowledge is transferred from one group to another to create learning systems. Universities are a critical resource in this process' (ibid. 2000: 901). This, of course, is true but it does not solve the problem of finding a suitable theoretical framework. Various authors have argued that the concept of the learning region is not (yet) a coherent theoretical framework (see, for example, Boekema *et al.* 2000; Hassink 2001). Yet, the present volume agrees with Keane and Allison (2000) that the concept of the learning region is the best point of departure to conceptualise and analyse the role of HEIs in regional development. The following section, therefore, examines the learning region more closely so as to gain a better understanding of this concept.

Learning regions and the conceptualisation of knowledge creation

For the better part of a decade, the concept of the learning region has been one of the key ideas in regional economics. This work departs from the concept of learning regions as it focuses on the relation between regional economic development, on the one hand, and the characteristics of (actors and processes in) regions, on the other. The contribution that HEIs can make to the (economic) development of their home region depends on the ability (competencies) and willingness (strategy) of both HEIs and the business community to exchange and create knowledge. (Regional) authorities also play a role here as they can facilitate HEI–business interaction through a variety of schemes. The theoretical foundations of learning regions have been explained at length in a variety of publications (cf. Boekema *et al.* 2000; Florida 1995; Hassink 2001; Maskell *et al.* 1998; Morgan 1997; Simmie 1997). This volume does not intend to present an elaborate overview of the merits and flaws of learning regions as a concept in theory. Instead, this section addresses some of the key issues that characterise the current debates on knowledge creation and learning regions.

Knowledge and learning

The key aspect concerning learning regions is the relation between knowledge creation (or learning) and the economic development of firms and regions. In today's knowledge-based economy, knowledge is the key factor of production and knowledge creation is the key competence for companies trying to stay abreast of competitors. The literature on learning regions, thus, explicitly focuses on processes of learning, or knowledge creation, and, as such, fits in the broader stream of innovation literature. Particularly since the publication of *The Knowledge-creating Company* by Nonaka and Takeuchi in 1995, this stream of literature has found its way into mainstream economic thinking. The main debate in learning theory today, according to Easterby-Smith *et al.* (1999), centres on whether learning should be seen as a technical or a social process (ibid.: 8). The technical variant sees learning as interventions based on measurement. Learning, in this case, is about 'effective processing, interpretation of, and response to, information' (ibid.: 3). The focus of technical learning is on the outcomes (an effective response) rather than on the process of learning. A major contribution to this line of thinking was made by Argyris and Schön (1978) with their distinction between single-loop and double-loop learning. The social perspective on learning, instead, 'focuses on the way people make sense of their experiences' (Easterby-Smith *et al.* 1999: 4). One of the key arguments in this line of thinking is that individuals have the ability to learn from their experiences and that they learn from and with others in a social environment, e.g. a work setting. Learning, in other words, is something that follows from social interaction and much knowledge exists not on paper but in people's heads or in a 'community' as a whole. A recent example of this tradition is the above-mentioned work by Nonaka and Takeuchi (1995). The learning region is largely based on the social perspective on learning – as the discussions in this volume will show – though some elements of the technical school can be found also. Particularly as a policy concept (Hassink 2001; Morgan 1997), the learning region sets out to improve regional policy outcomes (technical learning) by improving the process of learning among regional actors (social learning).

With regard to learning regions, what is at issue is the conceptualisation of learning and innovation. Following the social perspective, learning is the process that leads to innovation. In today's knowledge-based economy, companies create competitive advantage by producing goods and services that offer more value to consumers/users than those of competitors. In order to do so, companies must make new combinations of knowledge, as knowledge has become the most important factor of production (Maskell *et al.* 1998). Knowledge is usually divided into tacit and codified forms (Nonaka and Takeuchi 1995), with tacit knowledge being the most durable source of competitive advantage since it is most difficult to transfer (Morgan 1997). In other words, through a process of knowledge creation, or learning, companies must develop new skills and competencies that are largely based on tacit knowledge, such as experiences, know-how, knowledge of consumers' preferences, etc., as this will lead to durable competitive advantage (Rutten 2002). In other words, in order to understand competitive advantage, it is important to conceptualise the process of knowledge creation, i.e. learning. This is done, as was argued, in the social perspective on learning. For the study of learning regions, this means that attention should focus on how regional learning, that is, learning between regional actors, can contribute to the establishment of a durable competitive advantage by a region's firms. Efforts should concentrate on understanding and explaining the process of regional learning. That, however, is beyond the possibilities of the 'learning region theory' given the present state of affairs, as the following section shows.

The learning region paradigm

Boekema *et al.* (2000) cautiously present the learning region as a paradigm rather than a theory, arguing that the learning region is far too wide a concept to allow for a meaningful definition. This approach has been criticised by Hassink (2001). His article is probably one of the most sophisticated theoretical discussions on learning regions to date. Hassink specifically sets out to develop a clear definition and a sound theoretical basis for learning regions. He argues that:

> Although I realise that aiming for a too narrow definition of the concept [of learning regions] would be a mistake, as it would not come to grips with the daily complexity and continuous change, the current situation is far from satisfactory ... In my view, a learning region can be defined as a regional innovation strategy in which a broad set of innovation-related regional actors are strongly but flexibly connected with each other, and who stick to a certain set of policy principles.
>
> (Hassink 2001: 226)

Hassink views the learning region as a concept for regional innovation policy. His conceptualisation of learning regions as a regional innovation policy concept is encompassing. For example, Hassink points to the following:

- carefully co-ordinating supply and demand for skilled individuals;
- developing a framework for organizational learning;
- carefully identifying resources in the region;
- developing mechanisms for co-ordinating both across departmental and governance ... responsibilities;
- developing an educational and research infrastructure for knowledge society.

(ibid.: 226)

These points are underlined in the present work. In contrast to Hassink, however, the present work does not associate learning regions exclusively with regional innovation policy. There are three problems connected to the learning-region-as-regional-policy view. First, successful regional innovation policy depends on whether or not a region has effective innovation networks. Cooke, for example, argues that: 'Intra-regional networking must be activated across a range of firms, private and public institutions ... to make an impact upon innovative activity' (1996: 62). Cooke argues in favour of a broader perspective on regional innovation, focusing not only on regional innovation policy but on the 'regional innovation system' in general. This line of thinking not only looks at regional innovation structure and regional innovation policy, but also at the institutional endowments of a region such as the rules, practices, routines, habits, traditions, customs, and conventions associated with innovation (for a discussion on regional innovation systems and related concepts, such as regional milieux and regional institutions, see Cooke and Morgan 1998; Hassink 2001; Maskell *et al.* 1998; Morgan 1997; Storper 1997). Regional learning is affected by much more than regional innovation policy. Second, and related to the above, regional authorities are not the only *animateur* in regional innovation networks (Cooke 1996: 166). By placing regional institutions in the centre of the analysis, regional authorities lose the central position that Hassink seems to reserve for them. As was argued, many actors, i.e. firms, knowledge centres, intermediary organisations, and regional authorities, affect regional learning and it is in their interaction that these actors can accomplish most. Viewing the learning region merely in terms of regional innovation policy risks having a poor conceptualisation of the role of regional actors other than the regional authorities. Third, looking for a 'set of policy principles' risks developing a static theory which would very likely fail to capture the dynamics of knowledge creation and innovation.

In sum, the present work has a broader approach to learning regions than Hassink (2001). Though many of the above arguments can be found in Hassink's article, his approach is different from the present work. In his account, a learning region cannot exist without the involvement of regional authorities whereas in the present work, it can. Rather than regional innovation policy, learning regions are institutional configurations that do not necessarily (but most likely will) include regional authorities. Learning regions, as institutional configurations, facilitate learning among regional actors. In terms of space, learning regions, therefore, connect to the economic space of actors rather than to administrative regions. The learning region, thus, has more to do with the innovation strategies of regional actors and the way the regional institutional context[3] facilitates knowledge exchange between regional actors than it has to do with regional innovation policy. In other words, the learning region is about establishing innovation networks between regional actors. From the perspective of the present work, the question is not how to define the learning region. Instead, efforts should focus on a conceptualisation of the role of regional actors in the process of regional learning and on the conceptualisation of the process of regional learning itself. As the dynamics of regional learning and the institutional context will differ from one region to another, it makes sense to speak of the learning region in terms of a paradigm rather than in terms of a theory. The complexities surrounding learning regions are too elaborate to capture in a single theory. Learning regions, for example, deal with knowledge creation between actors, whether they are companies, HEIs, or other actors. They deal with the characteristics and institutions of a region, such as social capital (Morgan 1997), the availability of labour and knowledge, etc. They deal with regional innovation policy. These issues are interconnected and mutually shape each other. Given only the various levels of analysis involved, it would be extremely difficult to develop a single theory of learning regions. Almost inevitably, such a theory would favour some issues at the expense of others and, thus, do injustice to the complexities of regional economic development.

Moreover, no region has ever been actually identified as a learning region. The literature has proposed several characteristics of learning regions (see, for example, Boekema *et al.* 2000; Cooke 1996; Florida 1995; Maskell *et al.* 1998; Morgan 1997), but these examples only illustrate the diversity of the subject. It would be extremely difficult to identify a region that has most of the characteristics put forward in the literature. Nor would trying to find one do justice to the economic, social, cultural, and institutional differences of regions. Again, the present volume argues that it is more productive to think of the learning region as a paradigm which draws attention to the characteristics of successful regions in the knowledge-based economy. It provides knowledge and innovation services, strong interfaces and exchange mechanisms between the business community and the knowledge infrastructure, horizontal and vertical collaboration on innovation within the business community, a pro-active innovation policy from regional authorities, and collaboration between regional actors at an institutional level. What successful regions have in common is their ability to create and share knowledge among and between regional actors. From the above characteristics, it is clear, though, that there are many mechanisms of knowledge creation involving several levels of analysis.

The present volume argues that the objective of the learning region paradigm is to understand and explain the process of regional learning. This means two things. First, from a social perspective on learning, science must focus on the process of inter-firm knowledge creation. In doing so, it must also account for the spatial dimension of this process. That is, science must address the issue of whether or not spatial proximity facilitates learning and knowledge exchange between actors. Storper (1997) and Rutten (2002) suggest that it does since it is difficult to transfer tacit knowledge over long distances as the exchange of tacit knowledge requires face-to-face communication. Second, science must focus on regional innovation networks and their institutional embeddedness. That is, science must understand and explain why regional actors cooperate in the creation of knowledge (learning) and innovation and how the characteristics of a region (such as social capital, regional knowledge infrastructure, etc.) affect this process. The key to understanding learning regions, thus, is the conceptualisation of why (strategy) and how (process) regional actors cooperate in innovation and how the institutional characteristics of regions affect this. In order to do this, science must draw on a variety of theories, for example, innovation theory, network theory, and regional development theory. This is a huge undertaking given the considerable differences between those theories. Their levels and units of analysis, for example, are different. Trying to develop one theory of learning regions, then, would undermine the explanatory power of such a theory as it would, inevitably, favour some issues and relations over others, for example, regional innovation policy. The present work, therefore, sees the learning region as a paradigm that needs to be explored and explained from the point of view of a variety of theories – those which are best suited to approach the research questions and which address the issues of space, learning, and networks.

Objective and research questions

Following the above reasoning, the present volume focuses on the relation between the knowledge infrastructure (and HEIs in particular) and regional development. The main objective of this study is to develop a conceptualisation of the role of HEIs in regional learning. The various authors in this study approach the objective from different perspectives. Some focus on regional innovation policy and the contribution that HEIs can make to it; others address the knowledge exchange between HEIs and the regional business community, and yet others discuss the role of HEIs in relation to regional learning from an institutional perspective. In this way, the present volume works along the lines of the learning region paradigm. That is, the present work does not depart from a dominant perspective but, instead, draws on the strengths of a variety of perspectives. This approach will allow one to develop a clear conceptualisation of the role of HEIs in regional learning that accounts for the many complexities surrounding this role. These complexities yield the research questions that are addressed in this volume. They are as follows:

- How do HEIs contribute to regional learning?
- Are HEIs 'ready' to take on the 'new' role in the learning economy?
- How can HEIs be encouraged to cooperate with the regional business community, and should they be encouraged to do so in the first place?
- What are the institutional factors affecting HEI–business interaction in regions?

Each of the contributions in this volume addresses one or more of the above research questions. In addition, every contribution, of course, has its own research questions. Therefore, the discussion in this volume can benefit from a rich flow of ideas and insights. We believe that such a discussion on the role of HEIs in learning regions is both relevant and necessary. It is relevant because a conceptualisation of the role of HEIs with regard to learning and regional development is lacking. This volume fills a void in academic literature. In the practice of regional innovation policy, the role of HEIs has been the focus of debate for a long time (Cobbenhagen 1998; Technopolis 2001) but academic literature has only recently taken a serious interest in discussing the role of HEIs in the knowledge-creation process (see, for example, Gibbons *et al.* 1994; Dill 1995). This is a most unsatisfactory situation given the important contributions that HEIs can, and in many cases do, make to regional economic development. In a world where knowledge has become the key factor of production, we cannot be left in the dark regarding the role of HEIs, which are, after all, one of the key centres of knowledge creation. As academics, we owe it to ourselves to develop a better understanding of our own role in the knowledge-based economy.

Table 1.1 Contents of the book

	Chapters	Conceptualisation	Case study/ Empirical	Policy examples
	1	X		
HEIs, regions and the production of knowledge	2	X		
	3	X	X	
	4	X	X	
	5		X	
	6	X		
HEI–Industry collaboration	7	X	X	
	8	X	X	
	9		X	
Policy response	10			X
	11			X
	12	X	X	
Conclusions	13	X		
	14	X		

Outline of the book

As already mentioned, this volume aims to make a contribution to the conceptualisation of HEIs and their role in learning regions. In pursuit of this aim, it brings together a selection of international authors who have a history of publications in this field. As Table 1.1 shows, most of the contributions have a specific conceptual focus. Views on and arguments in support of these conceptual considerations can be found in a variety of case studies and empirical studies in the various chapters. The remainder of this work is structured as follows.

Part I, 'Universities, regions, and the production of knowledge', is a mainly theoretical discussion of HEIs, on the one hand, and learning regions, on the other. From several perspectives, this Part gives a sophisticated answer to the question of what role HEIs (can) play in regional learning. Though the emphasis in this Part is on theoretical considerations, the authors use several well-developed case studies to illustrate their arguments. In Chapter 2, Chatterton and Goddard focus their discussion on the question of how HEIs should respond to regional and local needs. This chapter provides a thorough theoretical discussion on the role of HEIs in regional economic growth and development. This contribution provides a much-needed theoretical framework for the central topics of this volume. Chapter 2, in effect, presents the theoretical groundwork for other contributions in this book. Goddard and Chatterton provide a sophisticated conceptualisation. It is necessary to stress the importance of Chapter 2 as a theoretical framework for the remainder of this book. However, other theoretical contributions in this Part also offer new, challenging, and promising insights into the learning region phenomenon. In

Chapter 3, Patchell and Eastham present the relation between HEIs and industry with further theoretical substance. The authors discuss the governance structure affecting HEI–industry collaboration and use a case study of the Hong Kong University of Science and Technology to support their points of view. This contribution makes clear why and how governance structures and institutional characteristics affect relations between HEIs and the business community. The findings of this chapter are supported in various other contributions in the remainder of this volume. In Chapter 4, the role of vocational training is highlighted in detail as Vermeulen discusses the contribution of vocational education to regional economic development and growth. Many policy-makers and scientists have claimed that a relation exists between these in recent years. In this chapter, Vermeulen considers these claims from a theoretical perspective in an attempt to add substance to the discussion. In support of his arguments, Vermeulen presents research data from several Dutch regions. His analysis makes clear that human capital – involving both tacit and codified knowledge – is a crucial factor with regard to learning. Hence the provocative title of his contribution, 'Knowledge still travels on foot'. In Chapter 5, Vaessen and van der Velde elaborate on the contributions that HEIs can make to the (economic) development and growth of their home regions. Their approach addresses the subject of regional development from the perspective of HEI employees, that is, the teachers and researchers. They argue that knowledge transfer from HEIs takes place through the embeddedness of their teachers and researchers in professional and social networks. Their research draws on a case study of the impact of Nijmegen University in the Netherlands on its local and regional environment. The empirical results of this study are very interesting in the light of the central issues of this volume. In the final contribution in Part I, Chapter 6, Ernste discusses the process of learning in more detail and presents a further conceptualisation of learning and learning regions. According to Ernste, learning has a positive connotation and its presumed favourable outcomes are, therefore, often taken for granted. However, this assumption may represent a serious flaw in scientific innovation research which further stresses the need for a more elaborate conceptualisation of learning and learning regions.

In Part II, the emphasis is on HEI–industry collaboration in general and collaboration between HEIs and the business community in particular. Understanding these relations is a key issue when it comes to the contribution that HEIs can make to regional economic development. The chapters in this part are quite varied as regards content and nature. Nevertheless, each stands as a valuable contribution to the issue of HEI–industry relations. In Chapter 7, Maskell and Törnqvist present a thorough, theory-based contribution to the issue. Their contribution is a conceptualisation of the role of universities in the learning region. The authors use empirical data from the Øresund region in Scandinavia to support their arguments. This region became the focus of many research efforts since a new tunnel and bridge were built across Øresund Strait to connect Sweden and Denmark. Due to this infrastructure, many new developments can be witnessed in this region, among others, the emergence of a transnational learning region. In Chapter 8, Meeus, Oerlemans, and Hage discuss the role of universities in the knowledge infrastructure from an empirical perspective. This approach is quite unique since few empirical studies are available on this subject. The authors use mostly empirical data from a Dutch high-tech region in order to examine interactive learning between industry and the knowledge infrastructure. This contribution gives a clear insight into the learning processes that take place within a region. Working in a different way, Nieuwenhuis, Verhaar, and Hoeve discuss another case study on HEI–industry collaboration in Chapter 9. The authors focus on the collaboration between Wageningen University and the Dutch agricultural sector. This study is interesting because of the unique position of the Dutch agricultural sector. The Dutch agricultural knowledge system is world famous (responsible, among other things, for tulips and cut flowers) and is generally regarded as one of the key strengths of the Dutch economy.[4] Even in manufacturing and service-dominated regions, the Dutch 'agro-business' is an important player. From an international perspective, therefore, much can be learned from this agricultural-flavoured learning region.

In Part III, the impact of the learning region on policy is put forward in more detail. The discussion focuses on the policy response to the emergence of learning regions and the role of the knowledge infrastructure, in particular HEIs. In Chapter 10, Huijts discusses the response of the Dutch Ministry of Economic Affairs to the challenges presented by the knowledge-based economy. In Chapter 11, Bax conducts a similar exercise for the Ministry of Education, Culture, and Science. These two ministries are the key national agents involved in learning regions and, for that reason, they cannot be overlooked in this volume. Although these chapters seem to present more Dutch examples, their relevance is much wider. These chapters are, in fact, illustrations of the struggle of every (European) government currently. Taking this into account, both chapters are of interest to an international audience as well. In Chapter 12, Lagendijk and Rutten present a conceptualisation of the European Union's policy on learning regions. It can easily be argued that the European Union has been the main advocate of the learning region in practice. Since the early 1990s, several European Union policy schemes have encouraged regions to step up their innovation efforts. Lagendijk and Rutten put these initiatives in a theoretical perspective and raise several questions concerning the assumptions underlying European Union regional innovation policy. In this way, the authors identify several weaknesses of regional innovation policy.

In the final part of this volume, Part IV, the conclusions and a research agenda are presented. First, however, Gibbons presents his by now well-known case of the new production of knowledge in Chapter 13. Although the original publication of this idea took place almost a decade ago (Gibbons *et al.* 1994), we believe that the arguments used still merit a prominent position in a discussion on the role of HEIs (and the knowledge infrastructure in general). We are convinced that Gibbons' new mode of knowledge production deserves a more prominent and dominant role within HEIs and the knowledge infrastructure. Chapter 13, therefore, serves as a framework of reference for the final chapter. In the final chapter, Chapter 14, we answer the research questions proposed earlier on the basis of the discussions in this volume. Being a hub in knowledge creation and dissemination, we believe that HEIs could make a difference in the knowledge-based economy for many regions, but the question remains how to do so. From the findings put forward by the various authors, Chapter 14 proposes a more sophisticated perspective on HEIs and learning regions. *The Economic Geography of Higher Education*, thus, points to the role that HEIs can, and should, play in regional learning and identifies the key issues concerning this role in the years ahead.

Acknowledgements

This chapter draws heavily on the paper 'Problems of Systematic Learning Transfer and Innovation: Industrial Liaison and Academic Entrepreneurship in Wales', by P. Cooke *et al.* (2000).

Notes

1 This is one of the key findings of a recent study on the regional impact of Nijmegen University, the Netherlands (Buursink and Vaessen 2001).
2 The next two paragraphs are largely based on Cooke *et al.* (2000).
3 For a discussion see Cooke and Morgan (1998), Hassink (2001), Maskell *et al.* (1998), Morgan (1997) and Storper (1997).
4 In a keynote address on innovation in The Hague on 3 December 2001, Harvard professor, Michael Porter, again referred to the agricultural sector as one of the key strengths of the Dutch economy.

References

Argyris, C. and Schön, D. (1978) *Organizational Learning: A Theory of Action Perspective*, Reading, MA.: Addison-Wesley.
Best, M. (1990) *The New Competition: Institutions of Industrial Restructuring*, Cambridge: Polity Press.
Boekema, F., Morgan, K., Bakkers, S. and Rutten, R. (2000) *Knowledge, Innovation and Economic Growth: The Theory and Practice of Learning Regions*, Cheltenham: Edward Elgar.
Buursink, J. and Vaessen, P. (2001) *De Regionale Funktie van de Katholieke Universiteit Nijmegen* (The Regional Role of Nijmegen University), Internal Report, Nijmegen: KUN.
Cobbenhagen, J. (1998) *Cohesion, Competitiveness and RTDI: Their Impact on Regions*, Maastricht: Province of Limburg/European Commission.
Cooke, P. (1996) 'The New Wave of Regional Innovation Networks: Analysis, Characteristics and Strategy', *Small Business Economics* 8, 2: 159–171.
Cooke, P., Manning, C. and Huggins, R. (2000) 'Problems of Systemic Learning Transfer

and Innovation: Industrial Liaison and Academic Entrepreneurship in Wales', *Zeitschrift für Wirtschaftsgeographie* 44, 3/4: 246–260.

Cooke, P. and Morgan, K. (1998) *The Associational Economy: Firms, Regions, and Innovation*, Oxford: Oxford University Press.

Dill, D. (1995) 'University–industry Entrepreneurship: The Organization and Management of American-University Technology', *Higher Education* 29, 4: 369–384.

Easterby-Smith, M., Burgoyne, J. and Araujo, L. (1999) *Organizational Learning and the Learning Organization*, London: Sage.

Etzkowitz, H. and Leydesdorff, L. (1996) *Universities and the Global Knowledge Economy: A Triplex of University–government Relations*, London: Pinter.

Florida, R. (1995) 'Toward the Learning Region', *Futures* 27, 5: 527–536.

Gibbons, M., Limoges, C., Nowotny, H., Schwartzman, S., Scott, P. and Trow, M. (1994) *The New Production of Knowledge: The Dynamics of Science and Research in Contemporary Societies*, London: Sage.

Hassink, R. (2001) 'The Learning Region: A Fuzzy Concept or a Sound Theoretical Basis for Modern Regional Innovation Policies?', *Zeitschrift für Wirtschaftsgeographie* 45, 3/4: 219–230.

Keane, J. and Allison, J. (2000) 'The Intersection of the Learning Region and Local and Regional Economic Development: Analysing the Role of Higher Education', *Regional Studies* 33, 9: 896–902.

Kitigawa, F. (2001) 'Challenges to the Role of Universities in Regional Knowledge Development', in A. Maconochie and S. Hardy (eds) *Regionalising the Knowledge Economy: Conference Proceedings of the Regional Studies Association Annual Conference November 2001*, Seaford: Regional Studies Association.

Maskell, P., Eskelinen, H., Hannibalsson, I., Malmberg, A. and Vatne, E. (1998) *Competitiveness, Localised Learning and Regional Development: Specialisation and Prosperity in Small Open Economies*, London: Routledge.

Morgan, K. (1997) 'The Learning Region: Institutions, Innovation and Regional Renewal', *Regional Studies* 31, 5: 491–503.

Nonaka, I. and Takeuchi, H. (1995) *The Knowledge-creating Company: How Japanese Companies Create the Dynamics of Innovation*, Oxford: Oxford University Press.

Rees, S. (2001) 'Engagement Strategies for Universities with the Knowledge Economy', in A. Maconochie and S. Hardy (eds) *Regionalising the Knowledge Economy: Conference Proceedings of the Regional Studies Association Annual Conference November 2001*, Seaford: Regional Studies Association.

Rutten, R. (2002) *The Entrepreneurial Coalition: Knowledge-based Collaboration in a Regional Manufacturing Network*, Nijmegen: Wolf Legal Productions.

Simmie, J. (1997) *Innovation, Networks and Learning Regions?*, London: Jessica Kingsley Publishers.

Smilor, R., Dietrich, G. and Gibons, D. (1993) 'The Entrepreneurial University: The Role of Higher Education in the United States in Technology Commercialization and Economic Development', *International Social Science Journal* 45, 1: 1–11.

Smith, A. (1776, book I) *An Inquiry into the Nature and Causes of the Wealth of Nations*, London.

Storper, M. (1997) *The Regional World: Territorial Development in a Global Economy*, New York: The Guildford Press.

Technopolis (2001) *RITTS-Utrecht Implementation Project: Final Report*, Amsterdam: Technopolis.

Part I

Universities, regions and the production of knowledge

2 The response of HEIs to regional needs

Paul Chatterton and John Goddard

Introduction

Within advanced economies, there is a growing conviction that university teaching and research should be directed towards specific economic and social objectives. Nowhere is this demand for 'specificity' clearer than in the field of regional development. While they are located 'in' regions, universities are being asked by a new set of regional actors and agencies to make an active contribution to the development of these regions. These demands are driven by new processes of globalisation and localisation in economic development, whereby the local environment is as relevant as the national macro-economic situation in determining the ability of enterprises to compete in the global economy. Within this environment, the local availability of knowledge and skills is as important as physical infrastructure and, as a result, regionally engaged universities can become a key locational asset and powerhouse for economic development.

While universities have always contributed to the social and cultural development of the places in which they are located through a sense of civic responsibility, the emerging regional development agenda requires regional engagement to be formally recognised as a 'third role' for universities, fully integrated with mainstream teaching and research. The requirements for regional engagement therefore embrace many facets of the 'responsive university' which are generated by evolving priorities within the higher education system. These priorities include meeting the needs of a more diverse client population: for lifelong learning created by changing skill demands; for more locally-based education as public maintenance support for students declines; for greater links between research and teaching; and, for more engagement with the end users of this research.

For many universities, regional engagement is therefore becoming the crucible within which an appropriate response to overall trends within higher education is being forged. Responding to the new demands requires new kinds of resources and new forms of management that enable universities as institutions to make a dynamic contribution to the development process in the round. Within the university, the challenge is to link the teaching, research, and community service roles by internal mechanisms (e.g. funding, staff development, incentives and rewards, communications) and, within the region, to engage the university in all facets of the development process (e.g. skills enhancement, technological development and innovation, cultural awareness) in a region/university 'value-added management' process within the 'learning region'. In this context, the principal objective of this chapter is to provide an understanding of the ways in which higher education institutions (HEIs) are attempting to respond to regional needs. The secondary objective is to guide the formulation of policy by national and regional governments seeking to mobilise HEIs towards the achievement of regional development goals.

This chapter is divided into three sections. The first expands upon the discussion of regional development and the territorial dimension of higher education policy. The second discusses the response of HEIs to the changing context in relation to teaching, research, and community service. The final part provides the conclusions and recommendations. It explores some of the factors inhibiting and driving the adoption of a regional role by HEIs and includes some final remarks concerning the contribution of universities, through critical debate, to the creation of a common understanding of priorities for regional development among regional stakeholders.

HEIs and territoriality

The capacity of an HEI to respond to regional needs is influenced by conditions which result from the inter-relations between several geographic scales from the global to the local and also from the historical legacy of each HEI and its region. Policy-makers need to be aware of the demands made upon HEIs from each of these different spatial scales. These include restructuring in the global economy; changing national contexts for higher education; the particular characteristics of the region in terms of the regional economic base; regional policy; the regional educational system and the particularities of each institution. The first part of this chapter discusses the context for HEIs through a review of territoriality and HEIs.

Problematising territoriality

Territoriality is an extremely complex and problematic concept for HEIs. Universities, in particular, exist as autonomous institutions which are often characterised by low levels of local territorial embeddedness, regulation at the national level, and preoccupation with international and national academic and research communities. All HEIs embrace some notion of territoriality within their mission statements and institutional plans; these range from general notions of contributing to 'society' and international research to more precise commitments to local and regional communities. A report for the Committee of Rectors of European Universities stressed the growing urgency for HEIs to take engagement with external partners seriously:

in order to respond better to the needs of different groups within society, universities must engage in a meaningful dialogue with stakeholders ... universities which do not commit themselves to open and mutually beneficial collaboration with other economic, social and cultural partners will find themselves academically as well as economically marginalised.

(Davies 1998: 54)

Moreover, the UNESCO's *Framework for Priority Action for Change and Development for Higher Education* has stated that HEIs should 'develop innovative schemes of collaboration between institutions of higher education and different sectors of society to ensure that higher education and research programmes effectively contribute to local, regional and national development' (UNESCO 1998: 26).

In spite of these positive statements, the issue of how they should respond to regional needs is relatively uncharted territory for most HEIs, especially for the older and more comprehensive universities. Most HEIs strive towards teaching and research activity of national and international significance. A recent survey of UK universities asked senior managers to comment on how they could best describe the territorial role of their institution. Only 2 per cent described their university as 'a community-based institution serving the needs of the local area/region', while nearly half described it as 'an institution seeking to contribute to the local area and also develop international strengths', and one-third described it as 'an international research institution seeking to provide support to the local community where it does not conflict with international research excellence' (DfEE 1998).

Research within HEIs tends towards an international/national rather than a regional perspective and this reflects the priorities of governments and their research councils as the main funders of research. Clearly, research with a regional perspective can increase as the funding base of HEIs is diversified, but most universities are reluctant to increase regionally-based teaching or research as they see this as the role of the non-university higher education sector. Moreover, it is often the opinion of regional partners that the best way for HEIs to meet regional needs is by functioning as a national and international centre of teaching and research excellence. The institutional profile (such as subject mix, funding sources, balance between teaching and research, size, etc.) of an HEI is an important influence on its territorial focus. However, the connections between institutional profile and territoriality are extremely complex. For example, HEIs that are highly specialised as training or technical institutions may either be local or globally orientated institutions. Moreover, large comprehensive universities while developing strong international and national teaching and research activities also have the resource base to engage with the region. Consideration of territoriality also raises the issue of institutional independence. HEIs that operate within nationally regulated and funded regimes generally function as autonomous institutions and have control over the nature of teaching and research. However, the introduction of a regional agenda within such national systems is likely to require a stronger regional planning framework which brings together a number of regional stakeholders to co-manage and coordinate and regulate the management and funding of teaching and research. Such mechanisms may pose a challenge to institutional autonomy.

HEIs, then, operate within multiple and overlapping territories and usually manage a portfolio of activities ranging from the global to the local. The advantage of the presence of one or more HEIs in a region is that expertise from these different scales can be a major asset to the community. The challenge is to simultaneously manage the various territorial portfolios so that they reinforce each other and to establish mechanisms through which the national and international connections of HEIs can be mobilised to benefit the region.

Although many HEIs are adopting the rhetoric of regionalism within their mission statements, some academics equate the term 'region' with parochialism and see it as the antithesis of metropolitanism and cosmopolitanism – adjectives which are heavily associated with the historical development of many old universities. Moreover, the term region can refer to many different scales. It can refer to the immediate hinterland, a large part of a country, a state in federal countries, or wider pan-national areas. In particular, regions are emerging, or are being defined, which cross national boundaries and consist of elements from several national territories. Thus, there are pan-national regions such as the Baltic and Scandinavian regions, the Pacific region incorporating Australia and South-East Asia, and the European Community.

It is also important to appreciate the multiplicity of ways in which an explicitly regional role for an HEI can be interpreted. For example, a self-conscious regional HEI may be defined by associating itself legally or through its name with a particular territory; by operating within a regional recruitment area; by interacting with regional research partners and the regional industrial base; or by offering service and outreach facilities to the regional community. HEIs, then, have many justifications for calling themselves 'regional' institutions according to the way in which the relationship with the region, and its stakeholders, is prioritised. It is clear, then, that the issue of territoriality for HEIs is not unproblematic. It is vital for all those who work in, or come into contact with, HEIs to appreciate these issues of territoriality and the ways in which they are addressed within HEIs compared to most other public and private institutions.

Reconceptualising territorial development and governance

The changing role of HEIs in regional development must be seen within a broader context of globalisation and the changing nature of regional development and governance, notably the shift in emphasis from material to non-material assets (knowledge, skills, culture, institutions) and the resurgence of the region as an important arena for political and economic activity. This section briefly reviews this changing context and outlines new forms of territorial governance based upon the concept of the learning region.

Emerging patterns in regional development – the learning region

For effective regional engagement it is vital that those steering the regional interests of HEIs develop an understanding of the enormous transformations which have occurred in the capitalist world economy since the mid-1970s. This can be viewed in terms of a shift in phases of capitalist development from a system based upon mass production, Keynesianism, macro-economic management, and the welfare state to one characterised by widespread economic and political deregulation and the emergence of more decentralised forms of economic organisation. These changes have had major implications for economic development strategies and territorial governance especially in terms of the dynamics which have been brought to bear upon securing regional economic success from the twin processes of globalisation and localisation.

The post-war period until the mid-1970s represented a highly regulated economic and political regime, known as Fordism in the West which was characterised by the mass production of standard goods, a strong state-led social welfare system, and a strong division of labour tasks. However, it is posited that this system has now given way to an emerging regulatory system of post-Fordism characterised by a new, and more regional, geography of capitalist activity.

One approach to understanding this new economic environment can be found in the concept of the learning economy which emerges from studies of national systems of innovation (Lundvall 1992; Lundvall and Johnson 1994). Lundvall defines the learning economy as:

> an economy where the success of individuals, firms, and regions reflects the capability to learn (and forget old practices); where change is rapid and old skills become obsolete and new skills are in demand; where learning includes the building of competencies, not just increased access to information; where learning is going on in all parts of society, not just high-tech sectors; and where net job creation is in knowledge intensive sectors (high R&D, high proportion with a university degree, and job situation worsens for the unskilled).
>
> (Lundvall 1992: 73)

The learning region depends upon network knowledge, the transfer of knowledge from one group to another to form learning systems – the institutional infrastructure of public and private partnerships. Because network knowledge is highly dependent on interpersonal relations, it can most readily be developed within a particular region.

Moreover, the link between the information society, information communication technologies (ICTs), and learning regions is considered to be mutual and self-reinforcing. Regions with strong learning cultures that support the development and uptake of ICT applications may be able to develop competitive advantages and utilise the information society as a mechanism for growth, while the ICTs themselves are constructed through certain social networking processes and contexts to be found in particular regions (the Silicon Valley phenomenon). For less-favoured regions the implications are clear: without some attempt to make better use of ICTs the prospects of cohesion and convergence are poor.

A number of features can be discerned within this system, all of which have resonances for the management of HEIs. First, the economy itself is becoming more regionalised in that there is a new geography of capitalist activity associated with, on the one hand, the growing internationalisation of production and the mobility of global capital flows and, on the other, the declining regulatory capacity of the nation-state. This shift entails a resurgence of the region through the integration of production at a regional level and the decentralisation of large corporations into clusters of smaller business units and the greater role of smaller businesses as sub-contractors, suppliers, and franchisees. Economic activity, then, is dominated by inter-firm relationships, or what Sabel et al. (1989) termed 'collaborative manufacturing' which emerges at the regional level and allows both competition and collaboration to flourish. While nation-states remain the basic unit of economic and political organisation, they are losing their monopoly on policy-making, representation, legitimacy, and questions of identity.

Second, in the context of the lifelong learning agenda, learning and teaching activities have moved away from a linear model of transmission of knowledge based upon the classroom and are becoming more interactive and experiential, drawing upon, for example, project work and work-based learning, much of which is locationally specific. Within this changed context, learning and knowledge creation take on different characteristics. In particular, it is important to differentiate between codifiable knowledge (know-what such as data etc.) and tacit knowledge such as know-how (skills), know-who (networking), and know-why (experience). These latter forms of 'hybrid knowledge', then, become the most valuable types of knowledge depending upon interpersonal relationships, trust and cooperation and are most readily developed within the region. Moreover, according to the hypothesis presented by Gibbons et al. (1994), there has been a shift from Mode 1 knowledge creation which is homogeneous, disciplinary, and hierarchical and which characterises the autonomous and distinct academic disciplines, to Mode 2 knowledge which is heterarchical, transient, transdisciplinary, socially accountable, and reflexive and undertaken in a context of application.

Third, in the wake of the declining regulatory capacity of the nation–state, the institutions which regulate economic activity are being regionalised. At a regional level, then, an array of intermediate organisations are emerging which create in any particular locality an 'institutional thickness' (Amin and Thrift 1994) comprised of a membership of institutions which will typically include firms, chambers of commerce, government agencies, R&D laboratories, and training and educational institutions including universities. This membership constitutes the basis for 'associative governance' (Hirst 1994), which signifies a shift from state regulation to regional self-regulation. Moreover, these networks rely upon *animateurs* who generate dialogue between the various organisations. The success of this network of organisations is underpinned by a 'soft infrastructure' or what has been called 'social capital' (Putnam 1993) and 'untraded interdependencies' (Storper 1995), which includes aspects such as trust, norms, values, and tacit and personal knowledge. These are key elements of the socio-cultural milieu within which regional networks of inter-firm organisation are embedded (Cooke 1998: 9).

Universities in the learning region

So where do universities fit into this? First, in the light of this regionalisation of the economy, universities are confronted by a new client base in terms of both teaching and research. Traditional relationships with large corporations and nationally-based firms and research organisations are being supplemented by a new regional client base comprised of clusters of firms and the emergence of regionally-based supply chains of small and medium-sized enterprises (SMEs). Such trends have important implications for the skills required of graduates and the way in which universities manage the interface between degree courses and the labour market. In particular, there is a greater demand for the provision of vocational and professional education from universities, which reflects the needs of the regional economy. Universities have much to gain in adapting to these evolving realities of a more regional economy. Regional networking can be thought of as an institutional survival or strengthening strategy for universities. As Morgan comments, 'Learning, of course, is worth little if there are no opportunities to implement what has been learned' (1997: 501). In this sense, a strong and supportive regional economy will create a competitive university, and a strong university has more to offer a region. However, it should be emphasised that universities, whatever their missions, remain autonomous institutions with allegiances to multiple territories rather than specific regions. In this regard, their relationship with territory is more ambivalent than that of public authorities with a legally defined domain.

Second, the emergence of inter- and transdisciplinary research centres within universities which engage with external research partners and increasingly rely on external funding sources can be situated within the shift to a new mode of knowledge production (Gibbons *et al.* 1994). Because interactive forms of learning are inherently bound in time and space, university teaching and research show tendencies towards localisation, or regionalisation. It is within this new regional context for learning and knowledge that connections can be forged between the teaching and research agendas of universities. The university acts as a conduit through which research of an international and national nature is transferred to specific localities through the teaching curriculum.

Third, historically, universities have played a key role in nation building and continue to underpin a wide range of national institutions through the participation of academic staff in numerous public bodies. However, as the institutions which regulate economic activity become more regionalised, universities, through their resource base of people, skills, and knowledge, increasingly play a significant role in regional networking and institutional capacity building. Staff, either in formal or informal capacities, can act as regional *animateurs* through representation on outside bodies ranging from school governing boards and local authorities to local cultural organisations and development agencies. Universities also act as intermediaries in the regional economy by providing, for example, commentary and analysis for the media. Universities, then, make an indirect contribution to the social and cultural basis of effective democratic governance and, ultimately, economic success through the activities of autonomous academics. A key challenge is to enhance the role which universities play, through their staff and students, in the development of these networks of trust and civic engagement, and hence in the wider political and cultural leadership of their localities.

This new environment confronting universities from within higher education and from regions has important implications for institutional management. In the past, higher education in most countries was primarily funded by national governments to meet national labour market needs for skilled manpower and to meet national research and technological development needs. In terms of higher education management this has generally meant a single paymaster, relatively secure long-term funding, the education of a readily identifiable and predictable population of full-time students in the 18–24 age range who are destined to work in the corporate sector and public service, and the provision of a well-founded infrastructure to support the pursuit of individual academic research and scholarship. Such a regime imposed limited demands on university management and in fact supported the ethos of academic self-management and collegiality. The new agenda in higher education requires universities to act corporately and to respond to the demands of a new and diverse set of clients and agencies representing them, many of whom are directly or indirectly concerned with regional development.

Figure 2.1 attempts to summarise the above discussion in diagrammatic form. It focuses on the processes which link all the components of the university and the region to form a learning system. Within the university, the challenge is to link the teaching, research, and community service roles using internal mechanisms (funding, staff development, incentives and rewards, communications, etc.) which make these activities more responsive to regional needs. These linkages represent 'value-added management processes'. Within the region, the challenge for universities is to engage in many of the facets of the development process (such as skills enhancement, technological development and innovation, and cultural awareness) and link them with the intra-university mechanisms in a 'university/region value-added management process'. Put another way, the successful university will be a learning organisation in which the whole is more than the sum of its parts and the successful region in which the university is a key player will have similar dynamics.

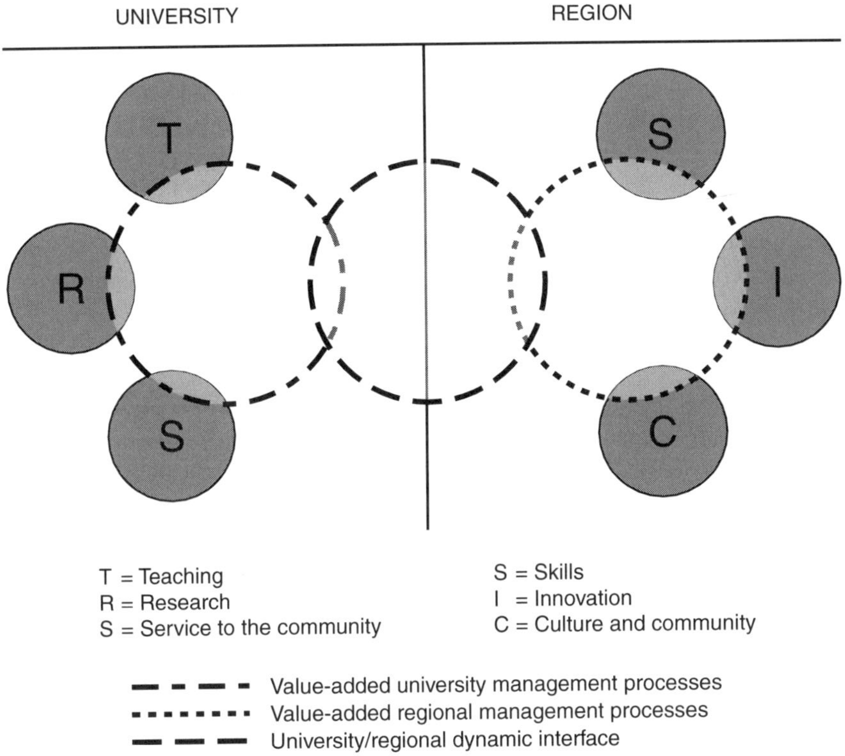

UNIVERSITY   REGION

T = Teaching   S = Skills
R = Research   I = Innovation
S = Service to the community   C = Culture and community

━ ━ ━ ━   Value-added university management processes
■ ■ ■ ■ ■ ■ ■ ■   Value-added regional management processes
━ ━ ━   University/regional dynamic interface

Figure 2.1 The university/region value-added management process
Source: Goddard and Chatterton (1999).

One issue which causes problems in the engagement of universities with their regions is the use of ICTs to harness new forms of educational provision. In particular, the idea of the 'virtual university' as an extension of the traditional place-based institutions and the development of the information society could be seen as a threat to the university wherein its potential role in a region is countered by its weakened setting as a 'place' of learning. Access to the Internet for students may affect the status and authority of university teachers, undermining their knowledge monopoly. The emergence of electronic manage-ment of university education with the 'hollowing out' of existing universities through online course provision by self-employed academics may disembed learning from its regional setting. All such major developments will pose threats and opportunities for regions struggling to adapt to the needs of the learning economy, and policies for education, training, innovation, research, and regional development all need to take into account how higher education (HE) systems might be affected by such developments.

Global economic and political restructuring and the concomitant emergence of new forms of territorial governance-based upon the 'region' are a vital backdrop, then, to the efforts of those steering HEIs to formulate strategies to meet regional needs. However, the extent to which the regional organisation of economic activity as set out above implies sustainable regional development is unclear, especially in the light of the dependency of many regional economies on footloose global inward investment and branch-plant activity. There are trends towards a heightened differentiation of performance between core and peripheral regions as a result of a more open and unregulated global economic and political system. HEIs can play an important brokerage role within regions in terms of promoting debate on the suitability of different models of regional development and their ability to meet the needs of the regional population.

Responding to regional needs

HEIs are responding to this changing environment by establishing new institutional management structures to meet more effectively the demands of various regional stakeholders. Such changes are occurring not only within the traditional teaching and research roles of universities, but also within their community service role. These three roles are discussed below.

Teaching

Universities have always played a role as a source of, and repository for, knowledge. Access to this knowledge base has been achieved through the development of teaching. A core function of HEIs, then, has been to educate through the dissemination of its knowledge base. While this teaching was initially offered to a national elite, of politicians, industrialists, the clergy, and civil servants, throughout the twentieth century access to knowledge has continually been extended to much larger groups. In spite of this, the development of the teaching function within long-established HEIs has not been influenced by regional needs as most still recruit from, and provide graduates for, national and international markets.

The context for education provision is, however, changing as a result of demands to create more regionally relevant education systems. Such demands are the result of policy changes from national governments, especially those associated with the concept of the 'learning society', and from impulses within regions to enhance the relevance of the teaching function. Newer institutions and those incorporated into the higher education sector from outside are creating or have inherited a tradition of providing locally relevant education. The challenge for all types of HEIs is to balance the need to meet regional labour requirements with the need to encourage the national and global mobility and competitiveness of staff and students and to position the institution in the global market. In order to realise the potential of HEIs for regions, all regional education providers must be brought together to reduce duplicative functions, enhance collaborative provision, and create a regional learning system by expanding the overall size of the education market. This agenda is problematic as there are tendencies towards localisation and delocalisation of teaching and learning as the regionally embedded HEI is renegotiated with the emergence of the virtual or placeless HEI. HEIs are adapting in a number of ways to anticipate the changing nature of teaching.

First, HEIs face choices in terms of prioritising different student markets. Most HEIs operate, or would like to operate, in national and competitive student markets. Larger comprehensive, urban universities and subjects such as medicine are generally very competitive and over-subscribed and, as a result, are more selective and nationally/internationally focused in terms of student recruitment. Many HEIs, then, would regard the attraction of the best students to the region from any source as a positive influence on regional development.

There are compelling arguments for making greater provision for more locally-based HEIs, not least because of the circumstances facing certain groups seeking higher education. For example, the steady shifting of costs in recent years away from the taxpayer and onto a full-time student's present or future family is a powerful reason why more full-time British students have each year chosen to go to a university close to their home. Further, most full- or part-time mature entrants (aged 25 and above on admission) are home-based and choose a local institution and most employed people seeking short courses or continuing professional development (CPD) activity prefer a relatively local supplier. Many HEIs already function as distinctly local institutions, or have histories which connect them with the regional community and those have consequently developed a strong role in educational provision for their region. Many national systems, such as the USA, have regionally defined catchments for student recruitment. Further, it is essential that rural, sparsely populated and old industrial regions retain the best students from the regional school system rather than lose them to other more prosperous regions.

Second, graduate retention is an important mechanism through which a region can retain people with innovative, entrepreneurial and management capabilities. The levels of graduate retention in a region reflect an interplay of several different factors such as the ability of HEIs to provide courses and skills training which reflect the needs of the regional economy; the robustness, diversity, and size of the regional economic base; the pull factor of 'core' regions; the current state of the national economy; whether the student originates from the region; the type of higher education institution attended; and, the socio-economic background of the student.

HEIs are a major influence on the functioning of the regional labour market. When considering their relationship with employers in a regional context it is useful for HEIs to consider themselves as being located at the head of an 'education supply chain' which produces educated people for the region. However, unlike a business enterprise situated in a similar supply chain position, HEIs devote relatively few resources to 'marketing' their products (graduates) or to responding to signals about what the market wants. This lack of marketing can be partly attributed to student funding regimes which reward 'production' but not 'sale' and the poorly developed mechanisms to undertake the marketing function outside careers services. If HEIs were in part rewarded for the delivery of graduates into employment, including local employment, they would clearly have an incentive to put more effort into marketing and economic development.

HEIs are confronted by a complex market place consisting of a variety of enterprises with a variety of skill needs which have to be catered for. These include the mature organisation (Type A) which provides well-established career routes and vocations for graduates, can choose to foster relationships with selected universities, and can influence the curriculum; the rapidly developing company (Type B) which will normally be inexperienced in graduate recruitment and may not have the sectoral coherence of Type A organisations; and finally, the traditional small enterprise (Type C) employing fewer than fifty people and probably fewer than twenty, which is unlikely to have mechanisms for selecting and screening graduates or to provide induction and this makes articulation of needs problematic. Such companies generally do not want or cannot cope with, 'green' graduates and there may be only the poorest coherence between traditional degree programmes and the skills/knowledge which Type C companies require.

Small firms with fewer than 250 employees account for the vast majority of firms in most national contexts. Increasing numbers of graduates are finding their way into such smaller firms via a number of routes such as pre-university placements, based learning and sandwich courses, vacation placements, part-time work, recruitment fairs, apprenticeships, teaching company programmes, recruitment at master's degree level, and schemes for unemployed graduates. Because of the great diversity of these small firms, it is very difficult to identify common needs. However, they generally require graduates to have acquired key transferable skills through their studies and work-based education, especially since SMEs do not have the resources, personnel, or time to undertake skills training. Yet, it is unrealistic to expect HEIs to have the ability or knowledge to prepare graduates for the diversity of employment situations which they may encounter within SMEs. A vast array of programmes has emerged to bridge the gap between the disparate worlds of HEIs and SMEs. Building partnerships and support mechanisms such as apprenticeship, matching and induction schemes, marketing and curriculum modification can ease the transition between the different institutional cultures and work practices. The challenge remains to develop a regional graduate Labour Market Information (LMI) system to systematically collect, process, and disseminate information on the movement of graduates in the region.

Third, HEIs can localise the learning process by drawing upon the specific characteristics of a region to aid learning and teaching. The creation of specialist locally-oriented courses which draw upon the characteristics of the region can give HEIs a competitive advantage in national and international student recruitment pools. Locally-oriented courses, especially those which are closely connected to growing industries in the region, can offer graduates greater chances of success and mobility in the regional labour market. Locally-based teaching, then, is an effective way of exposing the region to the work of

HEIs and the skills and talents of its students. Such teaching often draws upon representatives from local industry to add practical experience to the teaching process. Moreover, project and course work, particularly at the postgraduate level, can be undertaken collaboratively with regional partners and can be focused upon regional issues.

Overly localised teaching programmes can, however, have several short-comings; if tied too closely to the economic base of the region, courses can be susceptible to cycles of growth and contraction in the regional economy; regionally-oriented courses may have a limited appeal in terms of attracting non-local students and could also adversely affect the performance of students in national labour markets; and finally, many HEIs regard their role as generating expert knowledge and providing graduates of the highest quality. One cannot assume that young people in (or outside of) a region will be attracted to study those courses which are particularly focused on the region's economic interests. Indeed, there is evidence that in areas of economic hardship, home-based students will see a degree as a way of escaping from the region and will explicitly reject a course of study specific to their area. There is a real tension here. HEIs have always enabled young people to leave their home region in search of the kinds of jobs they want elsewhere, as well as being a means of matching the acquisition of knowledge and skills to the region's developing economy. HEIs, then, have to seriously consider the problems associated with localising the curriculum.

Fourth, HEIs are increasingly playing a regional role in meeting professional and vocational educational demand in the labour market. Technological change means that skills acquired are soon rendered obsolete and career progression is no longer linear. The implication is that there is a significant increase in the demand for adult and continuing education and a greater emphasis on lifelong learning, and on the critical role of skills development in maintaining and increasing national competitiveness. As a result of such changes, much effort has been made to ensure that HE provision more closely matches what are seen to be local, regional, and national skill needs, although adult liberal education and tailored and specialist continuing professional development courses for regional organisations are often undertaken in partnership with other local bodies. However, in the absence of intermediary agencies to articulate the skills needs of the region, it is often difficult for HEIs to organise suitable provision.

Finally, HEIs are moving away from traditional forms of course delivery and the standard three-year bachelor degree in order to provide flexible packages of higher education to a variety of audiences. Most HEIs have extended their teaching activities to offer access to HE for traditionally under-represented groups and, in many national contexts, HE provision is being tailored to meet the specific requirements of indigenous groups and ethnic minority/cultural groups. HEIs are also experimenting with new forms of course delivery to those located in rural or marginal areas hitherto poorly served by higher education.

As noted earlier, developments in telecommunications networks (such as broadcasting, cable, the Internet, the World-Wide Web) are challenging the role of the place-based university in the creation, preservation, and transmission of knowledge. Developments in ICTs enable a whole host of actors, including HEIs and other public and private institutions – individually or in partnership – to mould, and respond to, educational needs in radical ways. Thus, the monopolistic position of many HEIs in a regional and national context is being supplanted by external education providers, such as the Western Governers University and the University of Phoenix in the USA, who have entered the regional learning system and offer courses via mediums such as the Internet. HEIs are responding to such threats by offering web-based courses around the globe, creating a patchwork of internal and external HE provision in regions delivered by a range of actors. The concept of the 'virtual university', then, suggests that the role and remit of HEIs are in a period of complex renegotiation. It is unclear whether such developments represent a disembedding of HEIs from particular places and communities.

In sum, one of the most important challenges facing HEIs is the creation of a coherent learning system, in which regional stakeholders work together to develop the overall capacity of human resources in the region. The potential for developing such regional learning systems varies significantly between countries. There are few examples outside of the USA of systematic regional cooperation between different segments of the educational system, such as schools, universities, and other higher education institutions, and even fewer examples which demonstrate an awareness of the links between education provision and economic development at a regional level. At best, many HEIs display a reactive approach to linking teaching with regional development issues. The establishment of a national system which links FEIs and HEIs on a regional basis poses a particular problem as this has the potential disadvantage of blurring the distinctive missions of institutions within the two sectors.

Research management

Research within HEIs, especially the university sector, has traditionally focused on the generation of 'basic' knowledge for the national/international academic community and avoided the application of established knowledge for the local/ regional community. Some researchers in HEIs have been reluctant to seek external research sponsors and have often been guarded in their approach towards collaborative research activities. Many national funding regimes exacerbate inter-institutional competition rather than promote collaboration in terms of research activity and funding. However, there are a number of trends which are encouraging HEIs to develop mechanisms to commercialise their research base and link their research and expertise more closely to the external environment.

First, it is important to understand the ways in which the shifting production of knowledge (Gibbons *et al.* 1994) is being reconfigured and how this is altering the conduct of research within HEIs. HEIs no longer have a monopoly on knowledge production and must enter into strategic alliances with a range of knowledge producers in order to remain at the cutting edge of research. HEIs, then, are increasingly seeking external research partners to tap into wider knowledge networks and to meet the rising costs of research. This is being achieved by the expansion of research activities away from traditional academic units to new collaborative units such as research centres and science parks. These new vehicles for knowledge production have significant organisational implications for HEIs. Research centres often have an explicit regional *raison d'être* and function on a multi-disciplinary and collaborative basis. The expansion of such centres is also a strategy of HEIs to compete with the growing number of private research institutes.

Second, HEIs have responded to opportunities provided by, for example, the historical, cultural, political, or economic context of the region by developing research agendas which reflect these characteristics. The region is often used as a laboratory for research, which gives it a competitive advantage both nationally and internationally. A key question to pursue is the extent to which university research can draw new ideas into the region to aid its development. Research activities can also be directed towards promoting the growth of regionally-based industrial clusters. From the perspective of many development agencies, universities are seen as key actors in promoting the establishment and development of new clusters of economic activity.

HEIs have established a number of mechanisms to manage their research interface with the outside world. However, the transfer of research between HEIs and other stakeholders is a complex process. Rather than regarding research and knowledge transfer as a simple linear model between HEIs and their partners, there are a number of simultaneous flows between clusters of stakeholders and HEIs which occur on a spectrum from individual and *ad hoc* interaction and consultancy work to centrally organised activities. Explicit mechanisms through which research is transferred between HEIs and regional stakeholders include single-entry points such as regional development offices, research centres, spin-off companies, incubator units, advice and training services, science parks and mechanisms to exploit intellectual property rights (IPR). However, it must be recognised that the most effective technology and knowledge transfer mechanism between HEIs and the external environment is the teaching function of HEIs; that is to say, the staff and students via the teaching curriculum, placements, teaching company schemes, secondments, etc. This reinforces the intimate relationship between the teaching and research functions of HEIs.

Research interfaces such as University Research Centres can be considered as a developing 'dual structure' within most HEIs in which basic units such as departments are supplemented by new units and forms of activity linked to the outside world. They are responsible for introducing new ideas and promoting a more entrepreneurial culture in HEIs, including the more traditional units such as the academic departments. These interfaces depend more and more upon entrepreneurially sought, locally and regionally-based funding sources and collaboration with a wide range of partners. New research interfaces are challenging existing HEI structures and management forms, especially in terms of introducing entrepreneurialism into traditional disciplinary-bound departments.

Many HEIs have approached their contribution to regional development in a multi-faceted manner combining a number of the above mechanisms which, in turn, reflect the evolving needs of the region. The research relationship between an HEI and its region must, therefore, be a dynamic one utilising a diversity of tools – spin outs, science parks, centres of excellence and other gateway mechanisms, and last but not least, teaching and learning through work-based experience and professional development, which is linked to research. However, technology transfer between HEIs and regions should not be seen as a panacea for regional development. Initiatives need to demonstrate their 'added value' to the region; for example, do they lead to a net increase in innovation, employment, wealth creation, and linkages than would otherwise not have occurred in the regional economy?

Community service

The contributions that HEIs have always made to civil society through the extra-mural activities of individual staff (e.g. in the media, politics, the arts, advice to government bodies, socio-economic and technological analyses) and through providing liberal adult education and evening classes and access to facilities like libraries, theatres, museums, and public lectures are being bundled together and recognised as a 'third role' alongside teaching and research. Perhaps more than the other roles, it is this third role of community service which embeds HEIs in the region. In certain contexts, this role reflects the nineteenth-century paternalism of industrialists and philanthropists who gave endowments to establish HEIs in their home areas in order to create a 'cultured' and 'civilised' local and regional population. In other contexts, this role of service to the local community stems from the obligations on HEIs which arise from being major recipients of local taxes.

A number of trends are converging which are increasing this traditional service role of HEIs. First, the increasing awareness of the global, or pan-national, nature of many problems such as environmental degradation, poverty, and economic development has created a number of inter-connected local responses such as 'Local Agenda 21'. HEIs, because of their multi-territoriality and inter-disciplinarity, are institutions which are strongly placed to interpret global issues on a local scale. A second trend is the rise of the local state and local voluntary/community groups in response to the declining influence of national structures. Moreover, fiscal constraints at both local and national government are creating partnerships between the public, private, and voluntary sectors to meet community needs. In this context, HEIs, their staff and students, are heavily involved in community service through volunteer work, project work, mentoring, leadership, and commentary. In sum, through this third role of service, HEIs number among several actors involved in the governance of local civic society. What the third role highlights is the increasing embeddedness of HEIs in their regions and their duty as responsible local as well as national and international agents. This is evident in several ways.

First, regional development and promotional organisations are increasingly looking towards HEIs to provide leadership, analysis, resources, and credibility. HEIs contribute to the less tangible aspects of the development process by building social networks that link key actors in the local community and feed intelligence into these networks. HEI participation can inject an element of unbiased and informed realism into such networks. This 'partnership principle' is increasingly a prerequisite for securing certain forms of funding and for creating an effective platform for enhancing inward investment activity. Further, HEIs provide the region with commentary, analysis, information, and access to wider networks, through mechanisms such as media links and public lectures. They also provide a framework through which ideas and cultures can be shared and transmitted. In this sense, HEIs can play an important role in opening up and internationalising regions.

A second aspect of the third role of HEIs is their role in community and voluntary action in the region. The student population represents a significant resource to the local community in terms of volunteer workers. The USA offers many lessons for student community service through the 'education for citizenship' model. This partly reflects the historic legacy of municipality throughout the federal states and the tradition of Land-Grant universities which are dedicated to serving the community.

Third, HEIs own a number of facilities such as libraries, sports facilities, and arts and cultural venues which are often significant regional facilities offering public access. Since the funding for such facilities at many HEIs is discretionary and not provided for in earmarked government block-grants, their economic viability often depends upon partnerships, especially financial-based ones, with regional stakeholders. Regional access to facilities at HEIs may be a more pressing issue in lagging regions which have a less developed educational, social, and cultural infrastructure. Many regional cultural facilities are offered through students' unions, which often play a central role in entertainment in the region by providing comedy, live music, dance events, and late-night drinking and can increase the overall 'popular' cultural reputation of a city or region. As in the area of teaching and research, it is often necessary for HEIs within a region to work together with external partners in developing a portfolio of facilities and services which can be tailored to regional needs. Regional funding levered in this way can widen the range of facilities available on campus to students, thus enhancing the learning experience; at the same time active engagement in the community can enrich the life of both students and teachers. In short, the third role is not a one-way street.

Conclusion

This chapter has highlighted the ways in which HEIs are responding to regional needs in terms of teaching, research, and community service. But what are the drivers and barriers which each HEI has to confront when engaging with the region and what actions can and do various stakeholders take which can either enhance or inhibit greater regional engagement?

It should be apparent from the discussion that responding to regional needs is not a clear-cut process for HEIs, but is one framed by the history of individual institutions and the political–economic structures of both regions and nation-states? As a result of this, there are a number of drivers and barriers to greater regional engagement in terms of the ways in which the two main areas of activity within HEIs, teaching and research, are undertaken.

Amongst the drivers to greater regional engagement, those for teaching may include historical roots which link the institution firmly to its local economic base; a desire to increase the uptake of graduates into employment within the region; an increase in postgraduate, professional development and part-time teaching to attract more revenue; recruitment of senior management onto boards of regional agencies and initiatives; opportunities for undergraduate students to study from home and avoid debts; new 'ladders of opportunity' for students through access to knowledge, franchises, and other arrangements; and demand from mature and non-traditional students who are based in the region. In terms of research, drivers may include a renewed thrust of government policy towards promoting industrial links and clusters at a regional level; the regionalisation of national technology development and transfer policy; closer links between HEIs and the health sector; and in the context of Europe, funding accruing to the regions through the Structural Funds.

There are also significant barriers to greater regional engagement. In teaching, these may include historic patterns of nationally-driven subject provision and demand for courses which are not particularly congruent with the development needs of the region; academic promotion systems which do not sufficiently reward regional teaching and learning opportunities; the influence of external accreditation from professional bodies which pay little attention to regional development needs; lack of links between the formulation of regional policy initiatives by senior management team and implementation by teaching staff; and high start-up costs of regional collaborative projects and lack of regional 'seed corn' funds. There are also a number of perceived anxieties or threats associated with greater localisation/regionalisation of teaching, which include anxiety about the 'decline in standards' and a fear that enhanced skills will increase rather than decrease regional labour mobility. One of the most significant barriers remains the difficulty of matching the attributes of graduates and the skills needs of local employers, especially SMEs. In terms of research, barriers include the largely national-driven agendas of the research council; staff promotion mechanisms, peer hierarchies, and academic networks which, in a similar way to teaching, favour activity of a national/international significance; the distribution of funding according to the reputations of academics and HEIs rather than on the prioritisation of regional developmental needs. Most importantly, there are very few funds available at a regional level for substantial research programmes focused on regional needs. Funding from industry tends to come from R&D units at corporate headquarters. This is a particular problem in peripheral regions where there are very few R&D units belonging to big companies.

What actions can national governments, local and regional authorities, and HEIs themselves take to reduce the effect of the barriers outlined above? In the case of national government and unitary states without regional structures of governance, territorial development poses a fundamental challenge to the division of responsibility between ministries organised on a functional basis. In such situations, enhancing the responsiveness of HEIs to regional needs inevitably requires inter-ministerial dialogue and collaboration. (Goddard and Chatterton, 1999, provide an example for the UK.) While the primary responsibility for funding universities is likely to rest with the Ministry of Education or a quasi-independent funding body reporting to it, the regional agenda for universities is also likely to touch on the concerns of a number of different ministries – such as industry, science and technology, employment and the labour market, home affairs/local government, and culture and sport. Insofar as these ministries already deal with universities, it may be with different parts of the institution (e.g. one Vice Rector may be responsible for research and industrial liaison and another for cultural affairs). Thus, HEIs reproduce the functional divisions within the national government.

National governments can undertake a number of tasks to enhance the response of HEIs to regional needs. First, Ministries of Education can map the geography of higher education, for example, which courses are taught where, the home origins of students, and where graduates enter into the labour market. A particular concern of this mapping task will be to identify the steps between different levels of the education system – schools, further/vocational education/ community colleges, higher education, postgraduate institutions – in order to assess how far the regional pattern of provision assists/inhibits access and progress of students. In short, geographical analysis should highlight the fact that lifelong learning is an agenda that should be responsive to the needs of *people in places*. Further, inter-ministerial dialogue concerning higher education needs to be encouraged between, for example, Ministries of Employment and Industry to promote the notion of knowledge-based clusters, or between Ministries of Culture and Sport and Ministries of Education to promote understanding of the role of HEIs in regional cultural provision. Governments can also establish incentives and funding programmes to encourage HEIs to develop programmes/projects which have an explicit regional dimension and aim to strengthen cooperative activity within the region, and promote partnerships and dialogue between regional education providers such as schools, FE and HE, and other training providers.

Turning to public authorities operating at the local and regional scale, universities often remain a 'black box'. Central government has little understanding of what drives academics as teachers and researchers and the way in which HEIs are governed and managed. This has resulted in funding mechanisms that are poorly understood by the HE sector. Just as it is a key task for HEIs to explain this, so too regional authorities must attempt to learn about higher education. A useful way of building the relationship between public authorities and HEIs is through joint research. HEIs are a repository of knowledge about future technological, economic, and social trends and can be harnessed to help the region understand itself, and its position in the world, and to identify possible future directions. HEIs can also act as a gateway to global information and tailor this information to meet the needs of different sectors of the regional economy. Public authorities in cooperation with HEIs need to explore mechanisms for tapping into this knowledge base at both strategic and operational levels. In terms of strategy, an event like a regional future search conference involving staff drawn from across the university and the public and private sector within the region is one possibility. At an operational level, gateway offices which maintain an expertise database will need to be established if SMEs and small public and private organisations are to gain access to university knowledge.

HEIs also need to play a role in the formulation of regional action plans and programmes. In each of the main themes within a development programme there is likely to be a requirement for active university participation. For example, in the search for inward investment there will be room for university participation in overseas delegations; in regional technological development programmes there will be opportunities for universities to provide expertise to assist with product and process innovation through consultancies, student placements, and management development; in skills enhancement linked to raising regional competitiveness there should be a place for targeted graduate retention and continuing professional development initiatives; in cultural development, there will be scope for joint planning of provision of non-vocational education and of opening up of university facilities to the general public; finally, in terms of regional capacity building, university staff and facilities can be mobilised to promote public debate.

Finally, just as there is a need for national funding bodies to earmark specific funds to enable HEIs to pursue a third role, regional authorities will likewise need to underpin their requirements for new relationships with HEIs by financial support. This could take many forms but perhaps the most vital need is help for HEIs to establish mechanisms for regional interface that can be sustained on a long-term basis. As more and more sources of funding from national governments and bodies like the European Union relevant to the third role of universities are short-term and project-based, local or regional authorities could play a key role in ensuring the sustainability of university engagement by financially underpinning the bidding process.

What of HEIs themselves? This chapter has outlined a changing role for HEIs in their regions. The concern for HEIs is not only to identify their passive impacts in terms of direct and indirect employment but also to create mechanisms through which the resources of universities can be mobilised to contribute to the development process. This undoubtedly amounts to a third role for universities (after teaching and research), the pursuit of which can challenge established traditions of institutional governance.

To undertake this role, a number of requirements must be fulfilled. First, the starting point for engagement should be a straightforward mapping of regional links in terms of teaching, research, and participation in regional public affairs. A very basic task is to identify the home origin of students, what academic programmes they participate in, and the destination of graduates by occupation, industry and geographical location. With the judicious use of external data, the university should be able to establish its share of national and regional student and graduate markets, its contribution to raising levels of participation in higher education in the region and graduate skills in the regional labour market. The university should aim to establish mechanisms that track students on a longitudinal basis, including their careers as alumni and use this information to guide the shaping of academic programmes. On the research side, the geography of collaboration with the users and beneficiaries of research needs to be established. Again, external benchmarks will be required to make sense of these data, for example, to identify regional companies and organisations absent from the list. The mapping should identify the participating departments within the university, again to reveal possible missing links.

The contribution of the university to regional public affairs can be mapped by identifying university participation in employers' organisations, politics, the media, the voluntary sector, the arts, and other educational institutions. An important distinction will need to be made between, on the one hand, informal engagement where staff acts in an individual capacity and, on the other, formal university participation in partnership arrangements. It is also important to recognise the unique characteristics of each stakeholder, such as organisational culture, territorial remit, and funding sources. Documenting the present linkages and publicising them within the region will be an important first step in raising the profile of the university. Publicity within the institution will be equally important to draw the attention of all of the staff to the extent and significance of regional engagement. Such documentation is an essential prelude to a self-evaluation of the institution's desire and capacity to respond to regional needs. Ideally, this should be undertaken with the assistance of an external peer review group to gauge 'institutional capacity' to respond to regional needs (a good example of a self-evaluation followed by an external peer review is provided by Turku University, Finland – see Goddard *et al.* 2000). Such exercises can lead to a thorough re-evaluation of institutional culture, and a shift from a loosely coupled institutional form to a more managerial one. Regional offices and regional *animateurs* play a central role in such institutional reconfiguring. The challenge has been neatly captured by Duke:

> For universities, the learning region may be the best kept secret of the dying days of this century. In practical terms this implies blending and combining

competition in the "new enterprise environment" with collaboration; fostering and supporting "boundary spanners" who can work across the borders of the university in effective discourse with other organisations and their different cultures; fostering cultural change to enable universities to speak and work with partners from many traditions and persuasions as more learning organisations emerge and together enrich their various overlapping learning zones or regions.

(1998: 5)

Acknowledgement

This chapter draws heavily on a report by the authors for the OECD programme on Institutional Management in Higher Education, entitled the *Response of HEIs to Regional Needs* (OECD 1999).

References

Amin, A. and Thrift, N.J. (eds) (1994) *Globalisation, Institutions and Regional Development in Europe*, London: Oxford University Press.

Clark, B. R. (1998) *Creating Entrepreneurial Universities: Organizational Pathways of Transformation*, Oxford: Pergamon.

Cooke, P. (1998) 'Introduction: Origins of the Concept', in H.-J. Braczyk, P. Cooke and M. Heidenreich (eds) *Regional Innovation Systems: The Role of Governance in a Globalized World*, London: UCL Press.

Dahllöf U. et al. (1998) *Towards the Responsive University: The Regional Role of Eastern Finland Universities*, Helsinki: Finnish Higher Education Evaluation Council.

Davies, J. (1998) *The Public Role of the University. The Dialogue of Universities with their Stakeholders: Comparisons between Different Regions of Europe*, CRE, Geneva.

DEETYA (1998) 'Learning for Life, Final Report', *Review of Higher Education Financing and Policy*, Canberra, Australia: Commonwealth of Australia.

DETR (1997) *Building Partnerships for Prosperity: Sustainable Growth, Competitiveness and Employment in the English Regions*, London: The Stationery Office.

DfEE (1998) *Universities and Economic Development*, Sheffield: Higher Education and Employment Division, Department for Education and Employment.

DTI (1998) *Our Competitive Future: Building the Knowledge Driven Economy*, London: TSO.

Duke, C. (1998) 'Lifelong Learning: Implications for the University of the 21st Century', paper presented at the Fourteenth General Conference of IMHE member institutions, November, Paris.

Garlick, S. (1998) *Creative Associations in Special Places: Enhancing the Partnership Role of Universities in Building Competitive Regional Economies*, Southern Cross Regional Research Institute, Southern Cross University, Australia.

Gibbons, M., Limiges, C., Nowotny, H., Schwartzman, S., Scott, P. and Trow, M. (1994) *The New Production of Knowledge: The Dynamics of Science and Research in Contemporary Societies*, London: Sage.

Goddard, J. B. (1999) 'Universities and Regional Development: An Overview', in G. Gray (ed.) *Universities and the Creation of Wealth*, Milton Keynes: Open University Press.

Goddard, J. B., Charles, D., Pike, A., Potts, G. and Bradley, D. (1994) *Universities and Communities*, London: CVCP.

Goddard, J. B. and Chatterton, P. (1999) 'Regional Development Agencies and the Knowledge Economy: Harnessing the Potential of Universities', *Environment and Planning C* 17: 685–699.

Goddard, J. B., Moses, I., Teichler, U., Virtanen, I. and West, P. (2000) *External Engagement and Institutional Adjustment: An Evaluation of the University of Turku*, Helsinki: Finnish Higher Education Evaluation Council.

Hirst, P. (1994) *Associative Democracy*, Cambridge: Polity Press.

Howells, J. *et al.* (1998) *Industry-academic Links in the UK*, Manchester: PREST, University of Manchester.

Lundvall, B.-Å. (ed.) (1992) *National Systems of Innovation: Towards a Theory of Innovation and Interactive Learning*, London: Pinter.

Lundvall, B.-Å. and Johnson, B. (1994) 'The Learning Economy', *Journal of Industry Studies* 2: 23–42.

Morgan, K. (1997) 'The Learning Region: Institutions, Innovation and Regional Renewal', *Regional Studies* 31: 491–503.

National Committee of Inquiry into Higher Education (1997) Chapter 12; *The Local and Regional Role of Higher Education*, London: The Stationery Office.

OECD (1997) *The Response of Higher Education Institutions to Regional Needs*, Centre for Educational Research and Innovation, Programme on Institutional Management in Higher Education (CERI/IMHE/DG(96)10/REV1), Paris: OECD.

OECD (1999) *Response of HEIs to Regional Needs*, Paris: OECD.

Putnam, R. D. *et al.* (1993) *Making Democracy Work: Civic Traditions in Modern Italy*, Princeton, NJ: Princeton University Press.

Sabel, C. F., Herrigel, G. B., Reeg, R. and Kazis, R. (1989) 'Regional Prosperities Compared: Massachusetts and Baden-Württemberg in the 1980s', *Economy and Society* 18, 4: 374–404.

Storper, M. (1995) 'The Resurgence of Regional Economies, Ten Years Later: The Region as a Nexus of Untraded Interdependencies', *European Urban and Regional Studies* 2, 3: 191–221.

UNESCO (1998) *A Framework for Priority Action for Change and Development in Higher Education*, Paris: UNESCO.

3 Governance for university–industry collaboration in Hong Kong

Jerry Patchell and Tony Eastham

Introduction

Two positions dominate the discussion of university–industry interaction. The first is a search for means to promote interaction that is characterised by policy, legal, and institutional initiatives (Brett *et al.* 1991; Carboni 1992). This positive position implicitly and explicitly expresses a desire to use societal resources for business use and economic development. Indeed, some consider the failure to make a connection between universities and industry to be a squandering of national resources and indicative of falling behind in the innovation race (Fortier 1999). Obversely, the second position questions the societal costs and benefits of compromising the university's role as an independent third party and free disseminator of information for the benefit of private purposes (Bowie 1994; Feller 1990). In between these two viewpoints, a third examines the types, extent, and impact of university–industry collaboration (Cohen *et al.* 1994; Rosenberg and Nelson 1994). We contribute to this literature by examining how these positions are linked through a governance system.

The governance system of university–industry interactions is discussed as an internal governance issue when universities are considering developing new means of interaction such as entrepreneurship programs, consortia, directed funding, and so on. External governance issues are raised when governments exert pressure on universities to interact or when industry funding directs the activities of the university. External governance issues are also raised when government commissions and outside reviewers examine the costs and benefits of university commercialisation and academic entrepreneurs. However, although governance of the university–industry interaction, does occur, it might be carried out more effectively if seen as a means of constantly managing the tension between two diverging, yet complementary forces.

Our purpose in this chapter is to reveal the complexity of these governance issues. We do so by using the example of Hong Kong and its University of Science and Technology (HKUST). Hong Kong is a good example of external governance pressures because the government has made fostering university–industry collaboration a key part of its attempt to turn the territory into a technology and innovation center. It is also a good example because, although it is an executive-led government, it must still preserve the autonomy of the universities and can only indirectly lead them to take on an increased role in industrial development. Much less can it direct private firms. In the first section, we outline how this indirect governance of the universities and industry takes place.

The heart of the matter, however, is at the university level. Universities, whether public or private, are autonomous bodies whose missions and governance are primarily and overwhelmingly academic. It goes without saying that they cannot force companies to collaborate. Less obvious is the fact that they have little ability to force faculty members to collaborate with industry. While there is much contrast of interest between faculty and industry, they also have many common interests. In the second section, we investigate the mediation role a university's industrial liaison office (ILO) must play to reconcile the conflicts between university and industry to the mutual satisfaction of faculty members and companies.

The liaison office is the crucial institution of governance. It must, for example, devise means to reconcile the intellectual property rights concerns of companies with the university's role as disseminator of information. Furthermore, to achieve the university's role of technology transfer, it must also give a faculty appropriate incentives to work with companies and incentives for companies to adjust their bottom-line attitudes to the basic research perspective of universities, and so on. The complexity of mediation is underscored by the fact that the liaison office has to mediate between independent-minded publication/tenure-driven faculty members and autonomous market-driven private companies.

In the final section, we examine the ability of the liaison organisation of HKUST to accommodate both external and internal governance needs. HKUST is a good example of internal university governance because it spearheads university–industry interaction in Hong Kong.

External governance of university–industry interaction in Hong Kong

In the fall of 1999 Hong Kong caught high-tech fever. This fever was recorded on Hong Kong's most reliable thermometer, the Hang Seng stock index. Suddenly, any company with a technology element saw its value shoot up. Other companies quickly added dot.com identities to capture the same revaluation. The government also launched a new NASDAQ-type technology-oriented stock market. The first few firms to be listed rapidly escalated in value. The fever's most immediate cause was the government's announcement of support for a cyberport to anchor high-tech IT firms and define Hong Kong as the information services and technology hub of the South China region. Although the Cyberport Project played a key role in transforming the business mentality from skepticism to technology boosterism, the government and some industrial concerns had been trying to bring about this transformation for a decade. Exploiting the innovative and R&D capacities of universities to contribute to innovation and technology has been the major thrust of these efforts.

Most of the policy decisions and the practical application of those decisions that provide external governance to Hong Kong's universities are developed within the Education Department and the Industry Department. These departments report to and are directed by the office of the Chief Executive. External governance also comes from industry and community representation on university councils or boards of governors. These inter-relations are illustrated in Figure 3.1. Their respective impacts on governance are discussed below.

It is appropriate to begin with the Chief Executive's office because Hong Kong's attempt to transform its industrial base is a top-down effort. Hong Kong's Chief Executive is also chancellor of all the universities. His real impact on university policy is not directly related to the institutions, but filters through other organs of government. He is advised on university matters, not only by the Education Department, but also by various committees such as the Executive Council and the Central Policy Unit. However, the most important advisory unit has been the Commission on Innovation and Technology. This Commission, composed of technocrats, businessmen, and academics, was established in March 1998 to advise the Chief Executive on how to achieve the goal of making Hong Kong a center of innovation, which he had stated in his first post-handover, 1997 policy address.

The Chief Executive was pushed toward this high-tech policy by the growing numbers of opinions and studies decrying Hong Kong's reliance on real estate, financial services and low-end manufacturing, and warning of mounting competition from other regional service centers. High-tech and innovation could, it was claimed, solve these competition problems and create new value-added industries. The influential MIT report *Made by Hong Kong* (Berger and Lester 1997) and also a report by the Business and Professionals Federation (1999) exemplify the pressures mounting on the government to act. Both of those reports stated that Hong Kong should use its universities to help create a high-tech economy.

The Commission on Innovation and Technology (CIT) picked up both the general theme of improving technological and innovation capacity and the specific concern of increasing university–industry interaction. The Commission recommended increasing university–industry interaction in four areas: incubation of start-ups; technology transfer; R&D support; and undergraduate, graduate, and continuing education. To accomplish these goals it advocated, among a number of other initiatives, the creation of a HK $5 billion Innovation and Technology Fund (ITF) and an Applied Science and Technology Research Institute (ASTRI). Support for university–industry collaboration is one role of the ITF and universities are expected to work in close collaboration with ASTRI on joint R&D, cross-secondment of research personnel, sharing of equipment and facilities, internships, and the placement of graduates. The Commission also advocated the holding of 'sector events' involving universities, government, and industry to foster cluster development. The impact of this advisory governance

```
                        ┌──────────────────────┐
                        │                      │  Exec. Council,
 ┌─────────────┐        │                      │  Commission on
 │ Legislative │────────│    Executive         │  Innovation & Tech.
 │ Council     │        │                      │  Central Policy
 └─────────────┘        │                      │  Unit, etc.
                        └──────────────────────┘

              ┌──────────────┐        ┌──────────────┐
              │ Financial    │        │ Administrative│
              │ Branch       │        │ Branch        │
              └──────────────┘        └──────────────┘

 ┌─────────┐  ┌──────────────┐  ┌──────────────┐  ┌─────────┐
 │ Other   │  │ Trade &      │  │ Secretary for│  │ Other   │
 │ Bureaux &│  │ Industry     │  │ Education    │  │ Bureaux &│
 │ Depts   │  │ Bureau       │  │ & Manpower   │  │ Depts   │
 └─────────┘  │ Industry     │  │ Education    │  └─────────┘
              │ Department   │  │ Department   │
              │              │  │              │
              │ Funding      │  │ Research Grants
              │ Linkages     │  │ Council (RGC)
              │ Institutional│  │ University
              │ Linkages     │  │ Grants
              │              │  │ Committee (UGC)
              └──────────────┘  └──────────────┘

              ┌──────────────────────────┐
              │ Board of Governors       │
              │ (Ind. Representation)    │
              └──────────────────────────┘
```

Universities in Hong Kong		
Polytechnic Origin	Research Focus	Liberal Arts/Education
Polytechnic University City University	University of Hong Kong Chinese University University of Science & Technology	Baptist University Lingnan University Academy of Performing Arts Open University Institute of Education

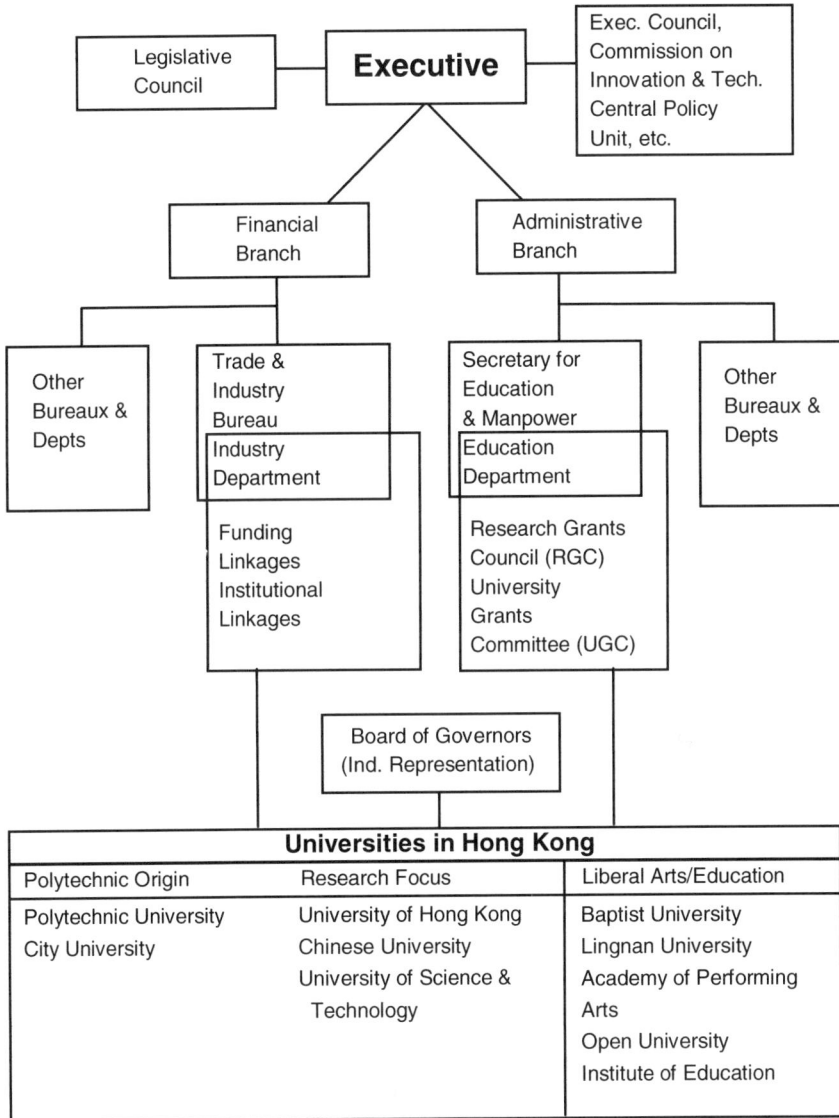

Figure 3.1 External governance of university–industry interaction in Hong Kong

has been rapid, and several of these proposals were implemented within one year. A further proposal, yet to be implemented, is the formation of a permanent high-level policy committee that would oversee innovation and technology. Importantly for universities, this committee would be convened under the authority of the finance branch of government and not the administrative branch which governs education. This committee, if not directly influencing education, then at least would be directly concerned with it.

The perspective of the business community should be noted at this point, because if the governance of university–industry interaction is to be effective, business must be convinced of its value. Policy initiatives pertaining to technology and innovation were not greeted with overwhelming enthusiasm by the business community. Although its manufacturers and traders have created remarkably flexible production systems on the mainland and elsewhere, and operate one of the most efficient trading and service centers, Hong Kong's business people have shown little interest in R&D. What had been strengths in business – hustle strategies, family management – do not easily accommodate the long-term investment necessary for R&D (Berger and Lester 1997: 82). High returns from property transactions have also diverted tycoons and school-leavers away from high-tech industries. The vested interest of traders importing other nations' high-tech into Hong Kong and doubt in Hong Kong's ability to compete against major global high-tech nations and companies also hindered acceptance of innovation policy. Furthermore, the business community has evolved within a policy regime of 'non-interventionism'. This is a regime that many economists still support as the system most likely to produce efficient results. Thus, although the government would like to instil a demand for R&D services, there is no guarantee that it will be forthcoming.

Yet this 'non-interventionist' policy and practice have been as much dogma as reality as the government has always supported monopolies and the Industry Department has developed many institutions and mechanisms to support industrial change. The HK Productivity Council was the precursor of these, supplying expertise in training, technology, and management across a spectrum of fields, while in the last decade centers focused on textiles, biotechnology, industrial technology, and other industries have been developed. The Industry Department has begun to use these facilities to foster university–industry collaboration, while the Industrial Technology Centre supports incubation facilities on two university campuses. The proposed science park is a more elaborate attempt at fostering university–industry interaction. According to the memorandum of understanding signed by the Provisional Science Park Co. and six of Hong Kong's universities:

> the following will be enforced in order to bring mutual benefits to the academia and HKSP and/or its tenant companies: in research programs, both parties will make their best endeavors to initiate and implement joint and/or complementary programmes in research and training, innovation, and technology development, technology transfer, and the development of related support services.
>
> (http://www.hksciencepark.com)

Other forms of collaboration include funding, staff appointments, student internship and training, professional service and facilities, and library use. It is important to note that the governance of this corporation brings together industry, academic, and government representatives.

The most significant foray of the Industry Department into indirect university governance is the funding it offers to universities and faculty members who collaborate with companies. It began in 1994 by encouraging universities to support manufacturing industries with the Industrial Support Fund (ISF) and in 1997 the Services Support Fund (SSF) was initiated to assist the service sector. In both cases grants were gained only when a commercial collaborator supplied (10 percent) matching funds. The CIT report stimulated a rapid evolution of this collaboration and through the ITF (successor to ISF and SSF) embarked on a number of new programs. Among them, the teaching company scheme allows students to work for a company while attending university, with university and company splitting the students' wages and with the work experience counting towards their degrees. In the Joint-Research Matching Grant Scheme a company can have half its research costs covered when the research is performed by a local university and it can negotiate with the university for intellectual property rights. The Industrial Research Chair Scheme matches corporate support for research efforts in technology fields not yet developed in Hong Kong. A company can gain IPR from the research of a distinguished professor whose teaching load has been reduced.

The CIT report, while acknowledging that it is neither 'appropriate or realistic to demand university researchers to focus on research near to the market end of the R&D spectrum' (Chief Executive's Commission on Innovation and Technology 1998: 58), is clearly stimulating universities to make a contribution in that direction. However, the CIT is not alone. The University Grants Committee (UGC) which governs Hong Kong's universities (all are public), and its sub-body, the Research Grants Council (RGC) which dispenses research funding, are also acknowledging the utility of linking university research to industrial needs and opportunities. They have accepted the premise that universities have a responsibility to enhance society's economic and social well-being through science and technology development, and have been influenced by the criticism that university research is too detached from the practical needs of industry (Tzang 1997: 61). However, with regard to society's need for expertise in science and technology, and indeed for a knowledgeable and creative workforce in general, the 1990s saw a revolution in Hong Kong's educational system.

Hong Kong strove to raise the quality of its human capital from that of a developing nation to that of a developed nation within a generation. Focusing primarily on tertiary education, universities proliferated from two in 1991 to six by 1995 and eight by 1999. HKUST is a new university; two polytechnics and one college were upgraded. The Academy of Performing Arts, the Open University, and the Hong Kong Institute of Education were given degree-granting status. In the late 1970s, only 2 percent of school-leavers enrolled for first year-first degree places. This percentage increased to 9 percent by 1989, but in that same year a decision was made to double the number of tertiary-level students to 18 percent by 1994 (French 1997). In 2000 the entrance rate was closer to 25 percent because many students went to overseas universities. The progress of this education revolution illustrates the simple fact that Hong Kong was not able to develop in high-tech because the expertise was not available to hire or to enable people to become entrepreneurs.

The production of science and technology students has increased quantitatively by increasing their enrolment numbers and qualitatively by upgrading diploma programs and facilities. However, the UGC has not seen its role limited to the production of human resources. In 1993 the RGC took the initiative to encourage industrial participation in applied research at tertiary institutions through cooperative research centers. Twenty-six such centers have been supported with about HK $90 million in four phases of this program.

The funding of cooperative research centers should be seen in the light of overall funding. Total expenditure on research rose from HK $183 million (US $24 million) in 1988–89 to HK $3,790 million (US $486 million) in 1997–98 (Tien 1998). These figures include institutional commitments to research and salary costs associated with faculty time devoted to research. This government-funded university research makes up the greatest part of Hong Kong's R&D expenditure, which was a modest 0.288 percent of GDP in 1998. Most of this money goes to the engineering, physical and health sciences because of their greater costs, and it remains oriented toward basic research rather than towards commercialisation. This orientation is governed by the terms of the grants given to the universities and faculty members and by the research assessment exercise. This exercise evaluates the research output of faculties in each university to inform its levels of recurrent funding. Assessments take place every three years.

The research evaluation exercise is a formal confirmation that Hong Kong's tertiary institutions are modelled on universities as research institutions. This is true not only for the older universities HKU and CU. HKUST was established with ambitions to become a world-class research university, and the upgraded polytechnics and colleges are compelling their faculty members to upgrade their qualifications to PhD and to publish. An informal governance maintains this basic research orientation. Hong Kong's universities inherited the British tradition of a separation between the academy and industry. The emphasis on this separation may have been stronger in Hong Kong because fewer resources were allotted to education and because tertiary education was primarily meant to supply the personnel needed in the colonial bureaucracy.

Yet, whether because of tradition or a lack of resources, the reluctance to engage with industry is still a legacy defining university activity. Hong Kong University, for example, has used a reverse taxation policy to dissuade its faculty members from engaging in non-academic activities; as external income climbed, payments to the university increased disproportionately. Faculty members also had to disclose all external income even when no university facility was used. These policies were adopted because HKU wished to maintain control over the activities of medical and law faculty members, but they were applied generally. Only in 1997 did HKU begin to adopt a more proactive attitude to industrial collaboration. Hong Kong Polytechnic University (HKPoly) also actively discouraged industrial collaboration. At one time it allowed no private consulting and, in fact, had two faculty members arrested by the Independent Council Against Corruption for engaging in such activities. Although all the universities feel the pressure to adopt proactive approaches to industry, they are all also very aware of issues such as public funds for private gain, conflict of interest, misuse and abuse of university facilities and position, unfair competition and feather-bedding of faculty and amateur entrepreneurs, and bad press due to failure and/or scandal. Some of the universities have been taught by experience to pay attention to these issues. They also feel that Hong Kong's government, funded universities, invasive government involvement, and media-transparent reporting make the American experience not particularly relevant in the Hong Kong context.

Whether a university will proactively encourage interaction with industry also depends on its board of governors and own executive. They are the bridge between external and internal governance. Although Hong Kong's universities are all public institutions and must abide by several UGC directives, they also have a great deal of autonomy, especially with regard to the proposals of the Industry Department and of industry itself. Industry representation on the board of governors may stimulate university–industry interaction and can also influence the culture and organisation of the university. This is certainly the case at HKUST, where the University Council selected a President who is very proactive in the promotion of university–industry interaction, and who has hired like-minded administrators. We will return to this issue later. However, irrespective of external governance promoting university–industry interaction, its success will turn on internal governance.

Universities as multilateral organisations

The external governance of a university can stimulate university–industry interaction through funding and publicly-funded institutions in particular can be enticed to interact with industry. However, because of the autonomous nature of the university and its faculty members, the ability to compel is substantially limited. Thus, when discussing how university–industry interaction can be fostered, the university cannot be regarded as a tool through which a government can interact with industry in a bilateral relation.

University–industry interaction must be considered from the perspective of the university as a multilateral organisation. The rationale for using this multilateral framework is that companies collaborate primarily with individual researchers in a university. They are interested in their ideas and access to facilities, not in the universities themselves. Faculty members are employed at a university, but they enjoy a high degree of autonomy. Although the university can tell them not to do non-university work, it cannot force them to do external work or to work with any specific company.

In relation to the university, the positions of faculty members and companies are comparable because they enjoy autonomy and they have to be given incentives to collaborate. This issue is not a problem when the traditional separation of university and industry pertains, but it becomes problematic when faculty members are expected to collaborate with companies. Thus, when a university takes on a technology-transfer role, its ability to create these incentives and to balance them against the other interests of faculty members and companies becomes crucial. If we are to understand the university's role in regional economic development or simply in technology transfer, we should not interpret its role merely as an employer offering the services of its staff to the community. Rather, we should view it as a multilateral organisation mediating the interests of autonomous parties within the community.

The defining characteristics of a multilateral organisation are the bringing together of several parties for common advantage through voluntary membership and consent to governance. These organisations are important in building the relational infrastructure within a region by providing informal opportunities for meeting and networking, and establishing trust and the rules of the game. They may provide other more formal functions such as training, research and information dissemination, infrastructure, standards, and financing. Some common types of multilateral organisations are industrial associations, cooperatives, chambers of commerce, and NGOs. These organisations provide not only venues and resources, but also governance. Governance may arise out of the agreement by members to abide by the rules or standards established by the directory body of an organisation such as an industry association. An attempt may be made to impose governance, such as an environmental NGO making a declaration of good corporate practices and haranguing companies to follow suit. A third party that has some direct authority over the relationship between two other parties may also impose governance. This is the case with universities and their industrial liaison offices (ILO). ILOs are the entities within a university with the responsibility for industrial liaison and partnerships, contractual work, technology transfer, IP protection, and licensing and business development.

Industrial liaison programs have existed almost as long as university–industry interaction. The predecessors of today's ILOs are the Division of Industrial Cooperation established at MIT in 1920 and the Wisconsin Alumni Research Foundation set-up by the University of Wisconsin in 1925 (Bowie 1994). The MIT program was established to secure research funding and to draw research closer to the needs of industry. The Wisconsin program was established to administer Professor Steenbock's patent for Vitamin D food irradiation and subsequently the office dealt with industry funding, disclosure of inventions, and patenting. MIT further developed its ILO in 1948, but this type of organisation was not widely adopted until the 1980s. The impetus for this popularisation was the double crises of stagnation in federal funding for university research and the Japanese challenge to American industrial prowess. These crises prompted calls to bring industry and universities together more effectively for the purpose of national industrial competitiveness. Coincidentally, in the fields of biotechnology and computers, the close connections between research and commercial application gave faculty members and universities the opportunity to profit (Bower 1992: 50). The Bayh-Dole Act of 1980, giving US universities ownership of intellectual property created with federal funding, provided universities with a greater incentive to commercialise their research (Bowie 1994: 19). Regional interests also began to push for technology transfer to promote their competitiveness (Feller 1992). Universities, industry, and government began to search for more efficient means to effect technology transfer. In the USA, federal and state governments initiated several experiments in university–industry collaboration, innovative examples being the NSF's University–Industry Cooperative Research Centers Program and Pennsylvania's Ben Franklin Partnerships. The USA, however, was not alone; Germany and Japan responded by developing their own forms of cooperation (Bowie 1994: 39–42), as did the UK, Canada, Australia, and other countries. ILOs in various forms evolved as a consequence of universities devising organisational means to deal with the new demands being placed on them, not only by society, but also by the entrepreneurial aspirations of faculty members and their own attempts to capture the economic benefits of research (Feller 1990: 345). Indeed, most university–industry cooperative research centers in the USA have been instigated by universities and faculty members in particular (Cohen *et al.* 1994: 1).

From the outset, it was realised that bridging the private and public sectors requires coming to terms with conflicting interests and building new units and governance systems. This process of multilateral organisation formation is depicted in Figure 3.2. The university's primary role is the dissemination of information through education and research, and especially in its research role, information should be freely disseminated as a public good. However, many see this role compromised by the role of technology transfer and industrial collaboration. Indeed, throughout the evolution of university–industry collaboration, at least in the USA, the conflict of interest debate has raged and the primary governance role of the university has been striking a balance between its traditional role and the new role of technology transfer. Essentially, this conflict pits the university and faculty members' roles as disseminators of information against the desire of industry to obtain proprietary control over information and the right to profit from it. Problems can arise from a company's desire to delay publication of research, the imposition of confidentiality in academic relations, and the withholding of professor-initiated innovations from the market if those are detrimental to the company's position. There is also concern about faculty members losing their ability to act impartially and 'venture forth from the ivory tower to contribute in a wide variety of expert, policy, advisory, or litigious settings' (Feller 1990: 346). A change in research emphasis from basic to applied, and the conversion of public funds to private uses and private gain are other potential problems that could arise when a faculty member consults or becomes an entrepreneur, or when a university re-orientates its efforts to work with business. Nor is the university an impartial party. The university has to consider the goals of technology transfer alongside the necessity of maintaining its reputation and its interests in securing infrastructure and research funding.

UNIVERSITY

information dissemination
&
technology transfer

FACULTY

academic
career
vs.
commercial
incentives

COMPANIES

spread R&D
risk
vs.
proprietary
control

INDUSTRIAL LIAISON UNITS

Institution Building

faculty–firm
&
centers/consortia
&
firm incubation

Relational Governance

contractual
&
monetary
&
informal

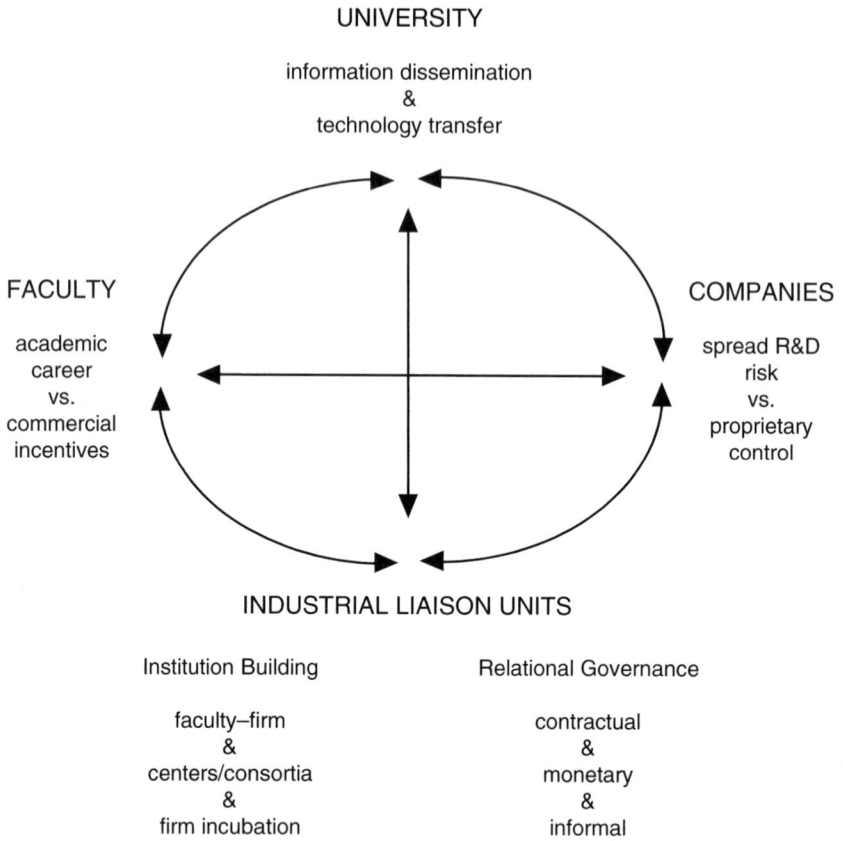

Figure 3.2 Process of industrial liaison unit building

These conflicts of interest have not yet been resolved; indeed worries about
'secrecy in science' are increasing. A university governs these interactions by
allowing or forbidding its employees to use their time and university facilities
for collaboration. Many universities, for example, allow their faculty members
one day a week for consulting or pay them on a ten-month basis, tacitly
encouraging them to find industrial employment or contract income for the
remaining two months. Similarly, a university may allow its facilities and
support staff to be used for industrial or private purposes. Universities differ
widely in how they balance these conflicts of interest. Some remain reticent and
reactive with regard to university–industry interactions. They maintain direct
governance, keeping university–industry interactions within the context of
academic relations by limiting any faculty–industry interactions to grants and
research contracts or by maintaining tight control over consulting. Other
universities are proactive in establishing liaison units. These units will be
granted various levels of funding, personnel, and autonomy depending on the
objectives of the institution. Some are granted independent legal status to

handle patents and other commercial relations. The meta-governance of the university directly influences the operation of the liaison units, but the liaison office can influence the creation of regulations by citing the needs for mechanisms of technology transfer.

The aim of this system of institution building is the governance of conflicts of interest between faculty members and the companies that fund them or their research. The conflicts of interest are felt directly by faculty members. Career advancement depends on research, teaching, and service to the community, and rarely is industrial collaboration explicitly recognised. Yet they are increasingly exhorted to interact with industry. The motivations for interaction include pressure to obtain research funding, pressure to interact with companies, desire to stay abreast of industry developments, and so on. These factors could be incorporated into career decisions, but direct commercial opportunities are more difficult to reconcile as they keep a faculty member from spending time on academic issues and reduce the desire to disclose information. However, despite this conflict of interest, a recent initiative of some technology transfer programs is to foster academic entrepreneurs.

Obtaining personnel, training personnel, access to facilities, prestige, and public relations are some of the reasons why business uses universities. Companies, however, are primarily interested in working with universities to spread the risk of engaging in research. Mounting research costs versus rapid technological change and the shortening of product life make cooperation with universities a cost-effective competitive strategy (Carboni 1992: xii). Multinational corporations use universities to inform their own R&D, whereas smaller companies expect cooperation to result in rapid commercialisation of products. Access to information is gained, however, with the purpose of obtaining an exclusive advantage, as companies would like to obtain proprietary control over new information. This control can be exerted through patents, but much of the information a company may derive from collaboration may be unpatentable. Companies are concerned about controlling these trade secrets derived through collaboration and also about the information they must divulge to university members. Thus corporate control conflicts with university and faculty members' interests in preserving the free dissemination of information. These conflicts challenge the governance of the university and the management of companies.

The lower part of Figure 3.2 depicts the main categories of industrial liaison units and governance used to promote technology transfer. The primary interface is direct interaction between faculty members and businesses, and includes specific grants, directed research, collaboration between company and university personnel, and consulting. These types are characterised by the various degrees to which a company can control the objectives of research. Contract research, for example, allows companies to sponsor specific research projects and to define what deliverables will be forthcoming. On the next level of interaction are affiliate programs, in which companies pay an annual fee to be kept abreast of occurrences in a department or university and which may lead them to work closer with a faculty member. Cooperative centers identify areas where a university has a core of expertise and facilities, such as electro-optics or biotechnology. Most universities will have many of these centers and they are the fastest developing forms of collaboration. In 1990, Cohen *et al.* (1994: 1) surveyed 1,056 centers on 200 US campuses and found that they accounted for almost 70 percent of industry support of academic science and engineering R&D. Centers may draw companies into direct relationships with university employees or they may be funded and operated as consortia. In consortia, several firms pool money to support research projects, and members have access to faculty members and students, tours through lab facilities, regular publications and newsletters, notification of developments, faculty visits, scientist/engineer residency and informal linkages. For a minimal investment they receive access to information which results not only from the pooling of corporate funds, but also from government and university funding. Another category of interaction is the use of the university's resources to support firm incubation and entrepreneurial activities, primarily for faculty members, students and staff, but also for businesses external to the university who are collaborating with it or using a university-developed technology. Support may include the provision of facilities, space on campus, venture capital, management, and the filing of patents and selling of licenses. Usually, a technology transfer office manages these activities.

The governance of these activities is crucial to their success, and the primary method of governance is contractual. The faculty member's contract with the university controls not only consulting, but also rights to patents and revenues from licenses. The key to collaboration is the research contract between the parties. From the company's perspective it identifies the principal investigator, what facilities and staff will be made available and the deliverables. The contract also can stipulate that information divulged to the faculty remains confidential and that the university must notify the company when filing for a patent or publishing results. Usually the right of the university to publish is assumed unless specific conditions are written into the contract. Universities may also assume intellectual property rights, although conditions of first right of use, limitations on other companies' use, or decreased licensing fees can be written into the contract. Liability can be a contentious issue between the parties; the university and faculty members wish to absolve themselves of any consequences of the use of their technology, while companies believe university researchers should stand by their findings.

Consortia governance is more complex as corporate members may have the right to advisory board membership or to attend review meetings of research projects. Consortia benefits (e.g. at MIT Media Lab) have to balance the interests of the members by, for example, specifying a set period of time for access to member rights, non-exclusive license to technologies, and geographical and negotiated time limits on the right to use licenses. Directed research can also occur within a consortium. Access, however, is graduated depending on the amount of funding provided; greater proprietary rights are granted to larger sponsors. Protection of faculty, staff, and student intellectual property rights must still be maintained in a consortium.

All sides in these agreements are concerned about money. The company wishes to minimise costs, while the university needs funding to pay for the direct and indirect costs of the research. Researchers want to obtain sufficient funding for the collaborative research and assistance for their primary research goals. Researchers may also be interested in deriving financial benefit from directed research or entrepreneurial effort. The university and the liaison directors are responsible for defining these parameters, and they vary widely. Investment may be provided to start-up firms by a university and the university's level of commitment can have a crucial impact on the development of these businesses.

Informal governance varies not only in universities but also in departments. Each department will have its own cultural attitudes towards the balance that must be struck between academic performance, industrial collaboration, and commercial activities. Departmental pressure not to interact with industry, or indeed to interact, will have an impact on the success of the more formal university or liaison governance. Building trust and ensuring that both sides of an agreement adhere to the spirit of collaboration are also important. Companies want to ensure that confidentiality is respected, while researchers do not want payments or future research to be compromised by pressure against publishing.

The modelling of ILOs described in this section is based primarily on the US experience. It is doubtful that it represents the complete range of liaison activities or, more importantly, the crucial separation between the interests of the academic world and business. In Japan, for example, this separation has until recently been mandatory, whereas in Germany university–industry interaction is obligatory (Bower 1992: 111 and 118). The US experience is, however, useful in understanding Hong Kong's attempt at fostering university–industry collaboration because Hong Kong is adopting the US model of university–industry interaction. Like the US government's initiatives in the Bayh-Dole Act, the Government–University–Industry round table, the NSF's engineering research centers, etc., the Hong Kong government is creating the institutional initiatives and funding opportunities to encourage university–industry interaction. Many of the Hong Kong government initiatives were described in the first section. These initiatives will be of no avail, however, if the internal governance described in this section is ineffective. The final section describes the efforts of HKUST to mediate a mission that incorporates an important role for technology transfer, while encouraging a high level of basic research output.

HKUST's industrial liaison office: balancing external and internal governance

The establishment of HKUST in 1987 was the Hong Kong government's first major step forward in improving its science and technology base and in promoting university–industry interaction. This action not only committed substantial resources to the teaching and research of science and technology, but also signalled the importance of those resources for Hong Kong's future. From the planning stage, the university was designed to cooperate with industry and to further Hong Kong's economic development. The dual missions of HKUST were given legal force in the ordinance which created the university, and which states that the objectives of the university are:

1 to advance learning and knowledge through teaching and research, particularly
   (a) in science, technology, engineering, management, and business studies; and
   (b) at the postgraduate level; and
2 to assist in the economic and social development of Hong Kong.

In the University Ordinance, the university is also given freedom of powers to achieve these ends, including the ability to enter into any contract; provide, for profit or otherwise, advisory, consultancy, research, and other related services; enter into a partnership or any other form of joint venture; acquire, hold, and dispose of interests in other corporate bodies and form or take part in forming corporate bodies. All of the above have become input ILO tools. Thus HKUST fundamentally differs from other universities in the clarity with which it has adopted its economic development role. Yet it is similar to the many that have adopted this role on an *ad hoc* or implicit basis.

Compliance with this ordinance is not measured by governmental review, but by the governance of the University Council. The Council composition makes a positive inclination to university–industry interaction likely, as its eighteen members must include at least ten from commerce and industry in Hong Kong. From the outset, a leading industrialist in Hong Kong chaired this Council and it has created policies favouring university–industry interaction. Not least of its actions was selecting a President who, through the executive and administration, could realise the substance of the ordinance and the policies which followed from it. The President, for example, although a physicist, lists technology transfer among his academic qualifications. Yet, despite a governing council and executive disposed to university–industry interaction, the academic ambition of the HKUST is to become a world-class research university. This ambition is proselytised by the President himself and reverberates through the culture of the institution. We will examine how HKUST mediates these potentially conflicting roles.

Academic governance

The academic mission predominates at HKUST. The goal is to replicate a US-style research university. The academic statement in the HKUST ordinance lends itself to this purpose by emphasising postgraduate teaching and research. Eminent scholars, primarily expatriate Chinese, were recruited to lead the executive, schools, divisions, and departments. Junior faculty members were recruited from leading research universities around the world (primarily the English-speaking world). The university boasts a 100 percent PhD-holding faculty, with two-thirds receiving their degrees from top research schools such as Simon Fraser and Surrey. The research focus is made possible by a modest teaching load of three one semester courses per year for the management and social sciences faculty and two semester courses for the physical sciences and engineering. The focus on research has enabled HKUST faculties to produce, per capita, a greater number of publications than the other Hong Kong universities.

The primary importance of the academic mission is upheld by the selection process in recruitment and the review and tenure procedures for remaining or advancing at the university. Interaction with industry is not given much weight. The appointment of Assistant Professors, in particular, is made predominantly taking research abilities into account and departmental selection committees maintain this perspective. Criteria increase when moving up the ranks to Associate Professor and professorial appointments, and industry interaction may then be considered as contribution to service. Deans, the Vice President-Academic, and the President have a greater input into these selections and thus there may be a likelihood of them being aligned to the dual roles of the university.

Most faculty members pass through two three-year contract periods in which they are expected to display their research, teaching, and service potential. Research is the first concern in these evaluations because there is a direct connection between the evaluation of the university, the department, and the individual. That is, individual performance reflects directly on the performance of department and university and can be counted as such. Teaching performance is evaluated rigorously, but is not deemed as objective a measure as publications, and the subjective nature of teaching evaluation does not readily couple individual performance to department performance. University, professional and public service are a third evaluation measure, and at HKUST it may encompass links with business and industry. Service, however, is not given the same weighting as research or teaching and, as there are several ways to fulfill the service requirement, there is no specific stipulation that faculty members contribute to industry. As with appointments, the governance of these criteria takes place at the departmental committee level for lower-ranking faculty, and as one rises higher, the university administration has more input.

After two contracts one must be promoted to substantiation (tenure) or leave the university. Substantiation decisions are made using the same evaluative criteria as contract review, but there is also an automatic review of all candidates by the VP-Academic and of professorial candidates by the President. However, although higher administrative levels can reverse positive endorsements of candidates, positive decisions cannot be forced upon the committees (by due process at any rate). Thus in all cases of appointment, contract review and substantiation, departmental committees exercise great influence over what standards are expected of all candidates and reflect the academic culture of that department. Driven by international academic standards, these committees remain overwhelmingly focused on research and teaching standards. At the higher levels external reviewers enforce global standards. It must be concluded that, to date, industrial interaction has had little influence on any career advancement.

Some concern for university–industry interaction can be brought into academic administration at the senate level. This body's primary function is to preserve the integrity of and enhance the quality of teaching and research. It can, however, also give guidelines to schools, divisions and departments regarding review and tenure standards. The senate is composed primarily of representatives of all the academic departments, but through the membership of the VP-R&D, the Director of the Applied Technology Center, and the Technology Transfer Center, consideration of university–industry interaction can be raised in academic decision-making. However, in comparison to the strength of research and teaching influence in the academic review process, this influence is unlikely to be a fruitful mechanism for promoting university–industry interaction. The ILO at HKUST has developed a set of institutions to reduce this resistance and fulfill the economic role of the university.

The Industrial Liaison Organisation

The university's executives and governors, in seeking to fulfill the directives of the ordinance, established a separate research and development administrative infrastructure designed to promote partnerships and technology transfer to the private sector. Although the R&D branch is organisationally distinct from the academic branch of the university, it has the dual role of facilitating academic research while promoting the application and commercialisation of advanced technical knowledge in Hong Kong and its region. The R&D branch is a direct output of the external governance discussed in the first section, but it is has also been a contributor to external governance. Members of the university and the R&D branch in particular have lent their voices to the shaping of government and industry opinion. The rationale which guides the organisational development of the R&D branch and their advice to the government is that it is necessary to overcome the gap between basic research and the ability of local companies to adapt the research to their commercial needs. Figure 3.3 schematises this gap and compares it with a closer linkage between university research and industrial capabilities in developed countries. The R&D branch is a substantive innovation in university–industry liaison. ILOs in other universities are organisation discrete units. At HKUST, a variety of these units has been placed under the governance of the R&D branch to enhance the interactions and feedback between them and to link basic research (where appropriate) to commercialisation and business development in a seamless manner.

Over the past decade, the R&D branch has been developing a multilateral organisation designed to bridge the unique issues of the university–industry-

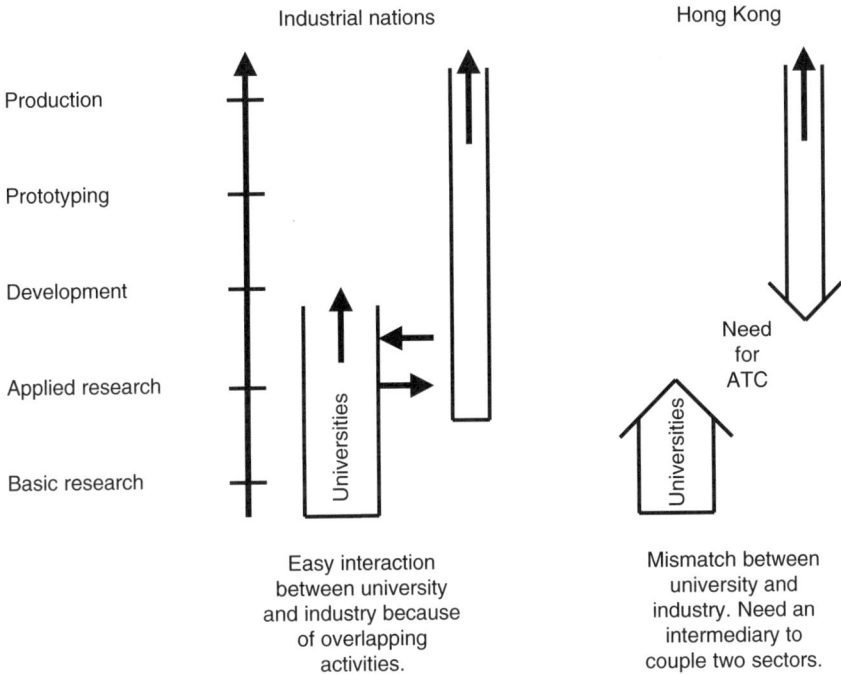

Figure 3.3 The need for an applied technology center at HKUST

government relationship in Hong Kong. Figure 3.4 illustrates the various components of this organisation and their relationships. The arrow labelled R&D spectrum illustrates in a simplistic fashion what the R&D branch intends to achieve for Hong Kong, i.e. to promote the developmental process of converting basic research into outcomes capable of commercialisation and wealth generation for society. These outcomes can be useful for the upgrading of existing businesses or the creation of new ventures. The area labelled branch responsibilities schematises the changing roles that academics and businesses perform as an innovation moves through the developmental process and concomitantly the changing roles of the Academic Affairs (AA) Branch of university administration and the R&D branch. The R&D branch sees its role as picking up where AA and faculty members' expertise, interests and conventional roles decrease. To compensate for this decreasing activity, the R&D branch has created new operational units and is seeking to take advantage of expanded funding sources. The intention is to promote technology transfer through interaction with existing business, to provide technology to create new businesses, and to give faculty members and students the opportunity to start up their own businesses.

As schematised in Figure 3.4, the various operational divisions within the R&D branch are designed to take faculty members' efforts step-by-step to commercial fruition. Their various roles are listed below:

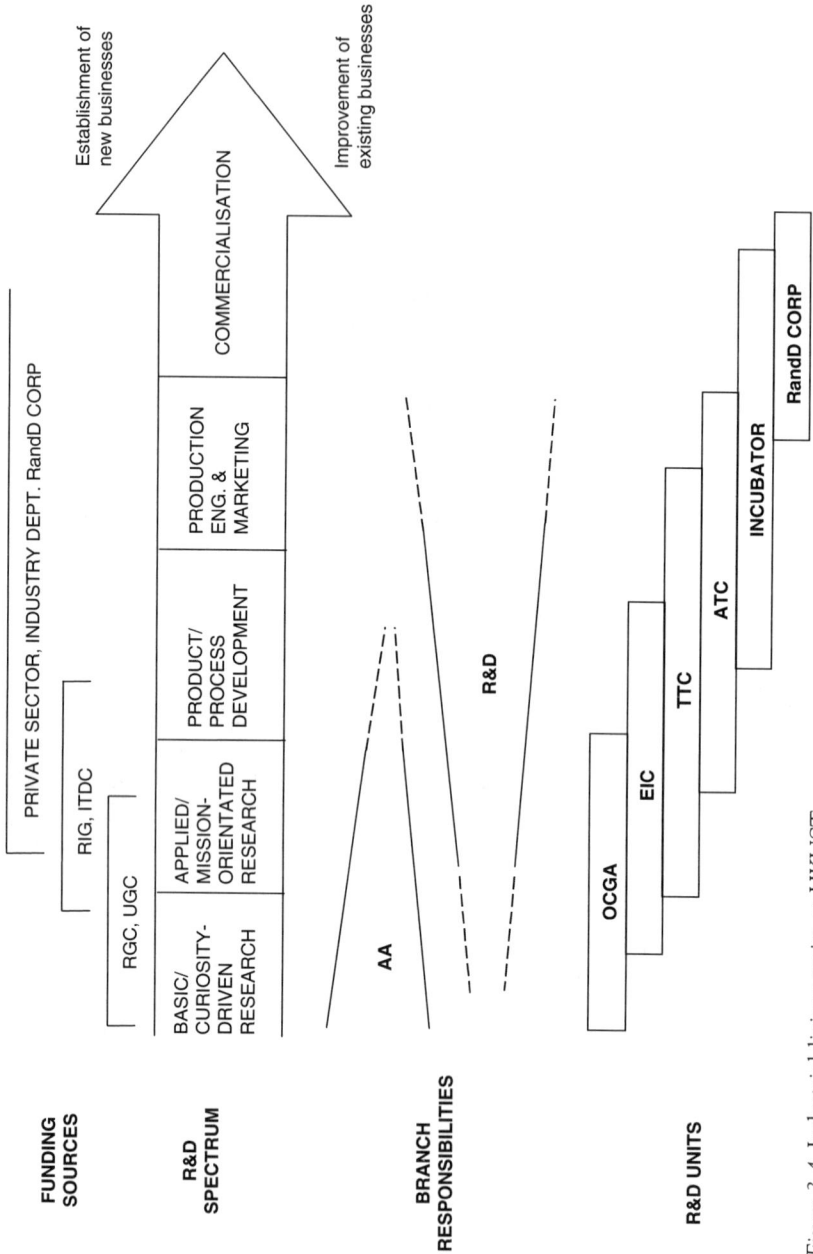

Figure 3.4 Industrial liaison units at HKUST

- *Office of Contract and Grant Administration* (OCGA) identifies and promotes sources of research funding; assists faculty members in preparing proposals; administers research funding; maintains research information databases; reports on research activities; and assists faculty members in preparing project reports and publications.
- *Engineering Industrial Consortium* (EIC) forms technology units in partnership with industries; organises professional development and training programs; builds collaborative research activities; and promotes technology diffusion.
- *Technology Transfer Center* (TTC) provides industrial liaison; helps establish industrial contacts and cooperation; assists faculty members in developing proposals requiring industrial collaboration; assists technology development activities; and facilitates technology transfer.
- *Applied Technology Center* (ATC) bridges the gap between applied research in academic labs and technology implementation by industry, by establishing technology development projects, demonstration programs, pilot plant operations, and pre-commercialisation activities.
- *RandD Corporation* assesses, protects, markets, and commercialises intellectual property as the separate business arm of the university; manages a venture capital fund; assists the establishment and growth of technology start-up companies and manages the Entrepreneurship Center (the university's incubation facility).
- *Research Institutes and Centers* are not illustrated in Figure 3.4, but are of critical importance in identifying areas of research strength to the business community. There are about twenty-five institutes and centers, including the Consumer Media Lab, Center for Display Research; Electronic Packaging Laboratory; and the Internet Business Consortium. Their roles are the promotion of interdisciplinary research collaboration; the establishment of a critical mass of research capabilities in defined areas of priority; the provision of an umbrella organisation to attract funding; the enhancement of the visibility of research efforts in particular areas; and the enhancement of interactions with industry. Many of these centers have Cooperative Research Center funding from RGC.

Full-time Directors administer each unit within the R&D branch. To ensure the effectiveness and growth of the university's technology transfer capabilities, much of their effort is expended on managing the interface between the university and the various funding agencies. These funding sources are indicated at the top of Figure 3.4 and, like the operational units, include a range of funding, from government-supported basic research to funds for commercialisation.

- *University Grants Committee* (UGC) is the governing body which provides general and recurrent funding to the tertiary sector in Hong Kong and entertains new proposals for changes in programs and infrastructure. It designates research funding to the RGC.

- *Research Grants Council* (RGC) determines how government funds for research by universities should be allocated. Currently, about 18 percent of funds are directly allocated to universities to support small-scale research projects. About 80 percent are allocated in response to competitive bids received from the universities, with as merit perceived by international peer review processes being the primary determinant. The balance is centrally allocated according to collaborative bids between two or more universities for major research facilities/equipment.
- *Research Infrastructure Grant* (RIG) is a component (approximately 2 percent) of the UGC grant that universities are expected to allocate internally to enhance research infrastructure or develop new initiatives.
- *Private Sector, Industry Department, and RandD Corporation* are funding entities whose monies are directly linked to the advancement of industrial R&D and the commercialisation of research. Businesses do this through contract research, consortia, consulting, licensing, etc. The Industry Department ties its grants to some matching funds from businesses. The RandD Corporation, in addition to handling the contractual interface between business and faculty members, supports faculty entrepreneurial efforts by searching for venture capital or supplying this from its own limited resources.

This organisational framework incorporates many technology transfer mechanisms discussed earlier, such as research contracts, industrial consortia, internships, incubators, and university supply of venture capital to faculty and student entrepreneurs. More than most research universities, however, HKUST devotes managerial expertise and capital not only to converting basic research into applied research, but also to propelling it further into commercialisation. The Applied Technology Center (ATC) plays an important role in bridging the gap between research and local industry that was schematised in Figure 3.2. These different liaison units were all innovations in Hong Kong, and although developed at university discretion they have often depended on coordination and resources from the external governance system. This is true for monies which faculty members have acquired through Industrial Support Fund matching grants, for the RGC money which supports the basic research infrastructure of the university, and for the initial start-up incubator facilities which were operated with the HKITCC.

University–industry governance

The units described above should not be considered simply as focusing, record keeping, or public relations administrative units. To complete the connection between external and internal policy promoting university–industry interaction, ILO governance must provide incentives for faculty members to cooperate with industry while not diverting their attention too far from their academic activities. This balance can be seen in the 'Principles governing commercial pursuits' (Figure 3.5), where the university encourages faculty commercial activities and industry interaction as a legitimate means of economic development, yet insists that a faculty retains open disclosure of research and does not compromise the research interests of students. There is also an admonition against the use of public funds for private means.

This balancing act is taken up again in terms of the contractual governance of faculty–industry collaboration. Here the focus is on retaining the freedom to publish. The university follows the standard practice of preserving the right to disseminate information, but can accept 90 days advance warning of publication or presentation and usually maintains the right to publish six months after completion of a research contract. It also protects its rights to intellectual property arising from research and protects itself from liability claims. The same conditions apply to consortia affiliates who have direct technical projects. An advisory board that includes industrialists, government officers, and HKUST academics governs the consortium to ensure the interests of all parties are voiced.

Although service to industry may be encouraged and academic freedom may be preserved, incentives to work with industry remain the key. HKUST has adopted the one-day a week allowance for consulting work, and compensation can be retained in full by a faculty member. This contrasts with other Hong Kong universities which levy a minimum of 15 percent on consulting

---

HKUST recognises its obligation to contribute to the economic and social development of Hong Kong and the region, and therefore encourages its faculty members to engage in appropriate activities that might lead to early commercialisation and/or implementation of the results of scholarly investigations.

(a) Appropriate and limited participation of faculty members in outside professional and commercial activities can make important direct and indirect contributions to the strength, vitality, and relevance of the university.
(b) Faculty members must regard HKUST as their primary place of employment and professional pursuit. Therefore, their commitment of time and intellectual energies must be primarily to the teaching, research, and service programs of the institution.
(c) As a public institution, HKUST has an obligation to ensure that publicly funded resources will not be used inappropriately for the private gain of any of its staff or for any private enterprise.
(d) In keeping with standards maintained in leading research universities throughout the world, HKUST maintains an open academic environment, in which all university research is governed by the tradition of free exchange of ideas and timely dissemination of research results. Proprietary investigations are permitted in certain situations when working with industry.
(e) Students must be able to choose research topics for educational reasons without being unduly influenced by the need to pursue investigations of direct interest to a particular firm, or by faculty members wishing to accrue personal financial gain from student-performed research work.
(f) Faculty members are expected to disclose their involvement in commercial pursuits.

Figure 3.5 HKUST principles governing commercial pursuits

irrespective of the use of university facilities. This levy is calculated to be proportional to the perceived conflict with the faculty member's teaching and research duties. In those cases where university facilities are used, the levy on consulting is more than 35 percent. All the other universities require prior permission to engage in consulting, whereas HKUST requires this only for extensive consulting commitments (in some universities Presidential permission is required). The university does, however, require a biannual disclosure of faculty consultation activities to ensure compliance with its guidelines.

HKUST distinguishes itself from the other Hong Kong tertiary institutions in its promotion of and liberal stance towards commercialisation and monetary rewards to faculty members. HKPU and HKBU do not allow faculty members to form companies and, while this is allowed at CUHK, it is not encouraged, nor will the university become involved as a shareholder. HKU has no experience in this activity, but will now consider faculty entrepreneurs as long as the university can take a majority ownership. CityU also requires majority ownership and tax incomes from ventures. These universities claim stakes and returns in these companies as payments for allowing the faculty to become involved in a venture. In contrast, HKUST takes a small minority stake of 3 percent to demonstrate its support of the spin-off firm. At the same time, it provides a package of services, including incubation facilities, to assist in the development of a company accepted into its new Entrepreneurship Program. An important aspect of HKUST's governance is that the RandD Corporation is incorporated as a separate legal entity. It takes over management of commercialisation of projects once they have been initiated through the ATC or the TTC, and manages the Venture Capital Fund and the Entrepreneur Program.

Formal governance would be ineffective if it were not accepted within the culture of departments. The liaison offices have to put a considerable effort into the promotion of industrial collaboration, in a research university in which most faculty members are young and concerned about increasing their publication records for career advancement. It does so through seminars, announcement of collaborative activities, and through departmental heads. To date, they have managed to involve 20 percent of faculty in TTC activities. On the other hand, faculty members occasionally need to be reminded to stay within the consultation time limit guidelines.

Conclusion: HKUST's role as a catalyst for university–industry interaction in Hong Kong

Considering its age, and by international comparison, HKUST's success in industrial collaboration is impressive. It has, for example, greater contract turnover than Britain's long-established University of Manchester Institute of Science and Technology (UMIST). Table 3.1 quantifies some of the results. With sixty-five patent applications filed and fourteen granted to date, HKUST is by far the leading patent producer in Hong Kong – private or public. As with

Table 3.1 Intellectual property protection, technology transfer and diffusion

No. of patents granted (to June 99)	13 (USA) 1 (UK)
No. of patents filed (to June 99) – in addition to those granted	41 (USA) 8 (European) 2 (others)
No. of technology licenses granted	30
No. of technology companies created	(Type I)[a] 2 (Type II)[b] 13
Total contract research with industry (to June 1999)	HK $72 million
No. of Master's students graduated	1533
No. of PhD students graduated	104

Notes
a A spin-off company that has acquired HKUST technology and is now operationally independent of the university.
b A start-up company established by HKUST staff or students (past or present) and which has been or is being incubated at HKUST.

any public or private institution, patents are no guarantee of successful commercialisation – indeed, there are few successes and they may be a financial burden. HKUST realises this, but commits funds to the patent effort to raise awareness of the importance of innovation in Hong Kong. However, in the future it will need to take a more business-like approach to the potential costs and benefits. The significant number of technology licenses granted (thirty) provides a direct indication of the market success of the university's innovations. The incubator facilities opened in 1998 have already assisted in the growth of thirteen (type II) start-up firms. Although there are only two formal (type I) spin-offs, one is Hong Kong's most successful university initiated business. The firm was Hong Kong's first Internet service provider and, when sold, returned the university more than ten fold on its investment.

Contract research is another direct indication of interaction with business. The total value of contracts, from 1994 to June 1999 stood at HK $72 million (US $9.3 million). Of that total, HK $30 million was contracted in 1998/99 alone, up from HK $4 million in 1994/95. Contract numbers have also grown from 40 in 1994/95 to 140 in 1997/98. While contract numbers fell to a hundred in 1998/99, their value rose. This reflects a shift from a high number of testing jobs to more research-oriented tasks with greater monetary and intellectual value to the university. The university is also fulfilling its more basic role of education and the supply of highly qualified scientists and engineers. In its six years of existence, 1533 Master's and 104 PhD students have graduated from HKUST. By 1998 the graduate student population had grown to 1,437, of which 247 were enrolled in Science, 590 in Engineering, 406 in Business and Management, 49 in Humanities and Social Science, and 100 in Joint Degree Programs.

Perhaps more important than HKUST's own direct impact on industry is the influence it has had on Hong Kong's other universities' relations with industry. The other universities, and especially those with strong science and technology faculties, are (at varying rates) transforming their attitudes towards industrial collaboration and technology transfer from negative or passive to proactive. In interviews, industrial liaison administrators of all universities in Hong Kong agreed that HKUST led the way in promoting university–industry collaboration and that HKUST had developed the most sophisticated means to achieve it. HKU and CityU are using the RandD Corporation as a model. CityU has also established a consortium. However, the other universities have yet to devote full-time employees to these university–industry interfacial issues. City University in particular is reaching out to industry, offering everything from access to faculty and scientific facilities to its swimming pool. HKUST's ILO, if not a model for their own collaboration initiatives, at least helped to make them aware of the reasons for undertaking industrial collaboration and the mechanisms to do so.

The attitude shift by the other universities is, of course, not mere mimicry of HKUST. It reflects their responsiveness to the increasing expectations of government, business, and the public for them to play an active role in Hong Kong's technological upgrading. Witnessing some funding become tied to obtaining matching funds from industry, and the need to find industrial money to fuel development as Hong Kong's rapid expansion of tertiary funding is affected by consolidation and cutbacks lend some force to the shift in attitudes. They are no doubt responding to the external governance signals that government and industry are putting out. Yet it is doubtful whether this external governance could achieve its desired effect if it were not for institutional competition and the resulting shift in resource allocation.

This chapter has argued that internal governance of university–industry interactions, occurring through an Industrial Liaison Office, is the key to understanding the governance of university–industry interaction in a region. External policy and funding can encourage university–industry interaction. From the executive, through both the industry and education departments, the Hong Kong government has tried to draw industry and universities closer together. These policies, however, may have little impact because of the autonomy of the universities and especially of the faculty members. To accomplish external governance goals it is necessary to focus on the internal governance of the university. That governance structure mediates not only the conflicts of interest between university and firms, but also between faculty members and firms, and perhaps most importantly between the academic and commercial incentives of faculty. This mediation will remain a tense balancing of academic and commercialisation goals. As an example, the ILO (specifically called the R&D branch) at HKUST has been developed as a complex multilateral organisation designed to promote technology transfer and catalyse the technological upgrading of industry in Hong Kong. However, together with other ILOs it should not be regarded simply as supplementary administrative units. There is little likelihood of governmental policies promoting university–industry interaction succeeding without an ILO or equivalent to resolve the internal tensions within a university.

References

ASAIHL *General Conference and Seminar on University–Industry Partnership in Economic Development*, (1997) Singapore: National University of Singapore.

Berger, S. and Lester, R. K. (1997) *Made by Hong Kong*, Hong Kong: Oxford University Press.

Bower, D. J. (1992) *Company and Campus Partnership*, London: Routledge.

Bowie, N. E. (1994) *University-Business Partnerships and Assessment*, Boston: Rowman and Littlefield Publishers.

Brett, A. M., Gibson, D. and Smilor, R. (1991) *University Spin-off Companies*, Savage, MD: Rowan and Littlefield.

Business and Professionals Federation Study Group (1999) *Hong Kong as a Regional R&D Center*, Hong Kong: Business and Professionals Federation Study Group.

Carboni, R. A. (1992) *Planning and Managing Industry-University Research Collaborations*, Westport, CT: Quorum.

Cohen, W., Florida, R. and Goe, W. R. (1994) *University-Industry Research Centers in the United States*, Pittsburgh: Carnegie Mellon University.

Cooke, P. (1996) 'Reinventing the Region: Firms, Clusters, and Networks in Economic Development', in P. W. Daniels and W. F. Lever (eds) *The Global Economy in Transition*, Harlow: Longman.

Chief Executive's Commission on Innovation and Technology (1998) *Chief Executive's Commission on Innovation and Technology*, Report, Hong Kong: The Commission, 1998–1999.

Dickson, D. (1988) 'European Companies Form Research Network to forge University-industry Links', *The Chronicle of Higher Education* 36, 17: 1.

Eng, I. (1997) 'Flexible Production in Late Industrialization: The Case of Hong Kong', *Economic Geography* 73: 26–43.

Enright, M. J., Scott, E. E. and Dodwell, D. (1997) *The Hong Kong Advantage*, Hong Kong: Oxford University Press.

Etzkowitz, H. (1994) 'Technology Centers and Industrial Policy', *Science and Public Policy* 21, 2: 79–87.

Feller, I. (1990) 'Universities as Engines of R&D-based Economic Growth: They Think They Can', *Research Policy* 19: 335–348.

Feller, I. (1992) 'American State Governments as Models for National Science Policy', *Journal of Policy Analysis and Management* 11: 288–309.

Fortier, P. (1999) *Public Investments in University Research: Reaping the Benefits*, Ottawa: Industry Canada.

French, N. J. 'Higher Education in Hong Kong: Recent Developments and Future Challenges', paper presented at the World Congress on Higher Education in the Asia-Pacific Region, Manila, Philippines 23–25 June 1997, Copyright © 1997 by: http://www.ugc.edu.hk/english/documents/ papers/nfheinhk.html

Goldstein, H. (1991) 'Growth Center vs. Endogenous Development Strategies: The Case of Research Parks', in E. M. Bergman, G. Maier and F. Tödtling (eds) *Regions Reconsidered*, London: Mansell.

Government-University-Industry Research Roundtable (1991). Industrial Perspectives on Innovation and Interactions with Universities. Washington, D.C.: Government-University-Industry Roundtable.

Hudson, R. (1994) 'Institutional Change, Cultural Transformation, and Economic Regeneration: Myths and Realities from Europe's Old Industrial Areas', in A. Amin and N. J. Thrift (eds) *Globalization, Institutions, and Regional Development in Europe*, Oxford: Oxford University Press.

Lundvall, B.-Å. (1992) *National Systems of Innovation*, London: Pinter Publishers.

Massey, D., Quintasp, P. and Wield, D. (1992) *High Tech Fantasies: Science Parks in Society, Science and Space*, London: Routledge.

Nijkamp, P. and Mouwen, A. (1987) 'Knowledge Centers, Information Diffusion and Regional Development', in J. Brotchie, P. Hall and P. Newton (eds) *The Spatial Impact of Technological Change*, London: Croom Helm.

Peters, K. (1988) 'Universities and Local Economic Development', in H.-J. Ewers and J. Allesch (eds) *Innovation and Regional Development*, Berlin: Walter de Gruyter.

Porter, M. (1990) *The Competitive Advantage of Nations*, New York: Free Press.

Rosenberg, N. and Nelson, R. (1994) 'American Universities and Technical Advance in Industry', *Research Policy* 23: 323–348.

Saxenian, A. (1994) *Regional Advantage: Culture and Competition in Silicon Valley and Route 128*, Cambridge, MA: Harvard University Press.

Storper, M. (1997) *The Regional World*, New York: Guilford.

Tzang, A. (1997) 'Creating a Close University-industry Partnership in Economic Development: The Need, the Challenge and the Approach', *ASAIHL General Conference and Seminar on University-Industry Partnership in Economic Development: 6–8 December 1996, National University of Singapore*, Singapore: National University of Singapore, 61–66.

Web addresses

www.hksciencepark.com/hksp/university/unimun.html
www.info.gov.hk/tib/roles/index_main.htm

4 Knowledge still travels on foot

An educationalist's perspective on regional development[1]

Marc Vermeulen

Introduction

Higher education is supposed to play an important role in the economic development of countries and regions. On a national level, central governments invest enormous amounts of money in education. From a regional perspective, the choice of location of large educational facilities is often substantiated by regional economic development-type arguments. For instance, in the Netherlands, the establishment of universities in Twente and Maastricht was supposed to provide a new impulse to the regional development of areas of industrial decline (textiles in the Twente area and mining in Limburg). However, the empirical evidence supporting this role is not very strong (Florax 1992; Vermeulen 1996). In this chapter, I will explore the role played by (higher) education in regional development and put education on the regional development 'map' again.

An important starting point for studying the role education can play in economic development was given by Gary Becker (1964), who is seen as the founder of the Human Capital theory. He determined that continuing economic growth could no longer be explained by the simple combination of the production factors of capital and labour (and land), but that, above all, the *qualitative* development of labour played an important role in economic development. The argument is as follows: as people become better educated, their marginal productivity increases. This increase in productivity means that employers are prepared to pay more for qualified labour than for unqualified labour, whereby it is also profitable to invest in education.

However, it is not always clear what the causal sequence is (do we have economic growth through good education or vice versa?), nor is the role that education plays in the increase of work productivity at the level of the individual, the region and the country always the same. In this chapter, I will first explore what roles are attributed to vocational education in the literature with regard to regional development. Then I will briefly look at the findings of an empirical study (Vermeulen, 1996) into these roles. As this study shows, the contribution of educational institutions to economic development in the recent past has been relatively modest. I will seek to redefine the contribution made by educational institutions to regional economic development. In order to do this, I will first look more closely at a number of changes in the economic process and in the labour market in order to explore how institutions of vocational education can adapt to these changes, and to examine how important geographical proximity is with regard to this.

Economic functions of education: what are we talking about and what mainly fits in with secondary vocational education?

As in many other countries, the Netherlands have a binary system of higher education, with both universities and colleges (HBO, higher professional education). Universities provide academic training and combine education and research. The colleges provide training for executive functions in trade and industry, in public authorities, education, health care, and the welfare service. Participation in both types of education has grown very strongly in the recent years. At the same time, a very radical form of upscaling has taken place in colleges, through which very large institutions have been established. There is also a positive striving towards regional distribution, so that one or more large educational institutions are based in every region. As in many other countries, there is a strong debate on the relation between universities and colleges. So far, both types of education are strictly separated in the Dutch system, although, following the declarations of Sorbonne and Bologna, closer relations will be established soon, perhaps even introducing the Anglo-Saxon system of bachelor's and master's degrees. I will come back to this discussion by the end of this chapter. First, I will explore the economic functions education may have.

Functions of education

The role which education can play in economic development, and the relevant spatial scales of education, are shown in Figure 4.1. The literature puts forward a number of economic functions which education can fulfil, mentioning clear differences in terms of the type of education and the scale.

Qualifications

The relationship between education and the economy is most strongly expressed in the qualifications of employees. The economic significance of this function of (higher) education is under serious discussion. It is said that the Dutch population is massively over-educated. From studies, it appears that the educational level of the population has risen much faster than the educational requirements of the workplace. This produces diploma inflation: over-educated people perform work which is below their level. Whether this is inefficient by definition is not certain, however: people are perhaps better able to do their work and think of all kinds of innovations. With regard to higher education, the

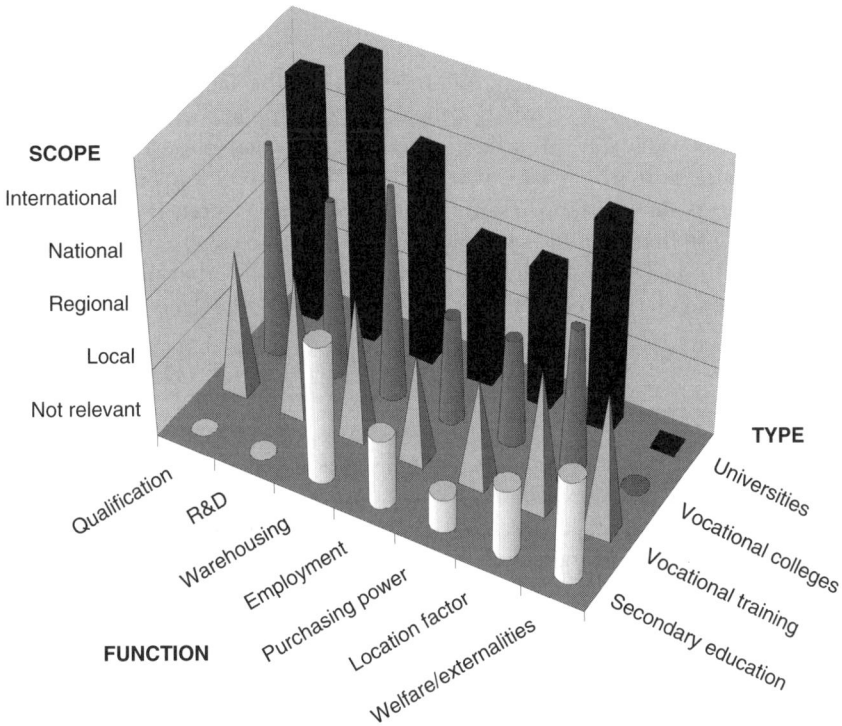

Figure 4.1 Functions and regional scope of education
Source: Vermeulen (1996).

fact that graduates are very mobile plays a role in *regional* analysis in all cases: students are often educated outside the region in which they live and after graduating move in a wide area.

Research & development

For the development of new technologies and products, a regional-scale level is not relevant: to a large degree this occurs on a global level. Apart from the fact that large R&D institutes bring job opportunities with them into a region, the knowledge generated here is directed at much broader markets than the regional ones. It is important that small and medium-sized companies, in particular, have easy access to new knowledge and that a regional infrastructure is in place for this. In my opinion, the role of education in an innovation-orientated region largely lies in the area of discovering and transferring new knowledge rather than producing it. Here too, the importance of good communications comes to the fore.

Warehouse for the labour market

Education often serves as a kind of storeroom for the labour market. If the number of vacancies is low, young people often postpone their entry into the labour market and stay at school. As a result, they also improve their qualifications, with which they can obtain a better position on the labour market. This is shown in American (Walters 1984) and Dutch (Herweijer and Blank 1987) studies. It is easy to imagine that this process also plays a part in regions with a high rate of unemployment. It also implies that in periods of a tight labour market, education has to compete with the labour market for students.

Internal job opportunities effect

Educational and schooling institutions themselves are employers; their presence in a region creates job opportunities. This mainly applies, of course, to the large educational institutions. In so far as such institutions 'draw' students, this also generates additional buying power in the region.

Location factor

The presence of a good educational infrastructure can make it attractive for a company to establish itself in a region, not so much because the company knows it is then assured of adequately qualified employees, but more from the point of view of attractive location features. In particular, companies which can choose their location and which have difficulty in obtaining adequately qualified personnel should let the general level of facilities in a region play a greater part in the choice of establishment location. If there are too few good facilities for the education of their children, this will deter new employees from moving to an area. In particular, personnel who are highly educated, and who generally attach great importance to the education of their children, will look critically at this.

External factors

In addition to the aforementioned effects, education often has a positive effect on all manner of social aspects in a region (social, cultural, health care, etc.). In turn, these effects often have, in an indirect way, positive repercussions on the socio-economic development of a region. However, the effects are often difficult to identify and are difficult to quantify (Haveman and Wolfe 1984).

In Figure 4.1, the spatial range of the functions is clearly different for the various types of education. For higher education, the qualifying function certainly has a distinct national range: after graduating, students disperse again and thus leave the region. In this way, the availability of higher education can even have a negative effect and lead to a brain drain. At the same time, the

R&D function is a much more regionally-based function for higher professional education.

The functional range of educational institutions is wider when it comes to higher forms of education. This also forms the basis of educational planning: primary schools have to be planned on a local level, while universities cover an (inter)national area. In formulating a course of action influencing the infrastructure of educational provision (increase in scale, distribution), a start must be made by naming and weighing up the functions of education in order, on the basis of this, to choose a particular level of distribution. It must be pointed out that the balance of functions is not constant. Depending, for example, on the situation in the labour market or the economic development of the region, different functions should be emphasised.

Empirical study

From an empirical study into the role education played in the economic development of the Netherlands in the 1980s (Vermeulen 1996), it appears that it did not play a very prominent role. In spite of the existence of considerable differences in participation in higher education between regions, it appears that there have not been any consequences for regional economic development: the regions characterised by a relatively high level of participation in education or by the presence of a strong higher education infrastructure did not 'perform' noticeably better than regions where this was not the case. The role of education as a supplier of qualified school-leavers for regional economic development was presumably restricted because of problems in the allocation of work (both due to displacement and mobility). Also, as far as the spreading of innovative knowledge is concerned, although there was talk of a number of new initiatives, these were not translated into a clear strengthening of the economic potential of regions. In contrast to what may have been expected, the study did not find a strong link between the regional unemployment rate and participation in regular education for the Netherlands. This, therefore, does not throw any clear light on the unemployment problem in the regions where there is a high level of participation in education.

Why the learning region?

From the last paragraph it appears that, although on the basis of a study of the literature a number of ways can be derived in which education can contribute to the economic development of a region, the empirical evidence shows that this contribution is actually very limited, or at least was very limited in the Netherlands in the 1980s. The question thus arises as to whether the role of education (educational institutions) is in need of redefinition: should we not look at other things or set another sort of process in motion in order to give education a role again in the economic development of regions? In the remainder of this chapter this question will be considered. Little or no empirical evidence is available, but I give a normative interpretation of the role which education *should have to* play. For this, I use the concept of the *learning region*, which I support by looking at learning regions from points of view: first, changes in the production processes and, then the associated changed orientation to regions.

Changes in production and labour supply

From mass production to tailor-made production

For the first point in the discussion of changing economic development, I refer to Bengtson (1991: Figure 4.2). In Figure 4.2, the vertical axis shows the development in the industrial manner of production. In the first instance, the product being manufactured determines, to a significant extent, what demand on the market can look like. In the early days of industrial production, only a very limited variety could be produced, but on a large scale. Henry Ford said: 'I can build all colours of T-FORDs, as long as they are black.' Profit is made mainly in economies of scale. In a following phase, more differentiation is applied to products: in the motor industry the variety of types and finishes is so great that a car brochure is as thick as a novel. Variation is a competitive force, but this means that much smaller series are produced and that planning requires much more care. In the last phase, only tailor-made work is supplied: the difference between production and service is then blurred. Series production is hardly carried out any

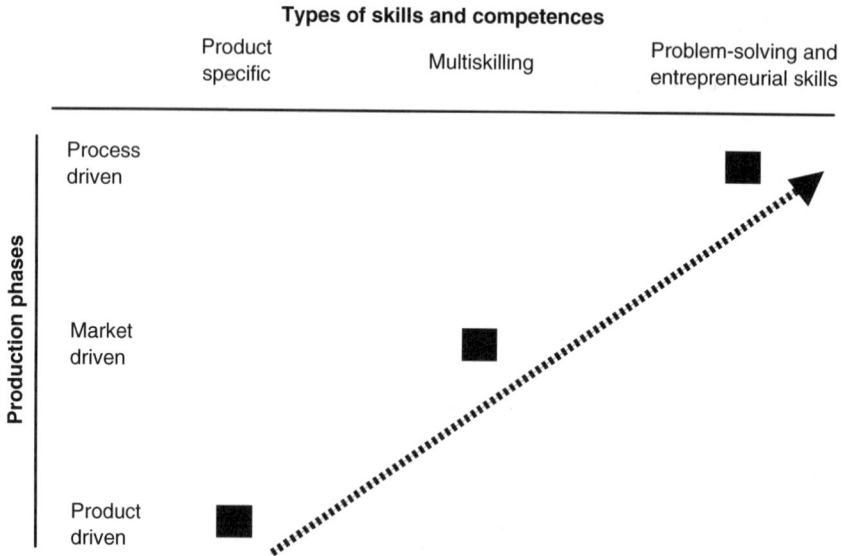

Types of skills and competences

| Product specific | Multiskilling | Problem-solving and entrepreneurial skills |

Figure 4.2 Interaction between factors behind education and training investment by enterprises and types of skills and competences needed

Source: Bengtson (1991).

longer, the amount of knowledge used in the manufacture of each product has increased enormously, and the production process operates on a project basis.

What does this mean for the qualifications required by employees? Initially, it was a matter of simple skill: a limited number of actions were carried out very frequently. The actions were easily visible and could be learned outside the production process. The control mechanism was that of monitoring the employees while work was in progress (supervisors). In the following phase, much more competence is required of the employees: they must have a broad range of skills which they must be able to use well, independently and alternately. Control takes place via planning and final inspection. In the final stage, problem-solving skills, communication skills (adapting to the wishes of the customer), and entrepreneurial skills are important. The most important steering mechanism is responsibility and trust (account management).

In my opinion, Dutch industry is slowly moving from the second phase to the third and this has consequences for the qualifications required of employees. In particular, there will be a shift from technical instrumental qualifications to social and normative qualifications such as loyalty, commitment punctuality, creativity, etc.

Efficiency and capital intensity

In most Western economies, the labour costs are relatively high. This certainly applies to a country like the Netherlands. If production is still to be carried out profitably under such circumstances, this must be done very efficiently, with high added value and with as little input of (costly) labour as possible. This means that the production processes are becoming very capital-intensive: there is investment in high-tech equipment which makes it possible to manufacture high-quality products quickly with low labour costs. A good example of this is the introduction of CNC (Computer Numeric Controlled) equipment.

Increasing attention is being paid to the internal efficiency of industrial processes. There is also talk of a radical change which is strongly linked to the necessity of being able to work quickly and flexibly. The essence of this development is that throughput times are shortened and 'intensification' occurs in the production chains. Just-in-time production management is necessary, as, on the one hand, stockpiling carries the risk of 'perishing' (being technologically out of date owing to rapidly changing trends in consumer demands), and, on the other, an unnecessarily large amount of capital is invested in the stocks. Among other things, the intensification in production processes is resulting in geographical proximity becoming important: semi-finished products must be quickly available and there must be great trust between the producer and supplier, as the risks of damage become greater through intensification. For example, Toyota obliges its suppliers to be based within a limited radius around the main factory. The Dutch motor works Nedcar (where Volvos are built) is very concerned about its competitive position as there is insufficient space in its immediate vicinity for supplier companies to establish themselves.

Both the use of capital-intensive equipment and the rigid organisation of production processes involve the taking of many risks: if something goes wrong, very expensive machines come to a standstill (and do not, therefore, make money), and a serious disruption takes place in the entire chain. Employers are very anxious to avoid such disruptions and therefore require highly qualified and reliable employees. The use of all manner of new production techniques means that professional requirements are changing radically: high-tech machines are taking over a significant proportion of specific (manual) skills, but, at the same time, good monitoring of the process and rapid reaction in the event of faults occurring are becoming more and more important. This is the responsibility of the process operator: when everything is going well, work is pretty dull and monotonous, but in the event of a fault occurring, stress level rises, management thoroughness, and integral knowledge are extremely important.

This integration of production processes occurs not only in the production of materials but also in the production of services, such as banking, insurances, Internet services, etc. All kinds of commercial services show a higher degree of integration and complexity as a result of having to deal with a steadily more individualistic and critical public (demand) and information technology. Also in these types of activities, minor actions or failures can have enormous consequences.

High-tech and ICT

Another, and very radical, change in production processes involves the introduction of information technology, a technological revolution which in many ways is without equal. Through the use of information and communications technology, new ideas are spread very quickly and a 'global village' is created. Enough has been said about this subject elsewhere. It is enough here to confirm the process of 'acceleration' of developments, whereby I think that the half-life of knowledge is sharply decreasing. This has a number of very far-reaching consequences for education, which I will only touch on briefly here:

1   The system in which people are initially educated and then work is in need of revision: it is important to come to a permanent alternation between learning and working.
2   In learning, the emphasis will shift from the transfer of knowledge to learning how to acquire knowledge by oneself. A number of educational changes also point in this direction (including self-regulated and independent learning).
3   The process of curriculum development is probably too slow to keep up with the rapid changes in the outside world. In the Netherlands, it takes about three to four years before changes in professional practice penetrate into the actual teaching practice of vocational education (think of the time required to translate the changes in production into educational objectives, to produce teaching materials, and to teach lecturers new methods). This

fact is illustrated by the fact that ICT is hardly used in education and that students often do much more with computers at home (often with more modern computers) than at school.

4 Rapid developments in computer technology have the effect that schools can hardly keep up and have to provide education on out-of-date equipment. Public finance is not sufficient (and will probably never be) to write off existing equipment and acquire new equipment at an accelerating rate.

Ageing of the labour supply

As a final development, I point to the ageing of the labour supply, in which two prominent processes are apparent: ageing and reduction of social security.[2] These developments mean that more attention will be paid to the in-service training of incumbent employees on a larger scale, as this is an important source of knowledge renewal. The traditional way of renewing knowledge through the inflow of school-leavers (with or without the simultaneous outflow of older employees) is steadily becoming less practicable. It can be expected that, because of this, a shift will take place away from teaching young people to teaching older people, and, as a result of this, educational arrangements will also change (consider, for example, how, where, and when learning will take place).

The developments described above also mean that companies will have to take much more responsibility for the knowledge renewal of their incumbent personnel. They must ensure that new knowledge regularly comes into the company and they must show themselves to be more active in this: the emphasis is changing from educational institutions which *come to bring knowledge* (supply-controlled), to companies which *come to fetch knowledge* (demand-controlled). Particularly for the small and medium-sized business sector, this can only work if the knowledge can be obtained nearby, without too many obstacles. Knowledge thresholds must be as low as possible for this sector. Specifically, colleges of higher professional education can play an important role in this: they are often the natural partner of the small and medium-sized business sector as they supply many graduates for SMEs and have good access to these companies through work placements and cooperation projects. Such colleges could develop good relations with universities and thus become an important partner in knowledge networks and provide a gateway for SMEs to those networks.

A change in the type of knowledge available is also seen, which is of crucial importance for good functioning in work organisations. This involves knowledge about processes, about integral insight, about the value of reacting rapidly to new situations, and about attitudes such as punctuality, quality awareness, etc. These new forms of knowledge are informal and difficult to codify ('tacit', see Nonaka and Takeuchi 1995): this kind of knowledge cannot easily be set down in books or on websites. It will not be possible to pass on this knowledge using the traditional teaching methods, which are very text-orientated. Personal contact will, however, remain very important. In education, knowledge and skills will be imparted largely via non-intentional teaching processes (the hidden curriculum) such as, for example, teachers acting as role models. It is clear that educational processes of this type are more difficult to plan and to influence.

It is also a question whether education can be of decisive importance in the acquisition of certain attitudes. Socio-psychological studies show that the basis for a number of important attitudes is formed at a young age, and that the possibilities of changing these attitudes at a later stage are limited (Kohlberg 1964). Education certainly is not the only influence on attitudes. The domestic environment and the peer group, in particular, play a very important role in this. Education, however, can reveal the attitudes of students and thus play an important role in the selection of new employees perhaps rather than actually forming or influencing those attitudes.

Regional integration

On the basis of the developments in production organisation and in the labour market set out above, the role played by educational institutions in regions can be re-established. As stated earlier, this is more about describing an ideal typical situation than about proven practice. However, this does not detract from the fact that there is not enough experimentation with regard to the reformulating of the position of educational institutions within regions.[3] Configurations that existed in the past, however, may prove to be valuable sources of inspiration.

The management of trust

Through chain integration in production processes, another kind of knowledge and experience is becoming relevant for companies. The introduction of innovations in production processes requires much more care nowadays than ever before (there is less time, the risks of damage are greater, and it must succeed the first time). Knowledge of and experience in implementation processes and organisational questions are, therefore, becoming more important. This is typically knowledge which can only be acquired on the shop floor. In this way, two-way traffic is created in the knowledge system: companies can easily 'fetch' knowledge from knowledge institutions (in this case, colleges of higher professional education and universities) in their area, and they can easily provide feedback about implementation problems. This information is then returned to the R&D establishments via the educational institutions. Physical proximity in a network of educational institutions also increases the trust therein. Recently, a great deal of attention has been paid to the role of 'trust' in the economic process (see Fukuyama 1995). As communication, coordination and interaction are becoming more important, the traditional planning and control cycle is making room for the management of trust (see also Van der Meer 1993; Stinchcombe 1979). People must be able to count on each other and trust each other. This explains the paradoxical development that companies are operating ever more internationally and at the same time orientating themselves more strongly to their local environment (act global, think local; glocalisation).

The increased risks of damage in production processes through greater capital intensity and chain integration mean that employers, when recruiting new personnel, find that having the right attitude is more important than having the required knowledge. In this way, the role of education will also drastically change and the emphasis will shift from the qualification function (the training of specialists) to the selection function. We now see examples of companies trying to establish contacts with young people before they finish their education and to build up a relationship with them (so-called campus recruitment). In this way, companies find out in good time 'what they are dealing with'. By entering into early relationships with students and their schools, they are bringing the selection aspect to the fore and making more accurate assessments of the new employees. Such forms of scouting can be seen in higher education as well as in the lower forms of vocational education, for example, in the recruitment of students for training in apprenticeships.

Just-in-time and low threshold

From the point of view of knowledge intensification of production processes, it seems obvious also to include knowledge suppliers in regional networks of companies working together. Knowledge, too, must be available just in time. If we pursue the production metaphor, knowledge can also no longer be 'stockpiled', as it, too, must be flexibly applied and the requirements for knowledge change rapidly.

This is not relevant for the new, high-tech knowledge required by large companies: such knowledge is available world-wide and large companies obtain their knowledge from all over the world. In regional networks, however, gateways must be developed so that smaller companies can find their way in a low-threshold manner.

The supply of knowledge which must be available in regional networks relates to the following:

1 the (permanent) education of employees of large companies in the region, involving the application of innovations coming from elsewhere in the world;
2 the renewing of knowledge for smaller and medium-sized suppliers in the regional cluster.

The just-in-time character of knowledge requirements makes low-threshold knowledge, available on request, necessary. The integration of working and learning springs from the process nature of production. This means that a bottom-up process of knowledge generation also occurs; in the literature, this is described as double-loop learning. In accordance with this, innovations can come about which, via the low-threshold knowledge centre, find their way 'up' in knowledge chains (as occurs, for example, in horticulture, see Grooters and Nieuwenhuis 1996). The advantage of a low-threshold knowledge centre, which is located in the immediate surroundings of companies, is that there is less mistrust with regard to innovations: the placement students, placement supervisors, and consultants are always present in the companies and form a natural bridge to the knowledge centre. In this way, innovative knowledge 'moves' up in the company.

A good low-threshold knowledge structure can also contribute to the *anchoring* of powerful and high-quality companies in a region. Hilpert (1991) shows that regional development is often not a direct result of a specific course of action, but is connected with the (co-incidental) presence of one or more powerful companies. Regional policy makes a contribution through making the best possible use of this advantage and ensuring that the companies in question are well established in their area. Thinking in terms of chain integration, this means that large promising companies should be strongly integrated into regional networks. Large companies with good prospects purchase their new knowledge throughout the world and, via their integration in the network, give a knowledge impulse to all (therefore also the smaller) companies in that network. Radical technological changes should, therefore, 'echo through' the entire chain, including the parts (e.g. small and medium-sized businesses) which have far fewer relationships with well-known knowledge institutions. They should acquire the new technologies partly through relationships with the (large/central) supplier/customer. However, numerous adaptations of the production process ('small' innovations), which are derived from the far-reaching innovations, should take place. In connection with increasing capital intensity and the associated risks of damage, the importance of such 'small' innovations is increasing. Colleges of higher professional education can play an important role, particularly in the *distribution of knowledge* on major innovations and the translation of this knowledge to practice after its distribution into the small and medium-sized business sector. It is well known that this type of education leads to a good relationship between colleges and this type of company (e.g. guest lecturers, work placements, graduates). Colleges in close cooperation with universities may become partners in 'small' R&D projects of both larger firms and SMEs. Universities, obviously, will remain relevant partners for the R&D activities of larger companies.

Colleges of higher professional education and universities themselves scarcely influence, in a direct way, the location decisions of large, promising companies (Vermeulen 1996). Rather, the presence of such large companies should be seen as a fact and an attempt should be made to optimise the location features of such companies (Van der Laan and Mevissen 1994). Thus, Philips was very much involved in establishing the Eindhoven Technical University. Colleges can certainly contribute to large companies feeling 'at ease' in a regional network and deriving maximum benefit from the presence of such large companies.

Older employees

If we place this development against the background of an ageing employee population, another argument arises which makes the spatial embedding of educational institutions important: 'incumbent' employees will require a completely different kind of education provision than traditional students: they will want to call on their lecturers at different times (in the evenings, shift-work, etc.), often pursue short-term education with specific reference to working practice.[4] Incumbent employees are also less mobile in terms of education (as, among other things, their private circumstances make this more difficult) and the education should be closer to home and available in a flexible and low-threshold manner (education on demand).[5]

Opportunities and threats for colleges and universities

Above, it has been constantly emphasised that low-threshold accessibility to new knowledge is of the utmost importance: in achieving this, colleges and universities can adopt a position in a regional network and contribute to the economic development. Now we focus on a number of opportunities and threats. We also look at the question of what is necessary in order to give the educational institutions a stronger orientation to the outside world and what may possibly stand in their way.

Opportunities

Ideally, the different business processes should reinforce each other in order to implement the mission of an organisation. Within higher education, organisations providing regular education and courses can, in this respect, be of great importance to each other (education content, transfer of knowledge, company network, course participation, labour market information, etc.). The question is, however, to what extent both business processes are actually aware of their mutual value, whether they can supplement each other, and/or are able to develop the necessary instruments for this.

Through their work placements, the colleges of higher professional education and universities have an extensive network of contacts with companies. This gives them the opportunity to access business life in a fairly natural way. College students, through placements, are more practically orientated than their colleagues from universities, which is particularly important in connection with the specific application of new knowledge in SME settings. It is, of course, also important that colleges and universities themselves invest adequately in new knowledge and thereby further develop their inter-relationships.

As many higher education institutes have a strong multi-sectoral composition, they are able to offer a multi-disciplinary approach. Innovation problems often have a multi-disciplinary nature (e.g. the combination of technology and ergonomics) and, to support such processes, a multi-disciplinary assessment is then also important. This, of course, requires that the internal organisation of educational institutions make such a multi-disciplinary approach possible.

The Dutch education system is gradually directing its attention to charting the results of its efforts. The output of organisations is becoming ever more important, not only for financing, but also in connection with choosing future students. This development matches the increased emphasis on *quality assurance*, which also plays a role in trade and industry. This consideration arises from the fact that education, increasingly, is looked upon as something that must 'work in one go', whereby the development and making visible of quality standards are becoming more and more important. Thinking in terms of quality in education is strongly dictated by reviews. Whether more attention should be paid to quality assurance in education, as is already the case in ISO procedures, has yet to be decided.

Another important development in connection with this is the so-called *investors in people* concept: as part of their quality policy, institutions show how they invest in personnel. This is, of course, mainly applicable in the sectors where personnel form a key factor in production, such as in-service provision and education.

Finally, through concentration and upscaling, providers of education are given the opportunity to communicate more professionally with the outside world (PR, centres for contact activities, etc.) and thus to become more recognisable players in the network.

The above-mentioned opportunities are also important for the ordinary educational processes of the colleges and universities. They offer the possibility of linking the curriculum much more to what happens in practice. In addition, there are various internal and external interactions which benefit education. A stronger anchoring of higher education in the surrounding area makes it easier to find work placements, to exchange personnel, and to make use of, for example, expensive equipment or laboratories. All in all, such anchoring fits in excellently with the idea that, both in the production and the distribution of new knowledge there is more talk of interaction than of the previous one-way traffic. Furthermore, these opportunities make it possible for learning in professional education to take place in 'real-life' situations more often.

Threats

In higher education, there are also a number of developments which could pose a threat to the role which the colleges and universities can play in (regional) economic development. The aforementioned concentration and increase in scale also embody the risk of bureaucratisation, which can work against attempts to increase the accessibility of the institutions. It is clear that the creation of bureaucratisation must be avoided: having to wait a long time for . . ., or going through a large number of procedures in order to . . ., does not in any way fit in with aspects of rapidly reacting to changes and being enterprising.

There is some concern in this regard: many colleges of higher professional education and universities are still under great pressure to bring their own internal processes up to date and are, therefore, still very inwardly orientated. Also, through a combination of ageing staff and budgetary problems, it is often difficult to achieve an optimum complement of personnel, which gives rise to two risks. Either the 'wrong' people are employed to carry out contract activities in the outside world and rapidly lose their position, or the 'good' people are used, but at the cost of the primary process (results being at odds with the aforementioned combining of different business processes).

A second threat to the role colleges and universities can play in (regional) economic development is specifically linked to the personnel of colleges of professional higher education: how up to date is the knowledge of those who are teaching in the institution? Education has to do with a considerable ageing problem and there is often no mention of a strategic course of education within the institution. It is, thus, entirely conceivable that personnel in colleges of higher professional education have out-of-date knowledge and have not been active in the business world for a long time. In this way, they are presumably not good contacts for companies.

A final problem, specifically in the academic institutes, is that the output of scientific work is almost exclusively measured by publications in international scientific journals. Practical work and applied R&D are almost overlooked, which does not motivate the scientist to put much energy in this type of activity.

Conclusion: costs, effectiveness, and the system of higher education

A redefinition of the role of colleges of higher professional education and universities in regional economic development presumably requires a considerable financial injection: institutions often have an ageing infrastructure and they have problems in finding and keeping good lecturers. This latter problem will become even greater now that the shortage on the labour market is increasing and companies and educational institutions are competing more with each other. In the Netherlands, it now seems to be very difficult to find, for example, technical specialists as lecturers. It is very difficult for universities to find new trainee research assistants (AIOs) and PhD students, which endangers both the research capacity and the new influx of staff. Part of the reason for this is that companies can pay higher salaries as they are producing more capital intensively. In this way, work productivity is increasing in trade and industry, and wages can also increase. In the public sector, and certainly also in education, it is not certain that a comparable increase in labour productivity is also possible. Two situations, both problematic, may occur:

- either the growth in salaries in education will continue to fall (even further) behind the growth in salaries in trade and industry, whereby it will become even more difficult to find personnel;

- or the salaries of personnel in education will keep pace, but then education will become relatively more expensive as there will be no simultaneous increase in work productivity. The latter is known in economics as Baumol's law of the costs, the disease of the public sector.

A recent study in the Netherlands into the effectiveness of market-oriented activities carried out by public institutions (IOO/EIM 1998) shows that higher education is not very effective in carrying out contract research and contract education.[6] This lack of effectiveness is, among other things, the result of poorly developed cost-awareness and cross-subsidising of unprofitable activities. A discussion of the effectiveness of market-orientated activities is, in itself, extremely important, but the question here is whether strict business economic interests should prevail. In any event, it seems sensible to take any warning of possible inefficiency seriously.

Only recently did the Dutch Minister of Education permit universities and colleges to enter into mergers (Ministerie van OCenW 1999). This might be seen as a first step in harmonising the Dutch system with the Anglo-Saxon bachelor–master's system, following the declaration of the EU Ministers of Education in Bologna. Discussion on taking these steps will probably be long and heated as there are a lot of vested interests. The merger of universities with colleges of professional training is faced with mixed feelings, especially in the academic world. Academic freedom is feared to be at risk; fundamental research could become more difficult and preparation for a profession is not intended to be the main objective for universities, where general academic training should prevail. However, in my opinion, from the developments described before, both higher education and (regional) economic development may have a lot to gain from closer cooperation or even a merger between universities and professional colleges.

In the production of knowledge, a larger input from the professional field fits in very well with the concept of Mode 2 knowledge production of Gibbons (1994). He shows that very innovative and creative new forms of knowledge production may follow bottom-up patterns, as problems faced in day-to-day reality pose new and fundamental questions. Putting those questions on the research agenda not only implies a new method of research (e.g. the reflexive practitioner) and of knowledge organisation, but also a more open attitude of higher education, responsive to practical issues. Colleges probably have more of a tradition and have better networks in this than universities. Because of their experience in practical work, they are better equipped to develop close relations with companies, including SMEs. A merger between academic institutes and colleges might take the form of back office – front office cooperation, in which the back office (academic institute) provides innovative impulses in the work of the front office (college). On the other hand, the front office may provide the back office with relevant questions to put on the research agenda, but may also provide many casuistries for the research and development function of the university. This will provide a system in which small but increasingly important inventions will receive more attention.

Interaction, process interventions, communicative skills, and an open eye on shop floor processes will be very important characteristics of future professionals. The development of such skills is much more of a tradition in college education than in many universities, in which education is still very cognitive and theoretical. For the *reflexive practitioner*, a combination between universities (reflection) and colleges (practice) is 'a match made in heaven'.

In my opinion, we are now in a position of putting higher education back on the map of regional development and high-tech economic activities. A great deal of reconsideration of the role of higher education, to start at the level of the institutes, will be necessary. However, if universities and colleges miss this chance, the discussion on the costs and benefits of higher education will (continue to) dominate the debate on higher education, a discussion that might rapidly erode public and political support for higher education.

Notes

1 This chapter was written for the conference 'Higher Processional Education in the Knowledge Infrastructure' (The Hague, 24th June 1998). The Ministry of Education, Culture and Science made a subsidy available for it. I wish to thank the personnel of the higher professional education department of the Ministry for their critical notes on the draft article. An earlier version of this chapter was published in the *Journal of Higher Professional Education Management* (THEMA, no. 1, 1999).
2 Both processes are closely connected. On the one hand, ageing will drive up the costs of pensions and thereby place the total (public) social security budget under pressure. In other words, a broadening of the economic basis should be aimed at by repressing forms of inactivity. It is expected that the labour supply will decrease (in some sectors this is clearly visible) so that is will be necessary to increase the general level of participation by the population.
3 A good example of this is the International Partnership Network (IPN), which provides a platform for exchanging practical examples of how the relationship between schools and companies can be intensified.
4 This is linked to the necessity of paying more attention to the transfer of skills which are learned in working practice. Estimates indicate that the return on vocational education is only approximately 20 per cent and that this low return is largely connected with the poor transfer.
5 One of the reasons why distance education is increasing is that it can be more easily adapted to one's personal agenda. For a number of skills, distance learning cannot offer a real solution (e.g. developing attitudes, acting in 'real-life' situations, etc.). What the influence of virtual education will be in this regard is as yet unknown.
6 According to researchers, there is a prosperity loss of 3 to 6 billion guilders. The market sector should be able to tackle the same activities much more cost-effectively through greater efficiency.

References

Becker, G. (1964) *Human Capital*, Chicago: The University of Chicago Press.
Bengtson, J. (1991) 'Human Resources Development', *Futures* 23, 10: 1085–1106.

Florax, R. (1992) *The University: A Regional Booster?*, Aldershot: Avebury.

Fukuyama, F. (1995) *Trust: The Social Virtue and the Creation of Prosperity*, New York: The Free Press.

Gibbons, M. *et al.*, (1994) *The New Production of Knowledge*, London: Sage.

Grooters, W. and Nieuwenhuis, L. (1996) *Beroepsonderwijs in de Kennisinfrastructuur*, Amsterdam: Max Goote Kenniscentrum voor BE.

Haveman, R. and Wolfe, B. (1984) 'Schooling and Economic Well-Being: The Role of Nonmarket Effects', *The Journal of Human Resources* XIX/3: 377–407.

Herweijer, L. and Blank, J. (1987) 'Onderwijsexpansie en Werkloosheid', *Tijdschrift voor Arbeidsvraagstukken* 3/3: 80–86.

Hilpert, U. (1991) 'The Optimization of Political Approaches to Innovation: Some Comparative Conclusions on Trends for Regionalization', in U. Hilpert (ed.) *Regional Innovation and Decentralization*, London: Routledge, pp. 291–302.

IOO/EIM (1998) *Economische Effecten van Concurrentie Verstoring door Organizaties met Exclusieve Marktrechten*, Den Haag: Ministerie van EZ.

Kohlberg, L. (1964) 'Development of Moral Character and Moral Ideology', in M. Hoffman and L. Hoffman (eds) *Review of Child Development Research* vol. 1, New York: Sage.

Laan, L. van der and Mevissen, J. (1994) 'Ondernemingen en Regionale Arbeidsmarkten', in L. Van der Laan and M. Vermeulen (eds) *Onderwijs en Arbeidsmarkt in de Regio*, Delft: Eburon, pp. 103–116.

Meer, P. van der (1993) *Verdringing op de Nederlandse Arbeidsmarkt*, Groningen: Interuniversity Center for Social Science Theory and Methodology.

Ministerie van OCenW (1999) *Hoger Onderwijs en Onderzoek Plan, HOOP 2000*, Zoetermeer: Ministerie van OCenW.

Nonaka, S. and Takeuchi, N. (1995) *The Knowledge-Creating Company*, Oxford: Oxford University Press.

Stinchcombe, A. (1979) 'Social Mobility in Industrial Labour Markets', *Acta Sociologica* 22, 3: 217–245.

Vermeulen, M. (1996) *Human Capital in the Hinterland*, Tilburg: Tilburg University Press.

Walters, P. (1984) 'Occupational and Labor Market Effects on Secondary and Postsecondary Educational Expansion in the United States: 1922 to 1979', *American Sociological Review* 49: 659–671.

5 University knowledge transfer through social and professional embeddedness

A case study

Peter Vaessen and Martin van der Velde

Introduction

Despite the fact that scientists, administrators, politicians, and virtually everybody else is convinced of the untold importance of a university for the well-being of local and regional communities, there is a feeling that we do not understand the machinery of this spillover process and that we are not able to control it. University environment research faces two major conceptual problems. First, notwithstanding the attempts made to master the subject, too many pieces of the puzzle are still missing. It could even be stated that the heart of the matter has been passed over. Second, university environment research lacks a comprehensive conceptual framework in which different research attempts can be linked to each other. Hence, the research field is characterised by a morbid growth of fragmented, idiosyncratic approaches and research issues, which does not allow any overview to be obtained. This is understandable, however, because of the complexity of the subject. After a brief historic sketch of several ideas in university impact research and recent developments in this field, we try here to present a more encompassing conceptual model in order to link different research lines. The empirical part of our contribution focuses on the most recent ideas, conceptualising the university as the pivot of a learning region. The case study of the University of Nijmegen (the Netherlands) is used to analyse different kinds of direct connections between the university staff and the local and regional environment.

Theoretical context

A brief historic overview of university environment research

The presumed role a university plays in local and regional development processes has changed continuously over time. This is partly due to the changing appreciation of the 'blessings' of the university for the host region or city. Originally, the idea existed that the significance of the university for its environment could be found mainly in the fact that it provided the city or region with a certain prestige. This could boost the labour market with a highly educated labour force, provided that the graduates stayed in the university home region (Verger 1978). However, little systematic research was conducted into the impact of the university upon its host society. It was not until the 1960s and 1970s that this situation changed. Universities were considered to be potential triggers of economic development with the emergence of new ideas in economic development theory about economic multiplier effects of backward and forward linkages of propulsive organisations. Research was conducted into the impact of money flows from the universities on local and regional economies, looking at the expenditures of the university itself, its employees, and its students. Recent examples of this approach can be found in Bleaney et al. (1992) and Armstrong (1993).

In the 1980s, views on the role of the university changed once more. The global economic crisis at that time led to the rise of the post-industrial knowledge and service economy. Universities were called upon to apply their distinguishing commodity, i.e. knowledge, for the benefit of economic development (Florax 1992). The remarkable successes of Silicon Valley and the Boston area served as triggers. The economic fortunes of these regions were thought to be based on so-called local *techno-transfers* from Stanford University and the Massachusetts Institute of Technology, respectively. Local and regional governments and universities all over the world tried to copy the achievements of these areas by focusing on the transfer of technological know-how from the university to the local and regional businesses (Van der Meer 1996).

These technology transfers were channelled through two main streams (Goddard 1997). First, through research and consultancy carried out by the university and commissioned by private and public organisations. Policy-makers and universities themselves created special infrastructure, organisations, and branches to encourage these kinds of transfers (science parks, technology transfer offices, local information centres attached to universities). A second major stream of technology transfer consisted of the university spin-offs. Students as well as university staff were vigorously encouraged to start their own businesses and infant companies were financially supported by either the university or the government or both. Furthermore, universities offered spin-off companies accommodation and support facilities (Goddard 1996; Vaessen 2001).

However, the Silicon Valley and the Boston area success proved not to be easily reproducible and critics pointed to the narrow techno-economic assumptions underlying the supposed university environment interchange (Goddard 1996, 1997). Applying notions like the 'learning society' and the 'learning region', the more encompassing nature of the interaction between the university and society was put to the forefront (Amin and Thrift 1994; Florida 1995; Goddard 1996, 1997).

Just like a private business company, a region has to continuously and persistently innovate in order to renew and improve itself. However, since innovations are rarely available on demand, first of all, in our view, the concept of the learning region implies continuity in the relationship between the university and its environment. An infrastructure has to be created to attain this goal, within which it is possible for learning processes to flourish and new ideas to emerge at any moment. This means that, from a learning region point of view, university–society linkage research has to focus on persistence in the relationship between the two rather than on incidental schemes like external research and consulting projects. This focus on persistence in the relationship between the university and the local environment simultaneously diverts attention from formal, collective, incidental institutional cont(r)acts towards informal contacts and interactions between individual university employees and representatives of external organisations. These day-to-day linkages make up the network infrastructure through which the university infiltrates the environment and upon which formal agreements and contracts can thrive. Hence, *recurring* external face-to-face contacts of individual university employees with organisations in the (local) environment constitute the first of the two pillars of the present contribution.

Apart from the external linkages of individual university employees, the notion of the learning region places a heavy emphasis on the importance of a coherent social and cultural foundation in a region. Terms have been created to express this 'soft infrastructure' of the socio-cultural milieu, within which regional networks of inter-firm organisation are embedded (Cooke 1998; Goddard and Chatterton 1999). These terms are 'social capital' (Putnam *et al.* 1993) and 'untraded interdependencies' (Storper 1995), which includes aspects such as trust, norms, values, and tacit and personal knowledge. Ideally, a common regional business culture comes into existence in which opportunistic behaviour is abandoned, inter-firm uncertainty is reduced, and actors share a common way of doing business and do not restrict themselves to their own private goals, but are devoted to community goals as well. Where a university exists, this socio-cultural base should be characterised by the thriving participation of the university population in the social and political life of the region. In line with this, the second characteristic of the present contribution is the incorporation of socio-cultural links between the University of Nijmegen and the community. We measure the leisure social participation of university employees next to their professional face-to-face contacts with organisations in the environment.

The role of socio-cultural preconditions underlying economic growth has become a hot issue among economists in recent times. This subject is omnipresent in explanations of the Dutch economic success, known as the 'polder model'. Following this model, Dutch economic achievement is the result of a deep-seated debating culture in the Netherlands between the government, employers, employees, interest groups, and other civil organisations. Usually, cultural growth is thought to be dependent upon economic growth. In the polder model debate, this causality is inverted: culture is the foundation, economy is the derivative. Important cultural preconditions underlying the Dutch polder model are a solid information network, a *common* commercial attitude (which strongly minimises transaction costs), cooperation on all fronts of society, and reliable institutions of trade (Delsen 2000; Visser and Hemerijck 1997). The ubiquity of information, thriving on dense network relations, is an important factor in 'the model' as it stimulates equality, discussion, and the reaching of consensus between social and economic parties. It is presumed that universities, their staff, and students (can) play a crucial role in the genesis and development of the cultural and political determinants of economic success in a region (Goddard 1997).[1] Simultaneously, it is recognised that this issue has barely been studied (Chatterton 2000). For clarity, this will not be the case in the present contribution. We will make an inventory of the leisure social activities of employees of the University of Nijmegen. Furthermore, we will examine whether academic knowledge is transferred to these associations. Whether and how this knowledge then contributes to regional economic development and seeps through into the 'professional system' is a subject in need of quantitative research (see note 1).

Universities, learning regions, and networks

From the above, the reader can infer that a university is considered to contribute to the emergence of a learning region by linking the local environment with the academic knowledge environment through an extensive and dense network of persistent external relations. Through these links, bits of academic information, knowledge, values, and conventions can seep through into the local region without restraint and at any arbitrary point in time.

The main aim of this chapter, therefore, is to estimate the extent to which employees of the University of Nijmegen connect Nijmegen and its regionally-based organisations to academic knowledge and research networks. Thereby, we distinguish whether an individual employee of the university is part of a narrow inner university network only, or an extended outer-university network as well. While the narrow network includes mutual connections between employees (internal professional relations) only, the extended network also consists of the professional relations of the employees with representatives of other organisations (external professional relations). The reasons for differentiating between inner and outer university networks are twofold. The first reason concerns 'network diversity'. Burt (1992) convincingly arguments that it is not the size of a network which is critical for providing useful information but rather its diversity. A university employee who, during working hours, only has contact with his or her colleagues at the University of Nijmegen is likely to meet people who have the same (kind of) information and so provide the same information benefits (information redundancy). In contrast, an employee who simultaneously maintains professional contacts with representatives of organisations external to the university is more likely to meet people from different institutional and social environments who provide him or her with new, unique information.

The second reason concerns what might be called 'integrated knowledge' and the 'toughness of knowledge transfer' (DfEE 1998). Here we apply in a specific way a distinction made by Gibbons *et al.* (1994). These authors draw a distinction between two kinds of university knowledge. These are 'Mode 1' and 'Mode 2' knowledge. Freely rendered, Mode 1 knowledge is autonomous, hierarchical, and created in isolation from its community context. In contrast to this, Mode 2 knowledge is, among other things, of a socially embedded nature, socially accountable, and undertaken in a context of application. Gibbons *et al.* hypothesise that there has been a shift from Mode 1 knowledge creation to Mode 2 knowledge creation. We suppose that the aforementioned differences in our research between 'narrowly' and 'extensively' connected university employees correspond to the differences between Mode 1- and Mode 2-created university knowledge. We hypothesise that the knowledge of the latter group of university employees is of a more integrated and socially embedded nature than that of the former. We expect the knowledge of the latter group to be moulded by and adapted to information from the 'real, outside world'. Hence, we suppose that the knowledge of university workers professionally embedded in the outer university environment is more readily applicable than the knowledge of university workers who are not (everything else being equal).

Given the exploratory nature of the present project, we did not examine this issue in depth in our questionnaire. The results should, therefore, be interpreted as suggestions for orientating future research on university–community interchange. In sum, the overall *research question* is in what way the University of Nijmegen contributes to a learning environment for organisations in the local region.

The present contribution proceeds as follows. First, we present the operational context of the findings. This consists of a brief description of the University of Nijmegen itself, and of the local region in which the university is situated. Second, we outline the research design, including its realisation as well as the fieldwork response. Third, we present the results in three sections: we analyse the leisure links of university employees with local organisations (social activities); then, we analyse the working hour links of university employees with local organisations (external professional relations); and finally, we integrate both approaches and link social networks to professional networks. A brief recapitulation of the findings follows.

The operational context

The university and the region

The University of Nijmegen was established in 1923 and is the only full or general university in the south-eastern part of the Netherlands. The university has a Catholic background and, as such, its primary aim was originally to contribute to the emancipation of the Catholic section of Dutch society. Although this aim has lost part of its importance, it is still important to keep this fact in mind. Unlike other relatively young scientific institutes, the primary goal of the university was not to boost the regional economy. Nowadays, this fact is still visible in the relations between the university and the city of Nijmegen. Much effort is now put into improving and extending these relations.

Its *c.* 13,000 students and about 4,500 employees make Nijmegen University one of the medium-sized universities in the Netherlands. The university accommodates seven faculties: Medical Sciences, Physics and Mathematics, Policy Sciences[2], Social Sciences, Law, Arts and Religion and Philosophy. Also attached to the university is a University Hospital, which is closely connected with the Medical Sciences faculty.

The regional context of the university is presented in Figure 5.1. Nijmegen is situated at the eastern border of the Netherlands. Formerly considered to be in a peripheral area, at present it tries to capitalise on its central position on the main corridor between the Randstad agglomeration in the western part of the Netherlands and the Ruhr area in Germany.

The city of Nijmegen is by far the most important city in its region. With a little over 150,000 inhabitants, by Dutch standards it is a medium-sized city and it outranks the second biggest town of the region, Wijchen, four times. The region around Nijmegen comprises fourteen municipalities around the city of Nijmegen itself and these municipalities are the main domiciles of the university personnel. In total, 230,000 people live in these fourteen municipalities.

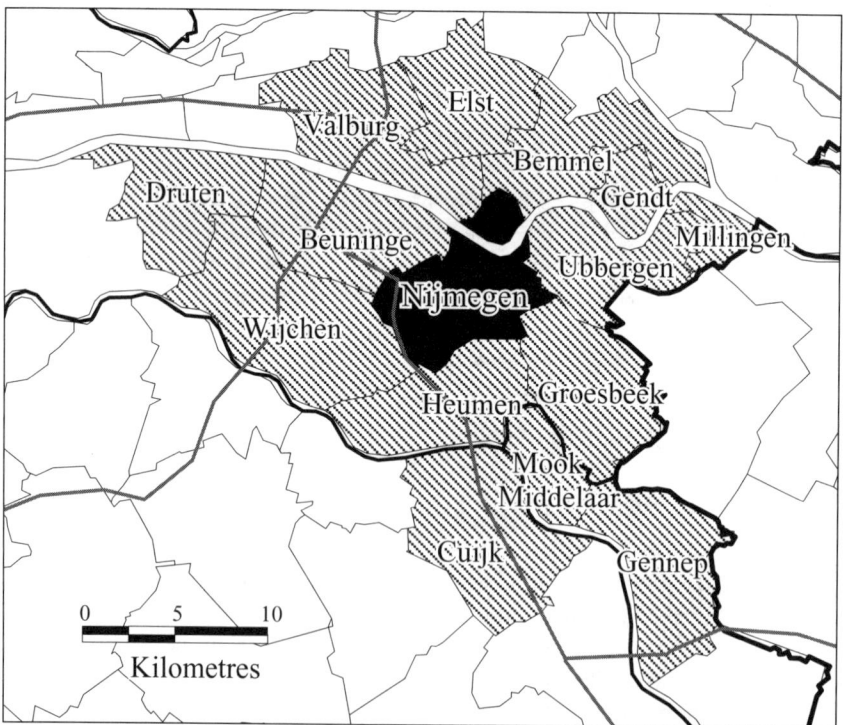

Figure 5.1 Nijmegen and its surroundings

Regional analysis of the University of Nijmegen

The empirical data used in this contribution are based on a larger study of the University of Nijmegen, carried out to determine the importance of the university for the city of Nijmegen and its direct surroundings (Buursink and Vaessen 2001). The central goal of this study was to determine the role of the university with regard to the economic system, and, more importantly, the social and cultural systems of the city and the region. The influence of the university is thought to consist of flows of money, on the one hand, and flows of services and knowledge, on the other. One of the most important additions to regular research into the interaction between universities and the regions is the fact that not only formalised institutional relationships are considered. The more informal personal contacts of university staff and students and their levels of participation in local and regional everyday life are also taken into account. Of course the scope of this contribution is not suitable to present all the results of this study. This chapter concentrates on the external job-related contacts of the university staff as well as on their participation in local and regional society. In order to be able to position this, inevitably partial, insight within the integral study, the conceptual framework of the latter is briefly presented.

The 'system' used to study the regional interaction of the university consists of three components. The first component is made up of the university's organisational units and the households of university personnel and students. The second component consists of the other households within the region. The last component is made up of all the organisations in the region not belonging to the university complex. Located within this cluster are, for instance, government institutions, private companies and interest groups but also all kinds of cultural and social organisations.

The interaction between the university and its surroundings is reduced to the outgoing flows from the university, originating from the organisation as well as its households. The remaining relationships or flows within the system are threefold. First, there are the money flows between the university and the region. Second, there are knowledge transfers. These flows are made up of the regular transfers, like contract research, consultancy, graduates and spin-offs. However, in this study, the external contacts of university personnel are also explicitly considered within this flow. The third type of flow between the components of the system can be characterised as service flows. Universities, especially in the Netherlands, are being more and more thrown back on their own resources. Several organisational sectors such as catering services, maintenance departments, print and copy services and security have become more or less privatised and are now charging for their services. At the same time, they are also offering their services outside the university. This leads to a completely different kind of interaction between the university and the region.

The 'system' described above is summarised in Figure 5.2. The complexity of this system is increased by the fact that these types of flows can, in principle, originate from the organisational units of the university as well as from the

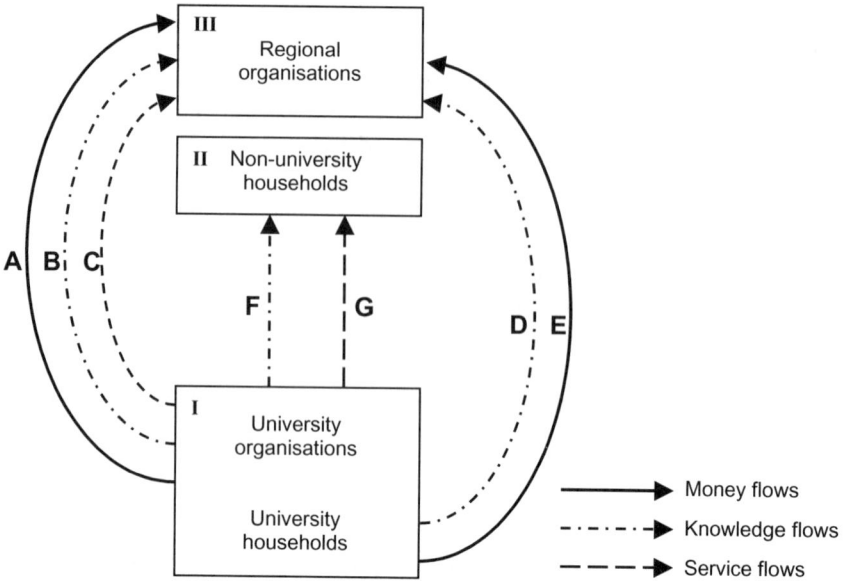

Figure 5.2 Interaction flows from the university

university households. Next to these flows directed towards external organisations, interaction between the university and local and regional households also exists. Regular education, university healthcare, and library services to non-students and non-employees could be included here. These interactions are not considered in the Nijmegen study, however. In total, seven flows are discerned in the model.

As mentioned earlier, we pass over external collective or institutional relations of the University of Nijmegen and limit the scope of the present contribution to the (face-to-face) relations of individual university employees. Furthermore, applying a learning region perspective, we disregard an inventory of monetary flows and focus on knowledge and service flows. Hence, two types of flows remain in our analysis; the knowledge flows from the university households (Flow D in Figure 5.2) and a subset of the knowledge flows from the university as an organisation (Flow B), namely, the external professional contacts of university personnel. By including these interaction flows, an attempt is made to determine the level of infiltration of the university in society as far as participation through the workforce is concerned and to what extent knowledge is transferred through this workforce.

In sum, two flows are dealt with explicitly:

• private knowledge flows through advisory activities and the participation of university personnel in social and cultural organisations in their spare time (socio-cultural participation);
• knowledge flows from the university to the external community through work-related (professional) participation.

The sample

The survey data for the present analyses have been collected through the administration of questionnaires to measure the economic, social, and cultural contribution of the University of Nijmegen to the city and the region. As well as some background questions, the questionnaire dealt with four subjects. These were consumer expenditures by university households, cultural and social activities of university personnel, and external professional contacts. We selected all employees of the University of Nijmegen with a contract of twelve months or longer. Research and teaching assistants were excluded, 4,743 university employees received a questionnaire, 1,444 (31 per cent) employees responded and returned a completed questionnaire. Guaranteeing the respondents' full anonymity, we did not identify individual questionnaires. As a consequence, it was impossible for us to send reminders in order to increase the response.

The respondents were, on average, 43.5 years of age. This figure is nearly identical to the average age of 43.9 years in the total population of university workers. Table 5.1 shows the age composition of both the response file and the population file of the University of Nijmegen. Table 5.1 tells us that 60 per cent of all respondents are men and 40 per cent are women. As we see, these figures are also quite similar to the distribution of the sexes in the population. Over 50 per cent of the university employees live in the municipality of Nijmegen itself. Nearly 28 per cent of the workers live in the adjacent municipalities. University personnel living outside the greater Nijmegen area were somewhat under-represented in the response data compared to the population data: 15 per cent

Table 5.1 Major characteristics of the sample and the population

	Respondents (%)	Population (%)
Age		
Younger than 30 years	12	12
30–40 years	23	24
40–49 years	31	30
50 years or older	35	35
Sex		
Men	61	60
Women	39	40
n.a.	< 1	
Domicile		
Nijmegen	54	52
Region	30	28
Elsewhere	15	20
n.a.	1	
Total	1444	4743

Source: Authors' questionnaire.

and 20 per cent, respectively. Finally, the check on the representation across university departments shows no major deviations of the respondent file from the population file. The department of Policy Sciences is slightly over-represented, whereas the Department of Natural Sciences, Mathematics and Computer Sciences, and employees of supporting service facilities are slightly under-represented in the respondents' file.

Socio-cultural participation

As mentioned before, in this chapter we consider two types of external personal linkages of university employees through which knowledge can be passed from the university to the (local) community. These are external professional relations as well as social participation activities of university employees in their spare time. We devote this section to the latter linkages, which are less commonly considered in university environment research, but are indispensable when considering the socio-cultural impact of the university. The external *professional* relations of university workers are dealt with in the next section.

The simplest form of social participation that is discerned in this respect is the membership of an organisation. Out of the total of 1,444 respondents, 73 per cent indicated that they belonged to a club or association. In total, the questionnaire registered 2,662 memberships. This is an average of 1.84 memberships per employee. Slightly over half of this social participation occurs in clubs located within the greater Nijmegen area (see Table 5.2).

Furthermore, 121 incidents of social participation in organisations located in Nijmegen itself stem from the 217 respondents living outside Nijmegen and its surrounding area. This is almost 9 per cent of all the occurrences of acts of social participation in this area and they can be attributed to the presence of the university.

However valuable it may be from a social point of view, membership of an organisation cannot be put on a par with active social participation. Active participation, in this contribution, involves organising activities, communication, cooperation, learning processes, and so forth. Hence, the respondents were asked to name all associations and organisations for which they had performed activities in their spare time for at least 25 hours in the past year.

A little over 30 per cent of the respondents indicated that they had spent at least 25 hours of their spare time during the last year in active social

Table 5.2 Number of memberships of organisations

Location of the organisation	Number of memberships	(%)
In Nijmegen and surroundings	1425	54
Elsewhere	1237	46
Total	2662	100

Source: Authors' questionnaire.

participation. These efforts benefited 693 associations. In total, the respondents invested about 58,000 hours in society this way. This is the equivalent of 36.1 man-years. Extrapolation of this figure to the social leisure time involvement of the entire university employee population, gives an estimated total of 134.0 man-years in the past year. For the city of Nijmegen, a total of 57.0 man-years is estimated.

Table 5.3 shows that university employees participate in several general types of social activity. The most important are cultural activities (religious associations, music associations, college groups, editing (club) magazines, radio and television work, etc.), sports and recreation, and social activities.

The geographical distribution of the social participation of the university employees shows, first of all, that there is no great difference between the spatial distribution of the participations and the invested time (see Table 5.4). In both instances, almost half involve associations located in the city of Nijmegen, and three-quarters involve organisations in the greater Nijmegen area. Both indicators show that, when compared to association membership, the active social participation of university employees concentrates to a much larger degree in the city of Nijmegen and its surrounding area. As mentioned in the previous section, memberships in the greater Nijmegen area only accounted for 54 per cent of the grand total.

However, compared to its share in the number of respondents (54 per cent), the Nijmegen municipality has a somewhat smaller share in the total amount of time devoted to social participation (Table 5.4). In contrast, regions outside the greater Nijmegen area receive more hours of social effort from staff of the University of Nijmegen than might be expected on the basis of their share in the number of university employees: 25 per cent compared to only 16 per cent of the personnel. This might be explained by the fact that, in general, the more highly educated employees prefer to live outside the city or even outside the region. They may possibly be more intensively socially active, thus leading to a higher activity rate in the immediate surroundings of Nijmegen.

A significant contribution to Nijmegen's social life stems from non-local workers. Non-local employees, being either employees living in the surrounding municipalities of Nijmegen or employees living elsewhere, reserve more than

Table 5.3 Type of activity

	Number of participations	(%)
Cultural	197	29
Sports and recreation	179	26
Social	126	18
Education	77	11
Otherwise	73	11
Unknown	37	5
Total	689	100

Source: Authors' questionnaire.

Table 5.4 Comparison of the geographical spread of social participations and the amount of time invested with the home addresses of all the respondents in the sample

Location of the social association	Number of participations		Invested hours	
	Absolute	(%)	Absolute	(%)
Nijmegen	329	47	27,468	48
Region	180	26	15,902	27
Elsewhere	184	27	14,441	25
Total	693	100	57,811	100

Source: Authors' questionnaire.

8,000 hours of their time for the benefit of Nijmegen associations. This is almost 30 per cent of all hours invested in the Nijmegen society by university employees. On the other hand, Nijmegen employees devote almost a quarter of the time they allocate to social participation activities (6,600 hours) to associations located outside the city of Nijmegen. A slight positive balance for the city of Nijmegen, therefore, exists between the incoming and the outgoing hours of social participation.

Going one step further, a distinction is made regarding the extent to which the active participation of a person is of importance for the organisation involved. Some activities, like participating as an implementer in the advertising campaign of a political party, which has already been planned and designed, seem of lesser importance than being on the board of that party. The latter appears socially more constructive. The question is whether or not a position on the board is involved. It turns out that, in 53 per cent of all cases of active participation, this was the case.

Furthermore, the data show that the geographical distribution of board functions is similar to the geographical distribution of other types of social participation activities. As stated earlier, about half of such activities occur in the city of Nijmegen, while the other half is distributed equally over the communities surrounding Nijmegen and elsewhere. Hence, it may be concluded that no additional spatial bias arises when analysing the qualitative nature of social participation in terms of board positions.

Professional contacts

A second important strand of links between university personnel and the external environment is made up of professional contacts. As the starting point for the discussion in the present section, we take it that universities have much to offer as gateways to global information resources (Goddard 1997). The main question we attempt to answer is what position the greater Nijmegen area holds in the web of professional external contacts of university employees. Stated differently, how well do university workers link up the Nijmegen region with the wider external (knowledge) environment?

Furthermore, we analyse the type of organisations university employees interact with professionally (private, government, civil). Finally, we will make a distinction between university departments.

University employees' linkages to inner and outer regional organisations

We asked the respondents to name all the organisations with which they had at least three face-to-face meetings within the past year, either at the University of Nijmegen or at the office of the external organisation. A quarter of the respondents actually indicated having been involved in such meetings in the past year (n = 336).

Although one might expect organisations located at a considerable distance from Nijmegen, and in particular abroad, to be under-represented in the present survey (given this built-in threshold of three face-to-face meetings), extra-regional organisations greatly outnumber regional organisations in the network of professional external relations of university employees.

Out of the 774 organisations named, 537 (i.e. 70 per cent) are located outside the greater Nijmegen area and 237 (30 per cent) within. Remember that these results are the opposite of the findings regarding social participation. Here, a mere 27 per cent of connected organisations were located outside the greater Nijmegen area and no less than 73 per cent inside (cf. Table 5.4). The inner-regional organisations participating in the web of professional connections of university employees are almost all located within the municipality of Nijmegen itself (see Figure 5.3).

On average, employees of the University of Nijmegen keep professional contacts with three times as many outer-regional organisations ($\bar{x}$ = 2.94) than inner-regional ones ($\bar{x}$ = 0.96). How should we interpret this over-representation of outer-regional professional relations among university employees relative to inner-regional relations? Does it indicate that organisations in the local environment are connected to a wide array of organisations in the national and international environment? Or should we infer that the university employees ignore organisations in the local environment?

In defence of the first line of thought, it is useful to note that the over-representation of outer-regional professional relations of the employees of the

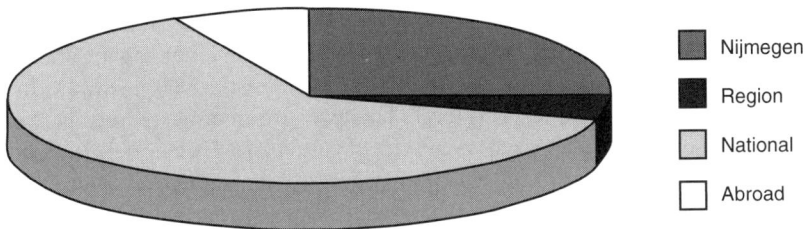

Figure 5.3 Location of the organisation
Source: Authors' questionnaire.

University of Nijmegen appears quite normal, since any arbitrary university employee has much more choice in contacting outer-regional organisations relative to local ones. Having a low proportion of inner-regional contacts may turn out to be more profitable for Nijmegen organisations in terms of the possible inflow of non-local information and ideas. It suggests, after all, that Nijmegen organisations have multiple rather than simple connections to a wider array of outer-regional organisations through university links. So, one should not focus on the relative figures (i.e. 30 per cent of the respondents' professional external contacts are with local organisations), but rather on the absolute number of 237 local organisations. Furthermore, the interaction with a smaller number of local organisations relative to non-local organisations might be counterbalanced by the stronger embeddedness of the former in the network of university contacts. This is true for Nijmegen organisations. University employees meet local organisations more frequently ($\bar{x}$ = 11.3, median = 5 meetings per organisation) than extra-regional organisations ($\bar{x}$ = 6.3; median = 4). This may stimulate inter-organisational trust and, as a result, the fluid passing on of (valuable) information.

However, opposing the foregoing positive explanation and in defence of the second, negative interpretation of the above finding, it is conceivable that inner- and outer-regional contacts are separated in the sense that quite different people may maintain each. In that case, information overflow from outer university networks into the local region could be seriously hampered. If this is the case, the above positive account of a smaller number of interacting local organisations relative to non-local organisations cannot be supported. Indeed, analyses show that out of the 339 respondents who reported having interacted professionally with at least one organisation three or more times in the past year, no less than 267 (79 per cent) do maintain either solely outer-regional or exclusively inner-regional contacts. The high number of respondents maintaining exclusively extra-regional contacts is particularly noteworthy (n = 175). Again, this appears quite normal from the perspective of the university not being founded as a local service organisation. That does not alter the fact that, from a learning region point of view, a switchboard function of the university personnel between inner- and outer-regional organisations, in our view, is of pivotal importance for allowing non-local, non-public knowledge to filter through into the local region. From this perspective, it seems worrying that the number of employees of the University of Nijmegen maintaining contacts with both regional and extra-regional organisations is lagging behind even the number of employees who exclusively maintain local contacts (n = 72 and 92, respectively). This poor interconnectedness between the inner- and outer-regional contacts of university personnel is put in perspective, to some extent, by the finding that employees maintaining exclusively extra-regional contacts do not confine themselves more to their own university department than do employees maintaining contacts with only regional organisations. Hence, in principle, the opportunity exists within the departments for non-local information to switch from employees maintaining exclusively extra-regional contacts to locally embedded employees and find its way into the local region.

Types of organisations university employees interact with

Another important question is what types of organisations employees of the University of Nijmegen interact with. Do employees interact more with the private business sector or with the government sector? Only 12 per cent of all organisations can be labelled as business organisations and 10 per cent as governmental or political. The bulk of the face-to-face meetings take place with organisations between these two opposites. Among these non-profit organisations, we find many so-called *civil organisations*.

If we exclude the academic research (11 per cent) and educational institutions (16 per cent), a long and colourful parade of organisations remains, for example, interest and lobby groups, youth care organisations, mental health and medical care associations, semi-state-controlled economic development organisations, professional societies, religious and legal organisations, the prison system, and so forth. The spatial distribution of business organisations and non-profit organisations excluding government and political organisations runs parallel to that of all interacting organisations. In both cases, the greater Nijmegen area accommodates about 30 per cent of interacting organisations. Governmental and political organisations, on the other hand, are concentrated in the local region to a much larger extent. No less than 49 per cent of these organisations are located in either the city of Nijmegen or its adjacent municipalities.

Finally, taking into account the overall predominance of meetings with non-profit organisations, Figure 5.4 reveals a marked division between departments. The Department of Social Sciences and, in particular, the Department of Physical Sciences, Mathematics, and Computer Sciences maintain the bulk of the external contacts with private business companies (46 per cent). The Law Faculty and the Department of Policy Sciences, on the other hand, account for 57 per cent of all face-to-face meetings with government and political organisations. The Departments of Linguistics and Literature, Medical Sciences, and the Auxiliary Services have contacts particularly with the non-profit organisations. These findings suggest that university employees participating in specialised networks have few interconnecting links between different types of organisations. Indeed, most university employees (65 per cent) have had professional meetings with only one kind of organisation, whether it is business companies, governmental and political, or non-profit organisations. From this perspective, Figure 5.4 suggests that the employees of the Department of Social Sciences participate in the most balanced networks, including different kinds of organisations. The empirical data show this to be true. The number of employees who have contacts with different kinds of organisations is the highest in this department (46 per cent), although other departments like the Law Faculty and the Department of Policy Sciences show comparable figures.

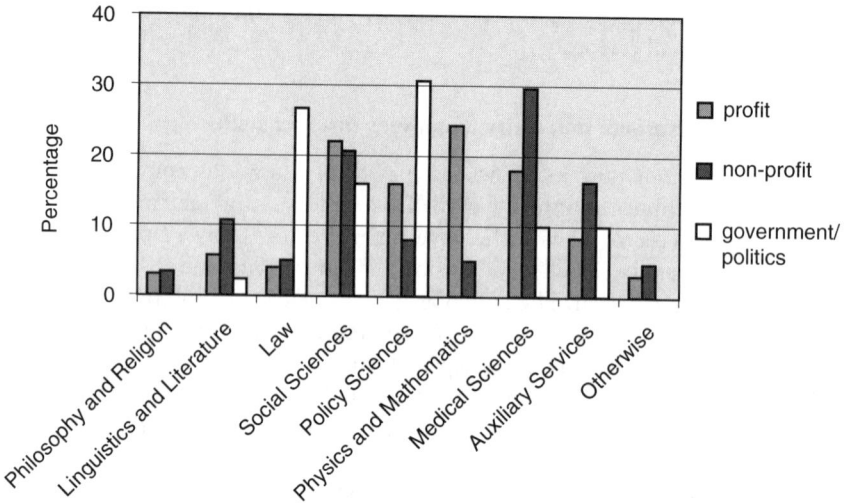

Figure 5.4 Type of organisation per department
Source: Authors' questionnaire.

Social activities and professional contacts links

Up to now, we have examined the leisure activities of university employees and their external professional contacts separately. In this final section, we raise the question of whether the University of Nijmegen serves a role as a link between these two types of networks in that its employees join both types of networks simultaneously. A major question we seek to answer in this analysis is whether useful information from the professional network disseminates into the local socio-cultural network of employees of the University of Nijmegen.

When analysing professional and social networks of university employees simultaneously, four groups of workers can be distinguished. We present them in order of increasing surplus value for the local region (see Figure 5.5).

The first group consists of employees connected to the inner-university network only. These employees did not report conducting social activities nor did they report recurring, work-related face-to-face meetings with non-university employees. As was stated earlier, these employees seem to lack both a well-developed social network and an external professional network. This is true for over half of the respondents (56 per cent). We estimate the surplus value of these employees for the local organisations to be indirect (they turn out graduates and research reports).

The second group consists of university employees who conduct social activities in their spare time but have no recurring face-to-face meetings with non-university workers during office hours (n = 200). This group of employees links spare time socio-cultural activities to the University of Nijmegen. Social activities may potentially benefit from these workers' expert knowledge and

Socio-cultural
(spare time-related)
external environment

Group IV
10%

Professional
(work time-related)
external environment

14%

20%

Group II

Group III

Group I
56%

Internal university
environment

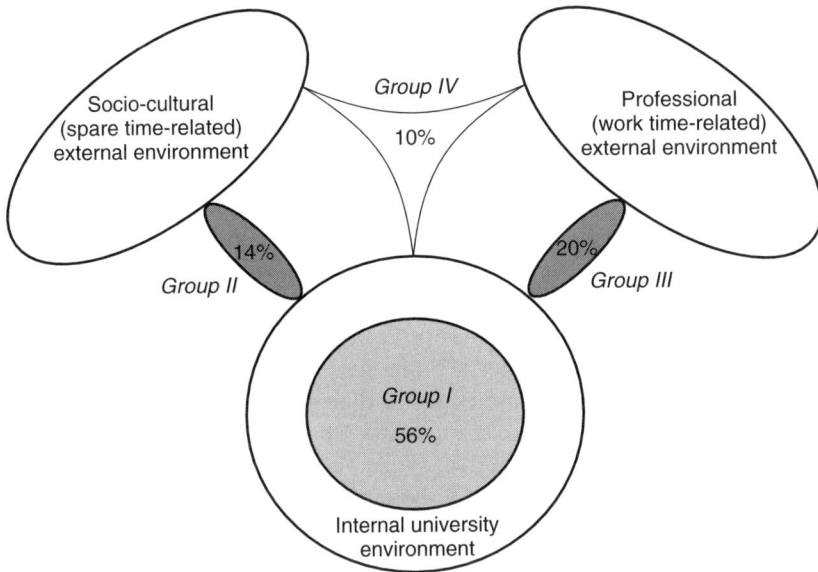

Figure 5.5 Employees characterised according to the type of their networks

Source: Authors' questionnaire.

skills. However, they cut off socio-cultural organisations from the diverse pool of professional outer university networks. As a consequence, we expect this knowledge to suffer from information redundancy and inadequate social embeddedness. By extension, this knowledge risks poor applicability (cf. Mode 1 type of knowledge, Gibbons *et al.* 1994). About 20 per cent of the employees can be ascribed to this group.

The third group consists of employees who reported being engaged in recurring face-to-face meetings with non-university employees during office hours, but simultaneously did not report conducting social activities in their spare time. Hence, we may conclude that, although these employees mingle with the outer-university environment, they do not venture outside their professional environment. So, while the external professional environment may have access to these employees' knowledge and skills, they do not contribute to the powerful development of (spare time) socio-cultural life, from a learning region point of view thought to be so important for social capital building (Putnam *et al.* 1993) and hence for social and economic development. Accounting for 14 per cent of the respondents, this group is considerably smaller than the former one.

The final group of employees is made up of university staff who are involved in both social activities and external professional face-to-face meetings. These employees link to both the socio-cultural (spare time-related) external and the professional (work time-related) external environment. So, while the preceding two groups of university employees may serve as 'bridges' in a *dyadic* (collective) network (linking either to the spare time socio-cultural or the external professional environment), this group of employees may serve as bridges in *triad* networks. From the perspective of the associations they work for in their spare time, following Burt (1992), these employees will most frequently provide new or non-redundant information. After all, the socio-cultural associations these employees are engaged in during their spare time may not only have access to their expert knowledge and their contacts with other university workers, but, additionally, to the infinite pool of diversified information and contacts from the outer-university professional environment. Therefore, we expect their know-how to be embedded in and adapted to the social environment and, hence, most readily applicable. However, employees in 'triad networks' appear to be rather rare at the University of Nijmegen. Out of 1,444 respondents, only 10 per cent conduct social activities during their spare time and are also part of external professional networks. On top of the general infrequency of these 'triad links' (n = 265), one must realise that, to the disadvantage of the local region, a considerable portion (37 per cent) of these organisations is located beyond the borders of the wider Nijmegen area (see Table 5.5).

In sum, of all social activities reported by the respondents, the greater Nijmegen region houses only 167 (25 per cent) that are connected to both the inner- and the outer-university professional environment.

Next, the question is raised as to whether socially active university employees can actually take advantage of their university jobs when performing communal activities. In other words, do academic knowledge and interpersonal linkages spill over into socio-cultural leisure time engagements? In the questionnaire, the respondents were asked whether the associations they work for in their spare time actually benefit from the web of relations connected to their university positions. From the results, it can be seen that no less than half of all social organisations benefit to some extent from the respondents' professional contacts (Table 5.6). Hence, the results indicate that academic knowledge flows over from the university into social life through these engagements. Teaching and research personnel report *frequent* spill-over advantages most often.

Table 5.5 Spatial spread of spare time socio-cultural activities of university employees and their integration into university networks

Location of assocation	Social activities connected to inner-university professional networks only		Social activities connected to both inner- and outer-university professional networks	
	Absolute	(%)	Absolute	(%)
Nijmegen	220	53	107	40
Region	120	29	60	23
Elsewhere	74	18	98	37
Total	414	100	265	100

Source: Authors' questionnaire.

Table 5.6 Types of functions and benefits from job-related networks

Function at university Benefits	Eductional and research		Managerial		Administr., technical, or supporting		Other		Total	
	Absolute	(%)	Absolute	(%)	Absolute	(%)	Absolute	(%)	Absolute	(%)
Never	177	49.4	21	34	105	55	20	32	323	48
Sometimes	133	37.2	38	61	73	38	38	60	282	42
Often	48	13.4	3	5	13	7	5	8	69	10
Total	358	100	62	100	191	100	63	100	674	100

Source: Authors' questionnaire.

Notwithstanding this, respondents indicated that spill-over advantages do not occur quite often. Only 10 per cent of all the social associations of the university employees benefited frequently from these employees' connections at the university. In 42 per cent of all cases, this overflow of benefits takes place only once in a while. However, we should be careful with this latter figure because we lack in-depth information about the gains reaped by social associations from the membership and involvement of specific university employees. It is conceivable that respondents under-estimated spill-over effects in our investigation as many of these may go unnoticed. A respondent may, for example, refer only to his expert knowledge contacts, but neglect his teaching, management, negotiation, or foreign language skills as well as his mental and methodical training. Subsequent empirical research should pay more thorough attention to the measurement of those items.

Regarding the spill-over of university knowledge and skills into spare time engagements, we found also that respondents who hold a board position in the association they work for after hours reported benefit from work-related connections more frequently than respondents who do not hold a board position. Out of the 433 respondents who named at least one association they work for in their spare time, 262 (61 per cent) hold one or more board positions in these associations. Of these, 169 (65 per cent) reported spill-over advantages. In contrast, out of the 171 respondents who are socially active without holding a board position, only 78 (46 per cent) report spill-over advantages.

The final question we wish to answer is whether it is beneficial for social associations not only to be linked to the University of Nijmegen itself but also to external university networks. We have already found that this kind of 'triad link' does not occur very frequently (10 per cent of all employees; 38 per cent of all socio-cultural engagements). The infrequency of these linkages contrasts with their potential additional benefits for the organisations in the network. Indeed, our research found some evidence for this. University employees who conduct social activities in their spare time and are frequently engaged in face-to-face meetings with non-university employees during office hours indicated that nearly two-thirds of their social activities benefit from their interpersonal contacts related to their university job (i.e. 63 per cent). In contrast, university employees who did not report having outer-university face-to-face meetings professionally indicated that only 45 per cent of the associations with which they are engaged benefit from their work-related contacts. Furthermore, of the 68 social associations that benefit *frequently* from the work-related interpersonal contacts of their university participants, the majority (i.e. 43) accommodate university employees embedded in outer-university networks.

These figures suggest that academic knowledge flows from the University of Nijmegen into the socio-cultural environment when links are established via the social participation of university employees. We found proof that it is more beneficial for a social association to have as members university employees, who are embedded in an outer-university professional network, than university employees who maintain inner-university contacts only. However, it appears that the University of Nijmegen does not have many such key workers who link the socio-cultural environment to both the outer- and the inner-university knowledge environment. This is very much to the disadvantage of the social and cultural life in the Nijmegen area, particularly in terms of lost opportunities.

Conclusion

However diverse the insights and approaches on studying the topic of the learning region may be, studies generally agree on the pivotal importance of the presence of a university in a region for stimulating learning processes underlying regional innovativeness and prosperity. We deduced two key characteristics for learning regions: first, the persistence or continuity of links between the local region and the university and, second, the existence of not only links between the university and the local economic environment but also between the university and the socio-cultural environment.

These insights led us to focus on recurring face-to-face contacts in the external relations of university employees. These relations we see as the central conduits between the university and the external environment, as we conceive of these meetings as the impulses of information transfer and learning. Two types of external relations were analysed. These were the work time or professional relations of university employees and their social participation and engagements in their spare time. In this way, we hope to have covered (face-to-face) linkages with organisations in both the economic and the socio-cultural environment. For our case study, we used the external relations of the employees of our own university, i.e. the University of Nijmegen.

The main results and their implications are summarised below. Out of 1,444 respondents, 438 (30 per cent) reported being actively engaged with 693 social organisations in their spare time for at least 25 hours per year per organisation. Furthermore, 336 (23 per cent) respondents reported having had at least three face-to-face meetings in the last year during work time with 774 organisations. Out of this total of 1,467 organisations, 746 (51 per cent) are located in the greater Nijmegen region. The respondents connected to the local environment to a much greater extent via social participation than via professional relations. No less than 73 per cent of social spare time engagements occur within Nijmegen or the surrounding municipalities, whereas this is the case for only 30 per cent of the work time-related professional contacts. Consequently, although slightly more professional relations than social engagements were recorded, the latter constitute the bulk of the relations with the local region. Out of the 746 relations reported between the university and the greater Nijmegen area, 513 (68 per cent) were established through spare time social engagements and only 237 (32 per cent) were established via professional relations during working hours. Furthermore, we found evidence that the actual knowledge transfer from the university to the social environment via these social engagements may be considerable. The majority of respondents engaged in spare time social activities (i.e. 250 out of 438) recorded having experienced advantages from their professional linkages to the benefit of at least one of their social engagements. In slightly over 50 per cent of all social engagements, it was indicated that these associations do benefit from the respondents' professional contacts. This occurred more frequently when respondents maintained outer-university professional relations as well as their professional contacts at the University of Nijmegen (triad links).

So, whereas mainstream research on university–community knowledge transfer focuses on direct professional linkages, and frequently reveals disappointing results (e.g. Fischer 2000; Florax and Folmer 1992; Huggins and Cooke 1996), the present investigation suggests that the stream of academic knowledge filtering into the local community via indirect connections through the spare time social engagements of university workers may be considerable.

It goes without saying that further research on this topic is required. Information originating from the university and entering the community directly and indirectly should be compared; and the volume of both streams should be established. Furthermore, it has to be examined whether and how, with quantitative underpinning, academic know-how that enters the spare time sociocultural environment finds its way into the professional, social, and economic system.

Note

1 For two illustrative cases regarding the interchange between a nation's economic performance and its culture, we refer the reader to two interesting publications. The first is a book about culture and prosperity during the seventeenth century in the Netherlands (i.e. The Golden Age) in 1650 – W. Frijhoff and M. Spies (1999) *Bevochten eendracht*. See also a review of this study by A. Th. van Deursen (2000). The second publication on this topic is a newspaper article on the economic chaos in Surinam, written by W. Donner (*NRC* 25 November 2000). Furthermore, we would like to draw the reader's attention to the fact that this subject is also mentioned in Fukuyama's book *Trust* (1995).

2 The 'Department of Policy Sciences' has recently been renamed 'Nijmegen School of Management'.

References

Amin, A. and Thrift, N. (eds) (1994) *Globalisation, Institutions, and Regional Development in Europe*, Oxford: Oxford University Press.

Armstrong, H. W. (1993) 'The Local Income and Employment Impact of Lancaster University', *Urban Studies* 30: 1653–1668.

Bleaney, M., Binks, M., Greenaway, D., Reed, G. and Whynes, D. (1992) 'What Does a University Add to its Local Economy?', *Applied Economics* 24: 305–311.

Burt, R. S. (1992) *Structural Holes: The Social Structure of Competition*, Cambridge, MA: Harvard University Press.

Buursink, J. and Vaessen, P. (2001) *De Regionale Functie van de Katholieke Universiteit Nijmegen*, Nijmegen: KUN.

Chatterton, P. (2000) 'The Cultural Role of Universities in the Community: Revisiting the University-Community Debate', *Environment and Planning A* 32: 165–181.

Cooke, P. (1998) 'Introduction: Origins of the Concept', in H.-J. Braczyk, P. Cooke and M. Heidenreich (eds) *Regional Innovation Systems: The Role of Governance in a Globalized World*, London: UCL Press.

Delsen, L. (2000) *Exit Poldermodel? Sociaal Economische Ontwikkelingen in Nederland*, Assen: Van Gorcum.

Deursen, A. Th. Van (2000) Niet één alleen, maar allemaal samen. Journal de Volkskrant, 78(22981), Amsterdam: PCM Uitgevers: 25.

DfEE (1998) *Universities and Economic Development*, Sheffield: Higher Education and Employment Division, Department for Education and Employment.

Donner, W. R. W. (2000) Chaos in Suriname komt door ontbreken van een echte elite. NRC Handelsblad, 31(48). Rotterdam: PCM Uitgevers: 9.

Fischer, M. (2000) *Knowledge Interactions between Universities and Firms*, Vienna: Department of Economic Geography and Geoinformatics, Vienna University of Economics and Business Administration.

Florax, R. (1992) *The University: A Regional Booster? Economic Impacts of Academic Knowledge Infrastructure*, Aldershot: Avebury.

Florax, R. and Folmer, H. (1992) 'Knowledge Impacts of Universities on Industry: An Aggregate Simultaneous Investment Model', *Journal of Regional Science* 32, 4: 437–466.

Florida, R. (1995) 'Towards the Learning Region', *Futures* 27, 5: 527–536.

Frÿhoff, W. and Spies, M. (1999) 1650: bevochten undracht. The Hague: SDU Uitgevers.

Fukuyama, F. (1995) *Trust: The Social Virtue and the Creation of Prosperity*, New York: The Free Press.

Gibbons, M., Limoges, C., Nowotny, H., Schwartzman, S., Scott, P. and Trow, M. (1994) *The New Production of Knowledge: The Dynamics of Science and Research in Contemporary Society*, London: Sage.

Goddard, J. (1996) 'Managing the University/City Interface', paper presented to the conference on Urban Universities and their Cities, 27–29 March 1996, Amsterdam.

Goddard, J. (1997) 'Universities and Regional Development: An Overview', background paper to OECD Project on the response of higher education to regional needs, University of Newcastle upon Tyne, Centre for Urban and Regional Development Studies.

Goddard, J. and Chatterton, P. (1999) 'Regional Development Agencies and the Knowledge Economy: Harnessing the Potential of Universities', *Environment and Planning C* 17: 685–699.

Huggins, R. and Cooke, P. (1996) 'The Economic Impact of Cardiff University: Innovation, Learning and Job Generation', paper prepared for the conference on Urban Universities and their Cities, 27–29 March, Amsterdam.

Meer, E. van der (1996) *Knowledge on the Move: The University as a Local Source of Expertise*, Amsterdam: AME.

Putnam, R. D., Leonardi, R. and Nanetti, R. Y. (1993) *Making Democracy Work: Civic Traditions in Modern Italy*, Princeton, NJ: Princeton University Press.

Storper, M. (1995) 'The Resurgence of Regional Economies, Ten Years Later: The Region as a Nexus of Untraded Interdependencies', *European Urban and Regional Studies* 2: 191–221.

Vaessen, P. (2001) *Kuncubator: Onderscheiden ondernemingen opgericht door alumni van de Katholieke Universiteit Nijmegen zich van andere ondernemingen en hoe sterk werkt de KUN in op de totstandkoming en het functioneren van deze ondernemingen?*, Nijmegen: KUN.

Verger, J. (1978) *Universiteiten in de Middeleeuwen*, Bussum: Unieboek.

Visser, J. and Hemerijck, A. (1997) *'A Dutch Miracle': Job Growth, Welfare Reform and Corporatism in the Netherlands*, Amsterdam: Amsterdam University Press.

6 About unlearning and learning regions

Huib Ernste

The subject of learning regions seems to take the concept of learning for granted. Learning certainly has positive connotations and is therefore easily included in the political and applied-scientific discourse on regional development. It does not call for intensive critical reflection. In this chapter, I will show that this lack of critical conceptual reflection can lead to serious flaws in scientific innovation research and can also lead to erroneous policies with respect to the strategic role of universities in the regional economy. First, I will describe the logic of the historical emergence of the concept of learning regions. This is followed by a theoretical reflection on the concept of learning. Finally, I will show what consequences this could have for the position of universities in the regional knowledge economy.

Innovation research and policy

Innovation research, and in particular geographic innovation research, is still a relatively new field.[1] Nevertheless, a number of different phases in the development of innovation research can already be distinguished. There is a certain logic in the way in which one phase follows the other, in the sense that each of them is clearly related to the respective economic and societal problems of a period. In the same way in which innovation research is closely linked to societal conditions and developments, innovation policy, as an application of the results of this research, is in line with modern trends. An overview of the above-mentioned developments is presented to make the main argument clear.

In the 1970s and in the first half of the 1980s, there was an upsurge of interest in innovation research. In economic circles, there was a growing awareness that Europe was technologically lagging behind countries such as the USA and Japan. From the beginning of the 1970s, economic growth had slowed down dramatically and Europe's competitive position had begun to crumble slowly but surely. It was soon found that this was mainly caused by the above-mentioned technological disadvantage. Initially, innovation research was therefore entirely focused on the process of technological innovation. The expectation was that technological renewal would be generated by large research and development establishments where people were working on new technologies, new materials, etc. Soon the whole process of technological innovation from invention to application or consumption was analysed in detail. The model of innovation associated with this approach can be described as a 'linear innovation model', which automatically brings to mind the epoch of the Fordist industrial and societal regime.

> According to the linear innovation model ..., the innovation process develops linearly from invention, via introduction in the market to diffusion of the new product. The model is characterised by formal research-based and codified knowledge, the involvement of large firms, and the introduction of national systems of innovation.
>
> (Hassink 1997: 162, my translation)

The most important problem in innovation research and policy in this period was 'How can these new techniques developed in R&D laboratories be made available to applicants and end users?' As developers and end users are usually spatially separated, this is essentially a geographical problem. Therefore, innovation always involves a process of spatial diffusion, including the transfer of both information and knowledge[2] (Hägerstrand 1967). It is only on the basis of this concept that we can speak of *spaces of innovation*, i.e. spaces in which innovation finds its origin or occurs more often compared to others. This implies that there are also spaces or regions with an innovation deficit. Although the origins of innovation policy can be traced back to technology policy, it was soon implicitly or explicitly connected with a spatial component. The main problem in innovation policy was what measures to take in order to support the transfer of technological innovations to regions with innovation deficits. One of the first instruments to be used was the direct influencing of potential actors through information campaigns and economic incentives. In this period, characterised by innovation-oriented regional policy (Ewers and Wettmann 1980a, 1980b) and transfer of technology, the emphasis was on *innovation for space*. The main concern in this phase was the generation of technological innovations in R&D laboratories of universities and large firms and the transfer of technology.

In this period of innovation research and innovation policy, such characteristics of early or late adopters as size, turnover, industrial branch, and organisational status within a corporation were analysed as determinants of the different innovation routes that were being followed by these actors. Generally speaking, innovation research in this period may therefore be characterised methodologically as rather behaviouristic in its approach. The specific socio-economic and institutional context in which these actors operated was largely ignored. Only in a later phase did these more contextual aspects become the focal point in innovation research and policy. Researchers and policy-makers became aware that it was not the characteristics of the adopters, but rather the whole context in which they worked, which caused them to be more or less innovative. This experience was mainly prompted by the development of new industrial structures which moved away from the Fordist mode of mass production towards increasingly knowledge-based, flexible, locally clustered network companies successfully operating in a global market. Innovation processes therefore needed to be conceptualised not as linear processes, but rather as non-purchasable cooperative processes between flexible regionally interconnected actors with decentralised decision structures and with a relatively strong client orientation. Innovation processes could not be understood without taking the institutional and cultural contexts into account. Moreover, the notion of learning had to be adapted to the post-Fordist learning economy. The reciprocal interdependencies within networks of innovation were embedded in regional labour market relations, personal experiences, moral values and institutions, which together constituted the regional 'milieu' (Hassink 1997: 162). The individual firm was no longer seen as an isolated actor, but rather as dependent on the regional environment (Kilper and Latniak 1996, cited in Hassink 1999: 10). Accordingly, a more action-theoretic approach focusing on the elaboration of the contextual aspects of relevant innovation decisions seemed to be more appropriate, also with regard to research methodology. Politically, this experience meant that innovation policy was moving towards a policy focusing on the improvement and support of the regional institutional framework within which the potential innovators have to operate. Innovations were not just imported from elsewhere but were to a large extent produced within a region, even if this entailed a connection with actors outside the region. Here we can speak of *innovation in space*.[3] This second phase in innovation research and policy is echoed in such concepts as 'flexible specialisation' (Ernste and Meier 1992; Pyke and Sengenberger 1992; Sabel 1989), 'innovative milieu' (Aydalot and Keeble 1988; Fromhold-Eisebith 1995), and 'regional clusters' (Enright *et al.* 1991; Enright 1996; Krugman 1999; Porter 1990).

It is not all that long ago that Europe entered the third phase in innovation research and policy. As the 'success stories' of regional clusters, innovative milieux, and industrial districts of flexible specialisation did not always prove to be as robust as expected on the basis of the theoretical model, and these models were often not generalisable, there was a growing demand for alternatives. Certain 'model' regions, such as for example, the Third Italy, began to show some cracks. The innovative milieu of the Swiss Jura region with its heavily networked watch industry revealed its weaknesses when the quartz technology was introduced (Ernste 1994). Furthermore, in terms of inventiveness, other long-standing clusters did not perform as well as theoretically expected. Finally, there were also regions that, according to the dominant conceptualisation, should not have been very innovative, but nevertheless proved very successful in this respect. In this situation, the idea of a *learning region* introduced by Florida (1995) and Morgan (1995, 1997) provided a promising alternative to the second-phase models. First of all, this concept draws our attention to the dynamics of the structuralisation and constitution of innovative networks and milieux. From the action theory perspective, this means the focus is not just on the network structures and cultural and institutional milieux in which they are embedded (or to put it differently: on the specific action situations), but also on the social actions of the actors themselves. It is these actions that make or break innovative milieux, for they constitute the core of what we call 'learning'. The concept of 'a learning region' helps us to explain theoretically why 'some regions learn by interacting and [why] collective tacit knowledge can turn from a strength into a weakness' (Hassink 1999: 12). On the other hand, however, this concept has never been defined very clearly and seems to draw its popularity more from the political economy of catchy slogans than from deeper scientific reflection on the actual learning process.[4] In this sense, it is not an already realised asset, but rather a promising concept. For more thorough reflection, I will elaborate on the concept of learning somewhat further in the following section (see also Vermeulen *et al.* 1997: 45–55).

There is learning and learning

What exactly do we mean by learning? First of all, learning is a basic concept in behaviourist psychology and systems theory. Here, learning is defined as a continuous growth of knowledge and understanding. In this respect, knowledge and understanding should be interpreted in a broad sense, not only including technical know-how, but also cultural, institutional and social knowledge. Experience promotes learning, and learning in its turn contributes to an increase in problem-solving capacity. Learning in this sense should be distinguished from maturing growth. Whereas maturing growth is generally an internal process that takes place without external interference, learning is explicitly initiated by the experience of external stimuli. As such, learning is basically a process of confrontation with influences that affect the existing condition. Furthermore, it is essential to learning that the reactions which were provoked by the stimulus are not forgotten but sustained in the stock of knowledge after the stimulus has disappeared, and also that they can be retrieved at will. Such lasting changes can only be expected if, in the actor's eyes, they do indeed lead to an improved problem-solving capacity.

The simplest representation of such a learning process is a simple feedback loop.[5] With a specific goal in mind, the use of means to reach that goal can be optimised by learning from the results of earlier actions. This form of learning may be called incremental learning. Step by step, the person in question learns to approach the target.

Within the context of innovative networks and milieux, we are dealing with learning actors in a specific social context. It is assumed that other actors, relevant to the learning actor, are also present and provide impulses for innovative change. They play the role of stimuli in the learning model described above. Spatial proximity increases the probability of interaction from which one can learn. An extensive milieu characterised by collective representations, common goals, shared cultural values, mutual trust, and a joint conception of legitimacy (Amin and Thrift 1994: 15) can facilitate these interactions considerably. Once such an innovative milieu has been established, one can in general distinguish a common goal. Furthermore, the most relevant interaction partners can then be identified. At this stage, the basic idea, joint project or specific mission of this regional innovative milieu is 'put on the rails', so that the wheels of innovation can be set in motion. When these basic features are lacking, there is no regional innovative milieu at all. The mere fact that an innovative milieu can be identified as such reveals that the innovation route has already been determined to some degree. This is hardly surprising, as innovative milieux are almost by definition path-dependent. An innovative milieu facilitates and speeds up interactions and innovations. It reduces the uncertainty and risk involved in collective innovative actions by embedding them in formal and informal conventions, shared cultural traditions and reciprocal expectations which are essential aspects of the innovative milieu. The fact that innovative actions are embedded in this way makes them more efficient and effective. The development of new technologies within the context of innovative milieux is not the result of 'a series of actions on spot markets, where the long term can be reduced to a series of disconnected instants', but rather of actions which are 'path-dependent, that is, truly historical' (Storper 1997: 18). However, there are two sides to every question. On the one hand, innovative milieux are tremendously important for accelerating the innovation process. On the other, they impede the realisation of innovations outside the 'project' of the innovative milieu. This is typical of the rather limited simple learning model with just one feedback loop. Argyris and Schön (1978) describe this as *single-loop learning*. Learning is thus confined to corrective improvement-learning or *reactive adaptation* (Hudson 1996).

Grabher (1993: 265) clearly underscores the limitation of this learning model by saying that 'single-loop learning is essentially the intelligence of a thermostat'. Basically, the assumptions and distinctions that are made by the actors in the innovative network on which the innovative project is based cannot be questioned within a single-loop learning situation. In this model, one cannot expect any fundamental changes to occur in the strategy, structure or culture of the innovative network, for it is exclusively oriented towards incremental improvements.

In situations in which single-loop learning does not lead to the desired result or the solution of the problem at hand, one has to take a totally different approach to reach one's goals. In this case, one may speak of fundamental or double-loop learning, in which joint local strategies as well as the basic assumptions and distinctions that could not be questioned in single-loop learning are brought to the forefront. Double-loop learning first of all focuses on the question *why* a specific strategy should be successful. Conflicts, contradictions, resistance, and uncertainties cannot be avoided in double-loop learning. As previous positions need to be abandoned before new ones can be taken, it is inevitable that various old and potential new insights and cultures will clash. Double-loop learning not only creates new knowledge, but also makes old knowledge obsolete. It involves not only learning, but also unlearning. Accordingly, the consequences are much more far-reaching, the number of actors affected is much larger and the process usually takes considerably more time. This kind of learning requires that one already possesses a substantial ability to reflect and relativise one's own actions. It is a real process of *renewal*.

Finally, there is a third level of learning. In this triple-loop learning, even the basic principles and goals of the innovative network are questioned. At this level, the identity of the innovative network and, consequently, the identity of the whole innovative milieu are totally renewed and reconstituted. This kind of learning focuses on the question what goals one wants to pursue and who one wants to be. If single-loop learning is described as *improvement* and double-loop learning as *renewal*, then triple-loop learning may be characterised as *development* (Swieringa and Wierdsma 1990: 41–46). However, because of their structural similarity, the last two types of learning often are not differentiated and therefore both denoted as double-loop learning. To avoid any misunderstanding, I usually prefer to use the term 'reflective learning' for both double- and triple-loop learning.

The cognitive learning model offers a totally different kind of representation of the learning process. Again a system is assumed which is confronted with problematic situations which have to be overcome. In this model, the relationship between the different kinds of learning mentioned above becomes even clearer. The essential difference between single-loop learning and reflective learning can be made clear with the help of the concepts of *assimilation* and *accommodation*.

Assimilation takes place if new experiences fit smoothly into an actor's world-view. This world-view is thus enriched, but its fundamental character has not been changed. On the one hand, there is an intensification of the stock of knowledge whereby the precision of this knowledge is increased. On the other, assimilation leads to an abstraction and generalisation of this knowledge, whereby the same structures of knowledge and the way of looking at things are caught in abstract and general categories so that they also become applicable to new situations. Piaget (1983) calls the knowledge thus gathered empirical knowledge.

Empirical knowledge is distinguished from operative knowledge, which is generated by the accommodation process. Operative knowledge is the ability to deal with empirical categories in an abstract way. This requires a higher level of abstraction. While the acquisition of empirical knowledge only requires the allocation of the object of our knowledge to existing abstract categories and/or discovering and adding new categories, operative knowledge requires new insights into the relationships between the empirical categories, transcending the concrete empirical situation.

Operative knowledge makes it possible to re-interpret the same empirical experiences from a totally different perspective. This may undermine certainties and can lead to a temporary disorientation, which may cause one to question one's own opinions, role, position, and identity. Existing world-views are consequently relativised. This is also the moment of what has been labelled 'unlearning'. This moment of unlearning creates a certain tension (cognitive dissonance) between experience and the cognitive schemes normally used (Festinger 1957). The tension initiated by the confrontation with new situations to which the traditional schemes do not seem to apply is a necessary condition for reflective learning.

On the one hand, one can react to these kinds of tensions by avoiding, doubting, or suppressing them or by stretching the existing cognitive schemes so that they still seem to be applicable. These kinds of reactions are quite typical and may block the learning process. On the other, one can take the abstraction somewhat further and adopt an even more general cognitive structure, which will enable the combination of the initially seemingly incompatible cognitive schemes. These new insights lead to the recognition of the common denominator of the different perspectives and the underlying general principles. Thus, the existing elements of knowledge are organised in a new way and combined to generalise their applicability in practical situations.

The balance between assimilation and accommodation is decisive for any learning process that is not limited to single-loop learning. If all new experiences fit seamlessly into existing cognitive schemes, an intensification and generalisation of knowledge will take place, but this usually means 'more of the same' and, consequently, there is no real renewal. If, on the other hand, the existing organisational structure of cognitive schemes is constantly questioned, the actor or network cannot develop an identity and position. A minimum degree of continuity and stability is a necessary condition for the constitution of a specific identity. Only a healthy relation between assimilation and accommodation in the cognitive structure enables learning on all levels. Such learning processes do not take place steadily, but are characterised by breaks and hypes. Periods in which assimilation within certain cognitive structures prevails are followed by periods in which cognitive structures undergo important qualitative changes through accommodation. Such 'quantum leaps' and fundamental changes can only be realised if the actors involved have developed sufficient competence to make them.

Grabher (1993: 256) uses the case of the German Ruhr area to illustrate how certain innovative milieux[6] can impede reflective learning: 'The initial strength of the industrial districts of the past – their industrial atmosphere, highly developed and specialised infrastructure, the close interfirm linkages, and strong political support by regional institutions – turned into stubborn obstacles to innovation'. In an earlier publication, I described a similar situation with respect to the traditionally very successful Swiss watch-industry region (see Ernste 1994). In both cases, one can clearly speak of *lock-in* effects. The same conclusion is drawn by Hudson (1994: 197) on the basis of an analysis of a large number of older industrial regions. The thick localised institutional layer, which had guaranteed a blooming and often also very innovative industry, suppressed the recognition and implementation of radical alternatives. DiMaggio and

Powel were probably the first to point out that these lock-in tendencies constituted a risk:

> in the long run, organizational actors making rational decisions construct around themselves an environment that constrains their ability to change further in later years. ... organizations may try to change constantly; but, after a certain point in the structuration of an organizational field, the aggregate effect of individual change is to lessen the extent of diversity within the field.[7]
>
> (DiMaggio and Powel 1983: 148)

Grabher (1993) seeks the solution to the lock-in problem in cross-boundary activities, which involve scanning the environment for new developments and tendencies, and the identification and mobilisation of external resources. These are mainly R&D and marketing activities. The relatively loose connections which are so typical of flexible networks and which result in a creative redundancy policy, especially in the field of cross-boundary activities, can indeed contribute to the learning capability of the actors involved. Although the importance of such activities cannot be denied, it should be stressed that they do not fundamentally question the strategies of the actors involved and, as such, these activities lead to nothing more than an increase in incremental learning.

In these kinds of solutions, the impetus for renewal always comes from outside the innovative milieu. It is not sought within the margins of the system, but rather beyond its boundaries. The socio-economic and cultural layer within the innovative network has to raise the efficiency and effectiveness of the innovation process. Often in passing, some of the parties involved also remember to mention that these systems should be open because important impulses for renewal are expected to come from outside the system. That the former and latter require totally different structures and processes is often ignored. For *reflective* learning, it does not suffice to demand openness; what is needed is an innovative milieu that is able to dynamically redefine its own borders and identity over and over again. This involves more than just crossing inner and outer boundaries: people should to be able to make creative use of the 'otherness' and diversity established in the border area. For fundamental learning, a regional *perestroika* culture is required which stresses the functioning of the innovative milieu. It is in this specific innovative culture that innovative milieux can constitute and change themselves. Furthermore, it is a culture that promotes experiments and creates *space for innovations*.

The *action-theoretic* perspectives associated here with the second phase of the development of innovation research and policy need to be developed somewhat further. It is not just the context of innovative actions that should be understood as important aspects of the structure of innovative milieux; the actual interactions that take place in these structures and simultaneously produce and reproduce them should also be analysed further. Research should therefore focus more on the dynamics of creative and innovative actions. Further reflection on the learning process, as in this chapter, might be a step in the right direction. The language-pragmatic action theory, which has already been applied to this context by Ernste and Meier (1992), may also prove valuable as it unfolds the actual process of the social construction and reconstruction of the action framework. Innovative action and interaction in this framework are seen as the production of new meanings and goals in the dynamic process of constant societal and economic renewal. This is more than the incremental optimisation of means to a given end and more than developing further steps on a given path. It involves the process of finding fundamentally new paths of development that involve a broader view of rationalisation and modernisation. It calls for reflexive modernisation (Beck 1994) or structuration (Giddens 1984) and a specific action setting stimulating creativity and fundamental learning. This introduces the 'cultural' factor into the innovation process. In the literature, this is also referred to as the 'cultural turn' (Barnes 1995; DiMaggio 1994; Lash and Urry 1994; Sayer 1994; Sayer and Ray 1999; Vaiou and Mantouvalou 1999). 'Culture' in this case denotes the broader societal context with its multiplicity of rationalities and meanings with regard to viewing and transforming a region's economy. In the context of reflexive learning and processes of creative fundamental renewal, it also stresses the role of the culture industries as an important source of change. Modern innovation research will increasingly focus on these cultural aspects within an action-theoretical framework.

Universities and space for innovations

Analyses of innovation processes and reflexive learning processes are, of course, important from the scientific point of view, but to stimulate innovation policy, regionally or otherwise, first of all a number of directives are required. In this book, which focuses on the specific role of universities within learning regions, these directives do not just concern innovation policy in general, but, more in particular, university policy within the context of learning regions and the local knowledge infrastructure. In this section, I would like to address these policy issues in the light of the foregoing analysis of the concept of learning. The main question in this section is therefore: 'How can universities contribute to the creation of more space for innovations and especially space for reflexive innovative learning in learning regions?'

As a result of the growing awareness among people involved in innovation research and policy of the fact that innovativeness is not just determined by technological research and development activities, the role of universities in this context has changed dramatically. Innovativeness was to a large extent determined by activities aimed at successfully introducing new products and services on the market and activities that had more to do with customer demand, product improvement, and the management of successful cooperative relations within a local innovative milieu than with fundamental research and development. Consequently, universities were not regarded as the primary sources of knowledge production. Gradually, however, the production of innovation-related knowledge was extended to other areas in society. Whereas many firms developed into open and flexible networks, universities became just nodes in a network of knowledge-producing institutions and organisations (Funtowicz and Ravetz 1993; Gibbons *et al.* 1994). This move from a relatively isolated elitist system of knowledge production to a much broader one seems to have eroded the awareness of the differences between learning processes and of the diversity of the knowledge produced within different parts of this system. Knowledge and learning were increasingly regarded as something that was the same to all the different actors involved. Universities were, for example, drawn into an extensive system in which there was a high demand for directly applicable technological know-how. At the same time, as a consequence of universities losing their monopoly position in knowledge production and the increased pursuit of efficiency gains in public funding, most governments drastically reduced their financial support to universities. This money was partly redirected to other knowledge producers that seemed to offer more directly applicable knowledge (e.g. institutions for higher professional education).[8] Unfortunately, the government having the sole responsibility for funding knowledge production was also questioned, which resulted in the total absolute amount of government funding for knowledge production being reduced. This increased the tendency of universities to compensate for the loss of the relatively secure long-term government funds by conducting more and more short-term contract research, facilitated by intermediary organisations such as technology transfer centres (Goddard 1997: 1). By doing so, they increasingly produced a rather one-dimensional type of short-term and easy-to-apply incremental knowledge for which there was a growing demand within the knowledge economy.

A reorientation was taking place, not only with respect to research and development (the generation of knowledge), but also in the field of the other important knowledge-producing function of universities, i.e. teaching (the transmission of knowledge). Here, the competitive struggle with institutions of higher professional education created an enormous pressure to deliver more focused and easy-to-apply knowledge which would facilitate uncritical incremental learning within future professional contexts. As a consequence, many universities implicitly or explicitly changed the basic philosophy of university teaching. Originally, the basic idea of *university* education was to organise teaching in close relationship with research. University education was in line with science and scientific thinking, while the basic idea of higher professional education was to provide an educational programme closely related to the professional praxis. Many research universities now became merely *schools* and critical and reflective learning, so crucial to the progress in science, was to a large degree replaced by uncritical and streamlined incremental learning, so important for quick progress along fixed routes. The former President of the University of Amsterdam, Jan-Karel Gevers, once characterised these school-like institutions as 'places where they serve the coffee that is made elsewhere' (Blokker 1999).[9] Currently, many European universities have divided their curricula into a praxis- and profession-oriented part and a more scientific part. Thus, not only the curricula, but in fact also the universities themselves have to a large degree been divided into a school-like and unscientific part similar to the schools for higher professional education and a part that resembles the erudite circles of elite graduate colleges. This may very well mean the end of the typical kind of reflective learning for which universities were originally created. Universities have thus opened up or are opening up their ivory towers. They now have become partners in an extensive network of players in the knowledge economy. However, by doing so, they showed a lack of sensitivity to the fact that, also in an innovative learning network, universities will have to play a very specific role, a role others cannot and will not play, if an institution is to play a role at all. By doing exactly what institutions for professional education are already doing, i.e. adapting to the rather shallow level of reflexivity of local professional and commercial organisations,[10] universities are becoming irrelevant within the local knowledge economy.

Given their differentiated view on learning processes and distinguishable levels of learning competence, universities could serve local innovative networks much more effectively, namely by redefining themselves as principal agents of change, as institutions providing the essential competence for reflective learning, and as generators of the fundamental reflective insights needed to accompany innovation in a regional context. This means that universities should not strive to become what others already are, but rather to externalise that part of the university that is focused on higher *professional* education, and to reconsider its *scientific* core competence (Mittelstrass 1997: 4). As argued above, the conditions for reflective learning are different from those for incremental learning. For the latter, the ivory tower of the traditional university was not functional at all, and in this respect the call to drive the scientists out of their ivory tower is certainly justified. For reflective learning, so important for overcoming path dependencies and lock-in effects in learning regions, it may be functional to turn away from the routine development paths, to take a long-term view, to reflect on what is really happening and – independent of direct commercial interests – to think through how things may be changed. Ironically enough, the ivory tower is very functional in this respect and perhaps scientists should be asked to go back into it. Of course, this does not mean that the ivory tower should not have connections with the regional knowledge economy. On the contrary, scientific research and teaching should address the current societal problems and developments as well as cultivate its reflective independency to be able to play its specific role within the local knowledge economy. As such, universities well rooted within these regional knowledge networks may develop into establishments of enhanced publicness in which society conceives itself, questions itself and educates itself (Kahl 2000). To suspend traditional ways of thinking and doing, to stop routines, stand still and think first, that is the main objective of every university. It is the place where society intelligently interrupts itself, unlearns, and fundamentally renews itself. Universities that pretend to play a role of significance within the region should create a place endowed with inspiration and reflective fascination, a place where scientific libido is generated, a place for reflective learning *par excellence*. The university should be the yeast in the regional dough. In this sense, the University of Oldenburg in Germany is an interesting example of how a grey inconspicuous provincial university can be transformed into a pioneering and highly esteemed university in only twelve years. Universities defined in this way can play a pivotal role within the regional context, not in the least as agents of change in the general *culture* of the regions in which they are embedded.

This is not just a question of repositioning the university in its totality within the regional learning network, but also of reorganising the production of knowledge within the university. The danger of lock-in effects and reduced incremental learning looms in each discipline. To be really innovative in a more fundamental sense, new kinds of knowledge are required. There is an increasing demand for transdisciplinary knowledge (Gibbons *et al.* 1994). The production of this kind of knowledge takes place in very dynamic and heterogeneous contexts in which people do not operate according to the usual disciplinary criteria or within the usual scientific hierarchies. In these inherently 'untypical' situations, the usual criteria for 'scientific quality' cannot be applied. In this kind of transdisciplinary knowledge production, not only the traditional standards for scientific quality, but also criteria that are much more sensitive to societal demands, need to be taken into account. Transdisciplinary research and education are more sensitive to external expectations, more reflective, and tend to be more socially accountable. Research problems are much less predefined, inspired, and jointly defined in a specific context by an extensive and heterogeneous circle of practitioners rooted in local society (Berkhout 1999; Nowotny 1997: 8). This linkage with the regional context should not be mistaken for 'doing what the local economy demands' in the sense of quick and efficient incremental learning. Experience shows that more and more actors within the local knowledge economy also demand assistance in the kind of reflective learning described above. Problems within this area are basically ill-defined due to the need to develop long-term vision, and situated at a conceptual and reflective rather than a direct practical level. Also, the integration of different development paths (e.g. for the purpose of technological and organisational improvements) is a typical issue addressed within these frameworks, which makes a higher level of reflexivity necessary. These are the problems of an organisation or network of organisations seeking fundamental learning and totally new development paths. Here, typically academic transdisciplinary research and university education firmly rooted in the learning region can play a very specific role.

Conclusions

What can be learned from this discussion?

1 The institutional approach of the second phase in innovation research and policy should be extended to a third phase in which the conditions for reflective learning in innovative regions should explicitly be addressed. An action-theoretic analysis of the main mechanisms in innovation processes might be fruitful in this respect.

2 The institutional approaches in the second phase have convincingly shown that innovative networks and the innovations processes taking place within them as well as their emergence, reproduction, and transformation are all firmly rooted in actions and interactions in the process of communicative rationalisation. The potentials of these processes are not yet fully realised. Reflective learning and reflective modernisation are not sufficiently taken into account in current policies on learning regions.

3 Regional innovation policies should as such be regarded as policies promoting the communicative reinterpretation and redefinition of the meaning of existing and future development paths and goals.

4 Classic innovation management is insufficient and sometimes even harmful. Innovation policy should not carry innovations *into* the region, but rather create spaces for creativity, spaces for inspiration, and spaces for reflection![11] Our society not only needs *innovative* milieux, but also *imaginative* milieux. What is required is a culture of change. The university can play a crucial role within learning regions as an inspiring agent of cultural change and as an establishment for reflective and creative thinking. However, to put it provocatively, this also implies that certain tendencies towards banning 'academic thinking' from universities as can be observed in a number of European university systems should be turned into a policy which makes universities institutions in which the regional society is constantly 'reconceived'.

Notes

1 For a historical overview, see also Windhorst (1983).
2 Below, I will try to show that this representation of spatial diffusion of innovation is based on a rather simplistic concept of 'learning in space', and that modern forms of spatial innovation can only be adequately conceptualised with a more complex model of 'learning'.
3 Variation of Lorenzen's (1997) term: 'Learning in space'.
4 A positive exception and first attempt is Grabher (1993) and the recently published book by Cooke and Morgan, on *The Associational Economy: Firms, Regions, and Innovation* (1998).
5 This is the typical realm of behaviourist theories of learning, such as Pavlov conditioning as a form of learning through the association of stimuli, and instrumental conditioning as learning from experimenting with reactions.
6 He prefers the concept of 'industrial district', but this does not change the line of argumentation.

7 This structuration process is described as consisting of four forces: (1) an increase in the intensity of interactions between partners within the network; (2) the development of power structures and of coalitions between the organisations involved; (3) an increase in the density of information with which organisations are confronted; (4) the development of a consciousness of being a part of a joint project.

8 In the Netherlands, these are known as 'HBO' institutions; in the German-speaking areas of Europe, they are called 'Fach-Hochschulen', comparable to the American college system limited to undergraduate studies resulting in a bachelor's degree.

9 In the same article, Blokker cites Professor Ed Elbers who notes that students also use a different kind of vocabulary to describe these kinds of institutions: 'studying' becomes 'learning'; 'lecturers' become 'teachers'; 'lecture halls' become 'class rooms' and 'universities' become 'schools'. 'The "homo academicus" is replaced by the "course participant" who is tempted by competing universities with the promise that one can expect a good return on investment from this course' (Blokker 1999: 37).

10 By saying this, I, certainly do not want to devaluate the role of local firms or other commercial players in the regional knowledge economy. Rather, I would like to emphasise that there is an important and flexible division of labour and a whole set of complementary products for which there is a need in regional innovative networks. If a partner in such a flexible network has nothing special and complementary to offer, there is no need for it at all! Commercial firms are not the main places for reflexivity, but rather the sites for efficiency and productivity. Even so, they have an important need for reflexivity and reflective learning at fixed moments and stages in their development. Here the specific role of universities in networks comes into the picture.

11 It is no coincidence that there is a course in the curriculum for policy studies at the University of Nijmegen which bears the title 'the inspiring place, space for inspiration' (see http://www.kun.nl/socgeo).

References

Amin, A. and Thrift, N. J. (1994) 'Living in the global', in A. Amin and N. J. Thrift (eds) *Globalization, Institutions, and Regional Development in Europe*, Oxford: Oxford University Press, pp. 1–22.

Argyris, C. and Schön, D. (1978) *Organizational Learning: A Theory of Action Perspective*, Reading, MA: Addison-Wesley.

Aydalot, P. and Keeble, D. (eds) (1988) *High Technology Industry and Innovative Environments: The European Experience*, London: Routledge.

Barnes, T. J. (1995) 'Political Economy I: "The Culture, Stupid"', *Progress in Human Geography* 19, 3: 423–431.

Beck, U. (1994) 'Towards a Theory of Reflexive Modernization', in U. Beck, A. Giddens and S. Lash (eds) *Reflexive Modernization: Politics, Tradition and Aesthetics in the Modern Social Order*, Cambridge: Polity Press.

Berkhout, A. J. (1999) 'De Universiteit in de 21ste eeuw: Multidisciplinaire Wetenschap in een Flexibele Netwerk Organisatie', *Tijdschrift voor Wetenschap, Technologie en Samenleving* 7, 3: 86–93.

Blokker, B. (1999) 'Slechte Ruilhandel op de Alma Mater: De Toestand van de Universiteit', *NRC-Handelsblad*, 29 January: 37.

Brown, L. (1981) *Innovation Diffusion: A New Perspective*, London: Methuen.

Cooke, P. and Morgan, K. (1998) *The Associational Economy: Firms, Regions, and Innovation*, Oxford: Oxford University Press.

Daxner, M. (1999) *Die blockierte Universität*, Frankfurt: Campus.

DiMaggio, P. J. (1994) 'Culture and Economy', in N. J. Smelser and R. Swedberg (eds) *The Handbook of Economic Sociology*, Princeton, NJ: Princeton University Press.

DiMaggio, P. J. and Powel, W. W. (1983) 'The Iron Cage Revisited: Institutional Isomorphism and Collective Rationality in Organizational Fields', *American Sociological Review* 48: 147–160.

Edmondson, A. and Moingeon, B. (1996) 'When to Learn How and When to Learn Why: Appropriate Organisational Learning Processes as a Source of Competitive Advantage', in B. Moingeon and A. Edmondson (eds) *Organisational Learning and Competitive Advantage*, London: Sage, pp. 17–37.

Enright, M. J. (1996) 'Regional Clusters and Economic Development: A Research Agenda', in U. Staber, N. Schaefer and B. Sharma (eds) *Business Networks: Prospect for Regional Development*, New York: De Gruyter.

Enright, M. J., Borner, S., Porter, M. and Weder, R. (1991) *Internationale Wettbewerbsvorteile: Ein strategisches Konzept für die Schweiz*, Frankfurt: Campus.

Ernste, H. (1994) 'Flexible Specialisation and Regional Policy', *Geografický Casopis* 46, 4: 351–382.

Ernste, H., Karuri, W. J. and Marquez, A. (1998) 'Cooperative Planning: A "Survival Kit"', *Salzburger Institut für Raumordnung und Wohnen (SIR)-Mitteilungen und Berichte* 26: 63–78.

Ernste, H. and Meier, V. (1992) 'Communicating Regional Development', in H. Ernste and V. Meier (eds) *Regional Development and Contemporary Industrial Response: Extending Flexible Specialisation*, London: Belhaven: 263–285.

Ewers, H. J. and Wettmann, R. W. (1980a) 'Innovationsorientierte Regionalpolitik', *Schriftenreihe 'Raumordnung' des Bundesministers für Raumordnung, Bauwesen und Städtebau* 06.042.

Ewers, H. J. and Wettmann, R. W. (1980b) 'Innovation-oriented Regional Policy', *Regional Studies* 14: 161–179.

Festinger, L. (1957) *Theory of Cognitive Dissonance*, Evaston, IL: Row & Peterson.

Florida, R. (1995) 'Toward the Learning Region', *Futures* 27, 5: 527–536.

Fromhold-Eisebith, M. (1995) 'Das "kreative Milieu" als Motor regionalwirtschaftlicher Entwicklung. Forschungstrends und Erfassungsmöglichkeiten', *Geographische Zeitschrift* 83: 30–47.

Fujita, M., Krugman, P. and Venables, A. J. (1999) *The Spatial Economy: Cities, Regions and International Trade*, Boston: MIT Press.

Funtowicz, S. O. and Ravetz, J. R. (1993) 'Science for the Post-normal Age', *Futures* 25, 7: 739–756.

Gibbons, M., Limoges, C., Nowotny, H., Schwarzman, S., Scott, P. and Trow, M. (1994) *The New Production of Knowledge*, London: Sage.

Giddens, A. (1984) *The Constitution of Society: Outline of the Theory of Structuration*, Cambridge: Polity Press.

Goddard, J. (1997) 'Universities and Regional Development: An Overview', background paper to OECD project on the response of higher education to regional needs, online available HTTP: http://www.newcastle.ac.uk/~ncurds/univ/imhe-97.htm

Grabher, G. (1993) 'The Weakness of Strong Ties: The Lock-in of Regional Development in the Ruhr Area', in G. Grabher (ed.) *The Embedded Firm: On the Socio-economics of Industrial Networks*, London: Routledge, pp. 255–275.

Hägerstrand, T. (1967) *Innovation Diffusion as a Spatial Process*, Chicago: University of Chicago Press.

Hassink, R. (1997) 'Die Bedeutung der lernenden Region für die regionale Innovationsforschung', *Geographische Zeitschrift* 85, 2 and 3: 159–173.

Hassink, R. (1999) 'What Does the Learning Region Mean for Economic Geography?', *Korean Journal of Regional Science* 15, 1: 93–116.

Hudson, R. (1994) 'Institutional Change, Cultural Transformation, and Economic Regeneration: Myths and Realities from Europe's Old Industrial Areas', in A. Amin and N. J. Thrift (eds) *Globalization, Institutions, and Regional Development in Europe*, Oxford: Oxford University Press, pp. 196–216.

Hudson, R. (1996) 'The Learning Economy: The Learning Firm and the Learning Region: A Sympathetic Critique of the Limits to Learning', *European Urban and Regional Studies* 6: 59–72.

Kahl, R. (2000) 'Mit Lust und Leid: Wie Michael Daxner wissenschaftliche Libido erzeugen will', *Die Zeit* 3, 13 January: 34.

Kilper, H. and Latniak, E. (1996) 'Einflussfaktoren betrieblicher Innovationsprozesse: Zur Rolle des regionalen Umfeldes', in P. Brödner, U. Pekruhl and D. Rehfeld (eds) *Arbeitsteilung ohne Ende? Von den Schwierigkeiten inner- und überbetrieblicher Zusammenarbeit*, Munich: Mering, pp. 217–240.

Knaap, P. van der (1997) *Lerende Overheid, Intelligent Beleid: De Lessen van Beleidsevaluatie en Beleidsadvisering voor de Structuurfondsen van de Europese Unie*, Den Haag: Phaedrus.

Krugman, P. (1999) *Some Chaotic Notes on Regional Dynamics* http://web.mit.edu/krugman/www/temin.html.

Lash, S. and Urry, J. (1994) *Economics of Signs and Space*, London: Sage.

Lorenzen, M. (1997) 'Learning in Space: Some Properties of Knowledge, Interaction, and Territory in Neo-institutional Geography', paper presented at the EUNIT Conference on Industry, Innovation and Territory, 20–22 March, Lisbon.

Mittelstrass, J. (1997) 'Abschied von der vollständigen Universität', *Unimagazin: Die Zeitschrift der Universität Zürich* 1, 1997: 4–6.

Morgan, K. (1995) 'The Learning Region: Institutions, Innovation and Regional Renewal', in *Papers in Planning Research* 157, Cardiff: Department of City and Regional Planning, Cardiff University.

Morgan, K. (1997) 'The Learning Region: Institutions, Innovation and Regional Renewal', *Regional Studies* 31, 5: 491–503.

Nowotny, H. (1997) 'Im Spannungsfeld der Wissensproduktion und Wissensvermittlung', *Unimagazin: Die Zeitschrift der Universität Zürich* 1, 1997: 7–9.

Piaget, J. (1983) *Jean Piaget: Meine Theorie der geistigen Entwicklung*, Frankfurt am Main: Fischer.

Porter, M. E. (1990) *The Competitive Advantage of Nations*, Basingstoke: Macmillan.

Pyke, F. and Sengenberger, W. (eds) (1992) *Industrial Districts and Local Economic Regeneration*, Geneva: International Institute for Labour Studies.

Sabel, C. (1989) 'Flexible Specialisation and the Re-emergence of Regional Economics', in P. Hirst and J. Zeitlin (eds) *Reversing Industrial Decline? Industrial Structure and Policy in Britain and her Competitors*, Oxford: Berg.

Sayer, A. (1994) 'Editorial: Culture Studies and "The Economy, Stupid"', *Environment and Planning D: Society and Space* 12: 635–637.

Sayer, A. (1997) 'The Dialectic of Culture and Economy', in R. Lee and J. Wills (eds) *Geographies of Economies*, London: Arnold.

Sayer, A. and Ray, L. (eds) (1999) *Culture and Economy after the Cultural Turn*, London: Sage.

Storper, M. (1997) *The Regional World: Territorial Development in a Global Economy*, New York: Guilford Press.

Swieringa, J. and Wierdsma, A. F. M. (1990) *Op Weg naar een Lerende Organisatie: Over het Leren en Opleiden van Organisaties*, Groningen: Wolters-Noordhoff.

Vaiou, D. and Mantouvalou, M. (1999) 'Guest Editorial of Special Issue: Spatial Disciplines in the Cultural Turn', *European Planning Studies* 7, 1.

Vermeulen, W. J., Waals, J. F. M. van der, Ernste, H. and Glasbergen, P. (1997) 'Duurzaamheid als Uitdaging: Wetenschappelijke Raad voor het Regeringsbeleid (WRR)', *Voorstudies en Achtergrondberichten* V101, Den Haag: Sdu.

Windhorst, H.-W. (1983) *Geographische Innovations- und Diffusionsforschung*, Darmstadt: Wissenschaftliche Buchgesellschaft.

Part II
HEI–industry collaboration

7 The role of universities in the learning region

Peter Maskell and Gunnar Törnqvist

Introduction

In contemporary society, there are clear links between *world-wide networks and local environments*, links that communicate information between different geographical levels. A glance at different forms of culture and sport, for example, indicate how both world-wide relations and local isolation characterise our modern view of life. The British geographer Doreen Massey used the expression *a global sense of place* to capture this notion in an article on the inhabitants of the shanty towns in Rio de Janeiro:

> Who knows global football like the back of their hand, and have produced some of its players; who have contributed massively to global music, who gave us the samba and produced the lambada that everyone was dancing to last year in the clubs of Paris and London; and who have never, or hardly ever, been to downtown Rio. At one level they have been tremendous contributors to what we call time-space compression; and at another level, they are imprisoned in it.
>
> (Massey 1995: 152)

The frequently small-scale production that is developed under both competitive and cooperative conditions in close regional environments would not be competitive or successful without close contacts to the world outside. The companies developed in these environments often sell their products in world-wide markets. They keep in touch with, and benefit from, the international flow of knowledge, capital, and ideas.

Universities in particular act as strategic links between world-wide networks and local environments. These links move in two directions. The university links up a place and a region with centres of knowledge throughout the world, thus acting as an international link. At the same time, the university mobilises local and regional competence in different ways to create an attractive environment in those places where they are situated.

Research and higher education have most probably been one of our most expansive sectors in recent years. At the same time, little research has been conducted on this sector. The lack of research in this area is remarkable when one considers the volume of research that has been devoted to, for example, the agricultural sector and industry. Research should, however, address the role of science and higher education in social and economic development rather than the internal operations of the sector itself.

The context of learning in universities

Universities and nations

Since the nineteenth century or, in some cases, even earlier, university research and higher education have been largely financed and regulated within a national framework. In many economically developed countries, the established churches, schools, health care, and public administration have been the principal sources of employment for university graduates. The career paths open to graduates have largely been within the borders of the nation-state.

As the American economist Nathan Rosenberg has clearly shown, the occupational divide between science and industry was almost complete right up to the end of the nineteenth century. Even after this date, and despite certain common origins, science and industrial technology developed along different paths that were easy to separate and that seldom crossed. It was not until far into the twentieth century that an innovation system was developed that indirectly drew universities and companies together. It was in the industrial research laboratories that the recruitment of university graduates began to bridge the gulf between science and industrial technology. In many respects, the situation is still the same today (Rosenberg and Birdzell 1986).

However, the major breakthrough occurred with the outbreak of the Second World War. A large part of the scientific and technical capacity of the warring nations was dedicated to total warfare. The Manhattan Project in the United States, which was devoted to the manufacture of an atom bomb, was in its time the most spectacular example of close cooperation between the war industry and research. Individuals from a range of ethnic backgrounds pooled their various skills and worked together in secret laboratories. Research that would normally have taken decades in peacetime was carried out in a couple of years. Entire industrial towns were quickly built to house applied research and development facilities. Never before had such large sums been channelled into research.

In a similar fashion, but under somewhat freer conditions, a gigantic space research programme was launched. During the days of the Cold War, cooperation between research and industry was further developed, not just in the USA, but in the UK, France, and other countries as well. The strongest ties between university research and industry still appear to be within what is known as the military–industrial complex. The foodstuffs and pharmaceutical industries are examples of other similar blocs of cooperation (Markusen et al. 1991).

As a result of these developments, the practical significance of academic research for society, particularly scientific research, became increasingly evident throughout society. The status and prestige of scientists grew in an unprecedented fashion. The growing stature of research spread from science and medicine to encompass all types of research. At present there appears to be a widespread view that the university is one of the major driving forces behind technical and industrial development. There is also considerable discussion of the idea that there is a fundamental relationship between research and education, on the one hand, and national competitiveness, on the other, influencing the economy, employment, and welfare.[1] By theoretically associating innovation and investment with growth, the literature on 'increasing-returns endogenous growth' has filled a vacuum by pointing out some hitherto partly overlooked policy areas where government-induced growth-enhancing improvements might be made.[2]

Universities and regions

While education and research are clearly the university's two most important tasks, the idea is gradually emerging that the university's cooperation with society is a third task it must undertake. Expressed in a narrow fashion, this third task is to disseminate information on the university's own activities and to sell research and educational services in the market place. In the general debate on the future of the university, this third task involving regional partnerships has gained in importance and has been extended to cover an increasing number of roles in society beyond the two mentioned above. This enlargement of the role of the university is naturally not without controversy.

University: A Regional Booster is the title of a book by the Dutch economist Raymond Florax (1992). As the title suggests, universities and university colleges are seen as 'help engines', 'locomotives', and 'start rockets' for regional developments. The establishment of new universities and university colleges has become an instrument of regional policy in Sweden in the past few years, as is the case in a number of other countries such as Norway, Finland, and the UK. At the local and regional levels, an increasing number of politicians and planners view universities and colleges as indispensable ingredients for creating attractive regional environments. However, the assessment of the actual importance of higher education as a driving force behind regional development is an extraordinarily complicated question. Further research will be required in order to find answers to this question. In the discussion below, some of the issues involved will be examined briefly.

Several regions that are widely thought of as being dynamic contain successful universities and research institutes. However, there are grounds for scepticism about loosely-based assumptions regarding the relationship between higher education and research, and regional development. If two phenomena appear in the same area, e.g. successful research and industrial expansion, this is not to say that there is necessarily a causal relationship between them.

A combination of fortunate circumstances in one region does not necessarily produce the same effect in another area. The few penetrating analyses that have been carried out indicate fairly clearly that these relationships are highly complex and that the effects of higher education and research vary greatly, depending on the place and region.

Types of multipliers

Universities and university colleges give rise to certain obvious consequences. They can attract new firms, frequently small, as well as the research-intensive departments of large companies. Research villages and science parks are examples of such concentrations. However, it would not generally appear to be the university's own research that acts as a magnet, but rather the opportunity of recruiting skilled graduates. From the Danish and Swedish experience, it is fairly evident that the new universities generally recruit students from their vicinity. It is therefore probable that regional universities manage to mobilise a skill reserve that would otherwise not participate in higher education. Regarding the supply of graduates, the picture is not quite so clear. The extent to which new graduates remain in the region or move outside depends in large part on the local labour market. In large densely populated regions, many graduates decide to stay on after completing their studies, whereas in more sparsely populated regions, new graduates tend to move. Particularly in small regions, the most important source of graduate employment is the university itself.

Universities and colleges naturally give rise to multiplier effects. In many areas, students and teachers form the region's largest workforce. Retail, culture, and other quality services become established in the vicinity of the university. University towns also become attractive places to live in both a physical and social sense. Even small universities and colleges can have an important symbolic value and raise the status of the region.

But the major question is whether the university can create a greater degree of dynamism in a region. Are there substantial synergy effects when research universities and companies group together in a region? An answer to this question may be found in recent research into well-known regional environments in the United States, Europe, and Japan. These environments have several common features. They are large population centres, contain large universities and research institutes, and have a strong element of entrepreneurship based on high-tech, electronics, and information technology.

On the basis of these studies, two different groups of environments may be clearly identified. The first group comprises the *London–Heathrow–Reading corridor*, the *Plateau de Saclay*, south of Paris, *Sophia Antipolis* near Nice, the *Munich region*, the *Kista-Arlanda corridor*, and *Tsukuba*, the science town near Tokyo. These areas are characterised by a heavy concentration of R&D-intensive companies and easy access to important universities and research institutes. However, the studies that have been carried out thus far have not provided any clear evidence of synergy effects between university research and entrepreneurial success. The contacts between them are few. Despite their close proximity, universities and research institutes live in one world, small companies in another.

In the other group, we find four different environments that have indeed experienced substantial synergy effects: *Silicon Valley* and Stanford University, the *Highway 128 complex* around Boston and MIT, *Aerospace Alley* and the California Institute of Technology, and finally *Cambridge* in Britain with its ancient, prestigious university. Here there are direct links and a substantial transfer of knowledge between research universities and clusters of companies. There are numerous institutional and individual networks. These networks are frequently held together by key individuals who know each other well. The regulatory framework is minimal and the environments are relatively unplanned and long-standing.[3]

The researchers who have studied these environments suggest that the following factors play an important role in explaining the remarkable differences between the two groups. It takes years for synergy effects to appear. It is vital that university research is in tune with the needs of industry, as was the case with the space programme and the Cold War military–industrial complex. Behind these successes are individuals whose early initiatives began a long-term process, a spark that ignited a chain reaction. Metaphorically speaking, there is a need for a 'precision-tooled' interaction between researchers and entrepreneurs. This interaction presupposes mutual understanding and trust. In this context, it is appropriate to remind ourselves of what we know today about *civility*, the *social tapestry*, and the *conditions for social communication* (Coleman 1984; Gambetta 1988; Putnam 1993; Törnqvist 1998).

In the literature, considerable attention has been devoted to the concept of *critical mass*. Underlying this concept is the belief that there are economies of scale in research. It is obvious that research in the natural sciences, technology, and medicine frequently requires advanced equipment. For economic reasons, this type of expensive equipment cannot be spread around. It is more difficult to say whether or not the same argument regarding critical mass also applies to human resources. The accumulation of competence in one place naturally creates opportunities for innovation. This is borne out by studies of creative environments. However, on the basis of the analysis carried out in writings about conditions for social communication, it would appear reasonable to assume that critical mass refers to *communication density* rather than the number of persons involved. It is perhaps not always the case that communication density operates in an optimal fashion in large university departments. In European geography, there are many good examples of how the social fabric is at its most dense in small and medium-sized environments, whereas the risk of blockages exists in very large environments. It is also obvious that innovative interaction and growth in knowledge-intensive industries are not the result of simple variables such as size or proximity between industry and university. Here we are confronted with the need for further research.

Creating learning regions

When striving to create new competitive advantages through learning, firms cultivate their ability to connect with others at the local, national, and even global levels (Ernst and Guerriei 1997). These geographically expanding business networks enable firms to gain access to new sources of information, skills, and production, thereby complementing a firm's own competencies and increasing the value of its assets. In a major and detailed study, DeBresson (1996) has, for instance, shown that of the 1,641 major Canadian innovations from 1945–70, less than 10 per cent were the result of a firm's 'in-house' activities only. The rest involved as many as seven, with an average of four, different independent organisations. Historical studies (see, for instance, Rosenberg 1972) have also emphasised the importance of interaction between users and producers in the USA. In Sweden, the Uppsala School, taking the economics of industrial marketing as their starting-point, has in a number of studies empirically shown how competencies were enhanced through networks involving informal cooperation between firms (Håkansson 1987, 1989). Others have demonstrated the importance of interaction with customers for successful innovation and competitiveness (Freeman 1982, 1991; Hagedoorn and Schakenraad 1992; Lundvall 1985, 1988). The recent literature on innovation systems has this interaction as its most basic building block (Edquist 1997; Freeman 1995; List 1841; Lundvall 1992; Lundvall and Maskell forthcoming; Mowery and Oxley 1995; Nelson 1993).

Such an innovative process – requiring a high level of interaction, dialogue, and exchange of information – may be conducted long-distance, but is often less expensive, more reliable and easier to conduct locally. Contemporary empirical studies strongly support this view (Jaffe *et al.* 1993; Malmberg 1996). The clustering of inputs, such as industrial and university R&D, agglomerations of manufacturing firms in related industries, and networks of business-service providers, often create scale economies in the creation of knowledge, and facilitate the transfer of knowledge to the firms in the area (Patel and Pavitt 1991; Patel 1995).

The practicality of being close to relevant organisations is not the only factor of importance. The ability to exchange otherwise purely internal information also constitutes an important part of the competitive advantage for industrial agglomerations (Lorenzen 1998; Malmberg and Maskell 1997; Maskell and Malmberg 1999a, 1999b). This ongoing process of geographically concentrated tacit knowledge-sharing and cross-fertilisation of ideas enhances knowledge creation at the level of the firm. Because of the uneven supply and huge economic significance of localised formal and tacit mechanisms for learning and knowledge transfer, a new entry is added to the list of currently important *locational* factors influencing the geographical pattern of industry. The issue of creating or improving an innovative regional milieu or culture has thus bit by bit come to attract major interest from policy-makers in the field of industrial development. It has also been a rapidly growing area of interest in the academic discourse of economic geography and business economics.

Receiving systems

Important elements identified in the formation of learning regions[4] are critical and knowledgeable customers, competent suppliers, trustful inter-firm relations and networks, and a high degree of intra-industry rivalry. The regional 'receiving system' which helps firms identify and utilise international technological innovations also appears to be very important in the making of a learning region (Mowery and Oxley 1995). A receiving system might be formally organised into public or semi-public bodies, or based on less well-defined but closely knit networks of information exchange between similar firms, or a combination of both. When firms in certain regions consistently lag behind firms in the remaining regions of a country, it can, at least in part, be attributed to deficiencies in the receiving system, regardless of its specific form. Such deficiencies might be surprisingly stable and long-lasting, making firms in the region unable to take full advantage of improvements otherwise available. This implies that the process of uneven economic development does in fact have an endogenous component where human assets or cultural factors, deeply embedded in the social fabric of the region, might play a significant role.

The need to unlearn

Sometimes the deficiencies in a region's capabilities are the outcome of past successful learning and adaptation. Extraordinary economically successful learning processes tend to beget routines of extraordinary durability: they are retained and might even be aggressively defended long after changes in external conditions have made them redundant. It is an established fact of life that it is a lot easier to challenge the orthodoxy of others compared with one's own, and regions can occasionally get caught in specific, initially successful, ways of doing things, which later events have converted into shackles hindering further progress. As Boisot explained:

> experiences work their way into the collective memory and expectations of a culture and remain embodied in institutional arrangements long after they have ceased to serve. They may then obstruct rather than assist the process of social adaption much as early childhood traumas become the source of phobias and pathologies in later adult life.
>
> (Boisot 1983: 161)

Almost all contemporary regions in high-cost countries contain elements of such 'childhood traumas' related to the institutional consequences of former successes in the bygone era of manufacturing industry. In order to restore the foundation for new rounds of successful regional learning, some 'unlearning' must take place in the region. One of the economically most important tasks performed by regional entrepreneurs is to facilitate such unlearning by breaking down redundant institutions and eliminating obsolete conceptions and antiquated shared beliefs.

Regardless of whether the unlearning of old ways and habits is relatively rapid or relatively slow, regional development policy is mainly a process of creatively 'making do' with the historical legacy of institutions and routines. We can never build entirely anew, and most economic processes are strongly path dependent (Arthur 1994; Krugman 1991).

The Øresund region

In many ways, the Øresund region is in a unique position to head a transformation from the traditional engineering industries of yesterday into a cohesive learning economy in the twenty-first century. In 2000, a 16–kilometre-long bridge and tunnel was completed between the cities of Copenhagen in Denmark and Malmö in Sweden, significantly improving accessibility within this built-up area of 2.9 million inhabitants, 1.1 million employees and 123,000 firms. The region contains eleven universities and university colleges with 17,000 employees, 7,000 of whom are teachers and researchers, and 120,000 students. The largest single units in the network are Lund University (38,000 students), the University of Copenhagen (30,000), the Copenhagen Business School (14,000), and Roskilde University (6,000) (Thanki 1998).

The combined scale of research is more difficult to estimate. The number of research reports published between 1994–96 can perhaps give us some idea. According to this rough measure, Øresund is ranked fourth among European regional concentrations of research, behind London, Paris, and Amsterdam/ Rotterdam. It should also be noted that 60 per cent of Scandinavia's entire pharmaceutical industry is located in the Øresund area.

The teaching units, research departments, administrative units, laboratories, databases and libraries of the various universities in the Øresund region are joined together in a computer network. Students are able to follow combinations of courses on both sides of Øresund. Cross-border research cooperation takes place in informal networks. At present there are a number of joint projects under way that will examine the growth of the Øresund region as a major social experiment. In order to coordinate these activities, there is a formal board which consists of the rectors of the various units that are part of the federation, an executive committee, and a joint secretariat.

The eleven local universities provide the Øresund region with a good supply of university graduates. The Scania region is particularly well equipped as it accommodates 39 per cent of the population and 40 per cent of the employees in the Øresund region, but 48 per cent of the graduates.

Both the Scania and the Copenhagen regions have, furthermore, been able to attract more graduates than they 'export', thus maintaining a positive 'balance of academic trade'. This is especially so for the Copenhagen region, which has benefited from a net immigration of graduates educated at universities outside the region (see Table 7.1). This net inflow has benefited private industry (3,566 graduates from engineering and business economics), as well as public administration and the legal profession (2,049 graduates from the social sciences, including law). A major outflow has taken place, however, within natural science (secondary school teachers, veterinarians).

However, in general, firms in the Øresund region do *without* university graduates. For instance, more than three-quarters of the firms in the Copenhagen region employ no university graduates in any capacity or function whatsoever (production, finance, marketing, human resource development, or public relations).[5]

As is the case in many other welfare societies, the majority of graduates from the humanities, as well as from the social and natural sciences, are employed in the Øresund region public sector as administrators, teachers or researchers. The majority of engineers work in the private sector in manufacturing, construction, and services. Previously, engineers typically occupied the senior positions in the larger firms in these industries, but it appears as if new groups of graduates with a more specialised education are gradually replacing engineers in many managerial functions. Young engineers entering these industries today are thus more likely to utilise their educational advantages in performing purely technical functions than was the case a generation ago.

The sectoral distribution of all university graduates in the Øresund region is shown in Table 7.2. Even here, obvious differences emerge as far more graduates in the Copenhagen region are employed in the private sector (outside KIBS) than in Scania, mainly because of the different division of labour in health services, etc., between the two parts of the region.

Not surprisingly, the R&D-intensive industries in manufacturing have five times as many graduates per thousand employees as their R&D-extensive counterparts. It is significant, however, that all sub-sectors of the manufacturing

Table 7.1 Graduates from universities inside and outside the Copenhagen region and working in the Copenhagen region in 1996

	Employed 1996	Emigrated	Immigrated	Balance
Engineering	13070	1660	4282	+ 2622
Natural Science	7297	3091	1642	−1449
Business Economics	5246	304	1248	+ 944
Social Science and Law	14616	1852	3901	+ 2049
Humanities	8457	1623	2057	+ 434
Medicine	9242	2832	2525	−307
Other	3957	–	–	–
Total	61885	11362	15655	4293

Note: 'Other' includes university level teacher training, officers training, etc. 'Employed' includes all university graduates working in the Copenhagen region in 1996. 'Emigrated' includes graduates from universities in the Copenhagen region working outside the region in 1996. 'Immigrated' includes graduates from universities outside the Copenhagen region but working in that region in 1996.

Table 7.2 Number of university graduates employed in 1996

	Graduates Copenhagen		Scania		Øresund region	
	Absolute	(%)	Absolute	(%)	Absolute	(%)
Primary sector	129	0	280	0	409	0
Construction, utilities	745	1	847	1	1592	1
Manufacturing	4620	7	5874	10	10494	9
R&D extensive	1493	2	2514	4	4007	3
R&D intermediate	1352	2	2174	4	3526	3
R&D intensive	1775	3	1186	2	2961	2
Public service & admin.	17850	29	32425	57	50275	42
Service (not KIBS)	15929	26	6761	12	22690	19
KIBS (see note)	9322	15	6205	11	15527	13
University, etc.	13290	21	4186	7	17476	15
Total	61885	100	56578	100	118463	100

Source: Statistics Denmark and Statistics Sweden (SCB)/NUTEK.

Note: As an average over the past 10 years, R&D-intensive manufacturing sectors have used more than 6 per cent of production costs on research and development in OECD. R&D-extensive manufacturing sectors have used less than 1 per cent. KIBS = knowledge-intensive business services. University graduates include all personnel in 'ISCED level 6+', which includes PhDs, etc.

industry in Scania generally have a higher proportion of graduates than the same sub-sectors in the Copenhagen region. Since many of the firms in these sectors compete in more or less the same international markets, this contrast in formal knowledge input might reflect a different division of labour between manufacturing and the knowledge-intensive business service providers. What a firm in Scania can provide in-house, a similar firm in the Copenhagen region might simply buy on the open market from a regional specialist. Such division of labour partly reflects the size of the local market. The larger a market is, the more specialised the services are that can be offered. As a consequence, the customers in industry do not need to maintain previous high levels of in-house knowledge to cater for less frequent technological, financial, organisational, or other managerial events.

The point made here is *not* that one regional industrial configuration characterised by the in-house availability of certain skills is superior or inferior to a configuration identified by outsourcing and a deepened division of labour between knowledge providers and customers. The only point is that they are different, and that adjustment costs must be expected in Scania or in the Copenhagen region, or in both, once they start to move towards one common, amalgamated Øresund region.

Informal learning in the Øresund region

The data presented above show that it is not the abundance of university graduates employed in industry that can explain the relative success of the dominant R&D-extensive, low-tech parts of the manufacturing industry in the high-cost environment of the Øresund region. However, knowledge intensity in firms is, of course, a much broader notion, and firms might possess huge stocks of accumulated knowledge without employing a single university graduate. In particular, the firms in the R&D-extensive industries might over the years have accrued and maintained a number of firm-specific valuable capabilities by relying heavily on in-house learning-by-doing and by interacting with customers, suppliers, and peers. Through a continuous process of trial-and-error, tacit and articulated (codifiable) skills and procedures are developed and refined and passed on from one generation of employees to the next as *the* way to do things.

While completion of an officially recognised educational programme will automatically appear on record in the relevant statistical database used in this chapter, no obvious trail is left regarding the learning that takes place on the job as part of just being employed. In order to cast some light on this issue, three different but inter-related measurements are applied.[6]

On-the-job training

Stability in the labour market goes beyond the broad categories used to characterise the industrial structure so far. A closer examination of job mobility in the Copenhagen region reveals that approximately one-third of all employees in 1996 held a position in the same establishment four years earlier.[7] Ten per cent of all employees in 1996 had even signed an employment contract with their present firm more than fifteen years ago. There is no doubt that such long contracts imply a very important element of on-the-job training for a core group of workers. It might, perhaps, be assumed that the international competitiveness of the dominant low-tech industries in this high-cost region is at least in part associated with the accumulated effect of incremental investment in the workforce, made possible by the lack of mobility.

Intra-industry learning

In some industries, long employment contracts are not common. Those previously short-term jobs found in the agricultural sector, in households, in harbours and the shipping industry are long gone, but in some industries – usually the ones with few sunk costs (personal and household services, transport, retailing) – employees seldom stay long for a very different reason: it is often not the jobs but the firms that come and go constantly, resulting in very short life spans. In other industries like construction, the ups and downs of the market cause firms to experience a succession of cycles, where hectic periods of hiring are followed by many redundancies once construction is completed. There are even certain manufacturing industries (e.g. the fish-processing industry) that are known for such successions of ups and downs. Many of yesterday's new high-flying firms in the information and communication (ITC) sector are also bound to become tomorrow's losers. In none of these industries is it likely that an employee will experience a twenty-five- or even a ten–year anniversary with the same firm. However, in order to utilise the personal investments made in the process of becoming familiar with the ways and language of a particular firm in an industry, many people who become redundant look for similar or better jobs in similar kinds of firms within that same industry. In the Copenhagen region, more than half of all employees worked within the same industry (NACE 2–digit) four years earlier.[8]

Individuals who remain within a specific industry gradually obtain all the skills and experience needed for a wide variety of jobs. Even without being based on formal skills, these accumulated experiences create their own segmentation of the labour market.

Final comments

This present study suggests that the economic role played by universities in one of the most prosperous and advanced regions in the world is mainly indirect, through the influence exercised on public governance, civic culture, and informal institutions rather than on private sector firms directly. Few university graduates find their way into business, and few firms employ university graduates while the region, nevertheless, has been able to sustain a long-term rate of economic growth, new firm formation, job generation, and welfare at or above the national average. These findings make it rather difficult to subscribe to any version of the popular notion of a chain of causality from universities to research to innovations to firm spin-offs and subsequent growth.

Before making any radical conclusions on the present and future economic role of universities on the basis of the findings presented in this chapter, we need further in-depth studies on the inter-relationship between regional economic performance and university–firm interaction. In particular, we need to understand how new ideas are born and how they disseminate through the economy to be picked up by entrepreneurs and incumbents alike. We need to learn about the ways by which the ethos of the university acts on the economy as a structuring force. We must, finally, recognise how university staff, graduates and dropouts actually function in the local and regional economy.

We are, admittedly, still in the very early stages of what will surely be a long and difficult process of disentangling causes from effects and developing new classifications and methodologies.

Acknowledgement

This chapter draws heavily and directly on a study commissioned by OECD and carried out by the authors with financial assistance from the Ministry of Education in Denmark and Sweden, respectively, and published in *Building a Cross-Border Learning Region* (OECD, 1999).

Notes

1 A current research project is conducting an analysis of these views. It is comprised of a base project conducted by Swedish researchers, along with an evaluation project containing work being conducted by foreign researchers. This research project, entitled 'The Role of Universities for National Competitiveness and Regional Development: The Case Of Sweden in an International Perspective', is led by Professors Sverker Sörlin, Department of the History of Ideas at the University of Umeå, and Gunnar Törnqvist, Department of Social and Economic Geography at the University of Lund. The following foreign researchers are participating in the project together with scholars in Lund, Stockholm and Umeå:

   - Manuel Castells, University of California, Berkeley
   - Henry Etzkowitz, State University of New York
   - Raymond Florax, Free University, Amsterdam
   - Peter Hall, University College, London
   - Nathan Rosenberg, Stanford University
   - Sheldon Rothblatt, University of California, Berkeley.

2 Recent advancements in the so-called 'increasing returns endogenous growth models' question whether all types of specialisation are equally advantageous for a country. These theories focus on the returns from inputs that can be accumulated, and treat the rent-seeking innovative efforts of firms as a cardinal mechanism of technological progress and productivity growth. Since the level of resources devoted to purposive knowledge creation is determined by the ability to appropriate the resulting Schumpeterian quasi-rents, and since this ability is not only the result of a given firm's own competencies, but also of the institutional endowment of the region or country in which the activity takes place, localised capabilities become an intrinsic part of the core of new endogenous theories of growth. However, in current versions of this new growth theory, the learning propensity is usually modelled by R&D expenditure only, thereby focusing scholarly and political interest on the development in each country's share of research and development intensive industries, i.e. its ranking and share within the so-called high-tech industries. See further: Grossman and Helpman (1991); Grossman and Helpman (1993); Rivera-Batiz and Romer (1991); Romer (1987); Romer (1990); and Sala-i-Martin (1990).

3 Analyses of these environments are available in the following studies: Castells and Hall (1994); Decoster and Taberies (1986); Hall, Breheny, McQuaid and Hart (1987); Hall (1997); Keeble (1989); Saxenian (1994); Scott (1993); and Tatsuno (1986).

4 The phrase 'learning region' was introduced in 1995 by Richard Florida in his contribution to *Futures* and later taken up by a number of scholars: Morgan (May 1995); and Asheim (1995).

5 This rate is, however, larger than in Denmark overall (where only 15 per cent of firms employ one or more university graduates). Many of the establishments with one or more university graduates on the pay role are very small, typically a law firm, a GP, a dentist, an auditor, a marketing bureau or, as a growing group, ITC firms, etc.

6 While sectoral stability has been investigated in both the Scania and Copenhagen regions, the latter two measurements have only been used on data from the Copenhagen region. However, it would be equally possible to obtain similar information from Statistics Sweden at a later date.

7 An establishment is the local unit of a firm. Most firms have only one establishment, but some firms have many.

8 Some 41 per cent of all employees in the Copenhagen region in 1996 worked within the same NACE 3–digit industry four years earlier. The Copenhagen region is slightly more stable than the rest of Denmark in this respect.

References

Arthur, W. B. (1994) *Increasing Returns and Path Dependence in the Economy*, Ann Arbor, MI: The University of Michigan Press.

Asheim, B. (1995) *Industrial Districts as 'Learning Regions': A Condition for Prosperity?*, STEP Report No. 3, Oslo.

Boisot, M. (1983) 'Convergence Revisited: The Knowledge of Diffusion of Knowledge in a British and a Japanese Firm', *Journal of Management Studies* 1: 159–190.

Castells, M. and Hall, P. (1994) *Technopoles of the World: The Making of 21st Century Industrial Complexes*, London: Routledge.

Coleman, J. S. (1984) 'Introducing Social Trust into Economic Analysis', *American Economic Review* 72, 2: 84–88.

DeBresson, C. (1996) *Economic Interdependence and Innovative Activity*, Cheltenham: Edward Elgar.

Decoster, E. and Taberies, M. (1986) *L'Innovation dans un pôle scientifique et technologie: Le cas de la cité scientifique Ile de France Sud*, Paris: Université Paris 1.

Edquist, C. (ed.) (1997) *Systems of Innovation: Technologies, Institutions, and Organisations*, London: Pinter Publishers.

Ernst, D. and Guerriei, P. (1997) *International Production Networks and Changing Trade Patterns in East Asia: The Case of the Electronics Industry*, Danish Research Unit for Industrial Dynamics (DRUID) Working Paper No. 97–7, Copenhagen: DRUID.

Florax, R. (1992) *University: A Regional Booster*, Aldershot: Avebury.

Florida, R. (1995) 'Toward the Learning Region', *Futures*.

Freeman, C. (1982) *The Economics of Industrial Innovation*, 2nd edn, London: Pinter Publishers.

Freeman, C. (1991) 'Networks of Innovators: A Synthesis of Research Issues', *Research Policy* 20, 5: 5–24.

Freeman, C. (1995) 'The National System of Innovation in Historical Perspective', *Cambridge Journal of Economics* 19: 5–24.

Gambetta, P. (1988) *Trust: Making and Breaking Co-operative Relations*, Oxford: Basil Blackwell.

Grossman, G. M. and Helpman, E. (1991) *Innovation and Growth in the Global Economy*, London: MIT Press.

Grossman, G. M. and Helpman, E. (1993) *Endogenous Innovation in the Theory of Growth*, Working Paper No. W4527, Cambridge, MA: National Bureau of Economic Research.

Hagedoorn, J. and Schakenraad, J. (1992) 'Leading Companies and Networks of Strategic Alliances in Information Technologies', *Research Policy* 21: 163–190.

Håkansson, H. (ed.) (1987) *Industrial Technology Development: A Network Approach*, London: Croom Helm.

Håkansson, H. (1989) *Corporate Technological Behaviour: Co-operation and Networks*, London: Routledge.

Hall, P. (1997) 'The University and the City', *GeoJournal* 41.4.

Hall, P., Breheny, M., McQuaid, R. and Hart, D. (1987) *Western Sunrise: The Genesis and Growth of Britain's Major High-Tech Corridor*, London: Allen and Unwin.

Jaffe, A. B., Trajtenberg, M. and Henderson, R. (1993) 'Geographic Localization of Knowledge Spillovers as Evidence of Patent Citations', *Quarterly Journal of Economics*, 63: 577–598.

Keeble, D. E. (1989) 'High-technology Industry and Regional Development in Britain: The Case of the Cambridge Phenomenon', *Environment and Planning C: Government and Policy*: 153–173.

Krugman, P. R. (1991) 'History and Industry Location: The Case of the Manufacturing Belt', *The American Economic Review* 81: 80–83.

List, F. (1841) *Das nationale system der politischen Ökonomie*, Basel: Kyklos (translated and published under the title: 'The National System of Political Economy' by Longmans, Green and Co., London (1841)).

Lorenzen, M. (ed.) (1998) *Specialisation and Localised Learning, Six Studies on the European Furniture Industry*, Copenhagen: Copenhagen Business School Press.

Lundvall, B.-Å. (1985) *Product Innovation and User-Producer Interaction*, Industrial Development Research Series 31, Aalborg: AUC.

Lundvall, B.-Å. (1988) 'Innovation as an Interactive Process – From User-Producer Interaction to the National System of Innovation', in G. Dosi, C. Freeman, R. Nelson, G. Silverberg, and L. Soete (eds) *Technical Change and Economic Theory*, London: Pinter Publishers.

Lundvall, B.-Å. (ed.) (1992) *National Systems of Innovation: Towards a Theory of Innovation and Interactive Learning*, London: Pinter Publishers.

Lundvall, B-Å. and Maskell, P. (forthcoming) 'Nation States and Economic Development: From National Systems of Production to National Systems of Knowledge Creation and Learning', Chapter 10 in G. L. Clark, M. P. Feldmann and M. S. Gertler (eds) *Handbook of Economic Geography*, Oxford: Oxford University Press.

Malmberg, A. (1996) 'Industrial Geography: Agglomeration and Local Milieu', *Progress in Human Geography* 20: 392–403.

Malmberg, A. and Maskell, P. (1997) 'Towards an Explanation of Regional Specialization and Industry Agglomeration', *European Planning Studies* 5: 25–41.

Markusen, A., Hall, P., Campbell, S. and Deitrick, S. (1991) *The Rise of the Gunbelt: The Military Mapping of Industrial America*, New York: Oxford University Press.

Maskell, P. and Malmberg, A. (1999a) 'Explaining the Location of Economic Activity: "Ubiquitification" and the Importance of Localised Learning', *European Urban and Regional Studies* 6 (Special Issue on learning regions, edited by Malmberg and Maskell), 1: 9–25.

Maskell, P. and Malmberg, A. (1999b) 'Localised Learning and Industrial Competitiveness', *Cambridge Journal of Economics* 23, 2: 167–186.

Massey, D. (1995) *Space, Place and Gender, Progress in Human Geography* 19: 152–153.

Morgan, K. (1995) *The Learning Region*, Institutions, Innovation and Regional Renewal Papers in Planning Research No. 157, May, Cardiff: University of Wales.

Mowery, D. C. and Oxley, J. E. (1995) 'Inward Technology Transfer and Competitiveness: The Role of National Innovation Systems', *Cambridge Journal of Economics* 19: 67–93.

Nelson, R. R. (ed.) (1993) *National Innovation Systems: A Comparative Analysis*, Oxford: Oxford University Press.

OECD (1999) *Building a Cross-Border Learning Region*, Copenhagen: CBS-Press.

Patel, P. and Pavitt, K. (1991) 'Large Firms in the Production of the World's Technology: An Important Case of "Non-Globalisation"', *Journal of International Business Studies* 21, 1: 1–21.

Patel, P. (1995) 'Localised Production of Technology for Global Markets', *Cambridge Journal of Economics* 19: 141–153.

Putnam, R. D. (1993) *Making Democracy Work: Civic Traditions in Modern Italy*, Princeton, NJ: Princeton University Press.

Rivera-Batiz, L. and Romer, P. M. (1991) 'Economic Integration and Endogenous Growth', *The Quarterly Journal of Economics* CVI: 531–555.

Romer, P. M. (1987) 'Growth Based on Increasing Returns due to Specialization', *Papers and Proceedings of the American Economic Association* 77, 2: 56–62.

Romer, P. M. (1990) 'Endogenous Technological Change', *Journal of Political Economy* (Supplement) 98: 71–102.

Rosenberg, N. (1972) *Technology and American Economic Growth*, New York: Harper and Row.

Rosenberg, N. and Birdzell, L. E. (1986) *How the West Grew Rich: The Economic Transformation of the Industrial World*, New York: Basic Books.

Sala-i-Martin, X. (1990) *Lecture Notes on Economic Growth (I): Introduction to the Literature and Neoclassic Models*, Working Paper No. W3563, Cambridge, MA: National Bureau of Economic Research.

Saxenian, A. (1994) *Regional Advantage: Culture and Competition in Silicon Valley and Route 128*, Cambridge, MA: Harvard University Press.

Scott, A. J. (1993) *Technopolis: High-Technology Industry and Regional Development in Southern California*, Berkeley, CA: University of California Press.

Tatsuno, S. M. (1986) *The Technopolis Strategy: Japan, High Technology, and the Control of the Twenty-First Century*, New York: Prentice-Hall Press.

Thanki, R. (1998) 'How Do we Know the Value of Higher Education to Regional Development?', *Regional Studies* 32: 84–89.

Törnqvist, G. (1998) *Renässans för Regioner: Om tekniken och den sociala kommunikationens villkor*, Stockholm: SNS Förlag.

8 Interactive learning between industry and knowledge infrastructure in a high-tech region

An empirical exploration of competing and complementary theoretical perspectives

Marius Meeus, Leon Oerlemans and Jerald Hage

Introduction

In the last decade, there has been an ongoing debate on the role of universities and the broader knowledge infrastructure (educational institutes, R&D organisations in the public sector) in the innovative performance of Dutch industry (Ministry of Economic Affairs 1995, 1997). Special attention has been given to the linkage between knowledge infrastructure and industry. On the one hand, the dramatic decrease in Dutch R&D investment in the early 1990s and the negative effects of this on the competitiveness of the Dutch economy intensified this debate. On the other, the attention given to the alignment of university research with the knowledge demands of industry resulted from the relatively large public expenditure on university research, compared to the smaller sums contributed by industry.

In recent work, we have reported that a majority of Dutch firms tend to underutilise university research and public research laboratories, whereas R&D collaboration in the value chain occurs quite frequently (Meeus *et al.* 2000). In Table 8.1, data from four different surveys are presented. We found a strong variation in types of R&D collaboration. In general, the involvement of buyers and suppliers in R&D collaboration was found to be the strongest. An exception was found in the data on man–machine Interaction, where 61 per cent of innovating firms were found to practise R&D collaboration with universities and professional education and simultaneously there is a significantly higher percentage of R&D collaboration with R&D centres. Furthermore, our surveys of 1997 and 1998 revealed that in the networks of organisations involved in image processing technologies and man–machine interfacing technologies, the Dutch universities and TNO (Dutch Centre for Applied Research) were considered to be very important knowledge suppliers (Meeus *et al.* 1997, Oerlemans *et al.* 1999).

In sum, these findings suggest a rather loose coupling between knowledge infrastructure and the innovation processes of innovating firms. This ambivalent relation between industry and the knowledge infrastructure was also found by Rosenberg and Nelson (1996) and Mansfield (1991). However, other researchers

Table 8.1 Percentage of R&D collaborators with external actors in four Dutch surveys

R&D Collaboration	MINT Survey (1992/1993) North-Brabant)[a]	CINT Survey (1996)[b]	Man-machine Interaction Survey (1998)[c]	Image processing Survey (1997)[d]
Competitors	5	8	8	0
Education (universities, professional education)	12	17	61	21
R&D centres	18	23	26	21
Buyers	48	47	37	28
Suppliers	43	47	50	66

Notes
a Listwise N of R&D collaborators = 420.
b Listwise N of R&D collaborators = 224.
c Listwise N = 47.
d Listwise N = 35.

reported that this loose coupling was not invariable and may sometimes be transformed into very intense collaboration (Mitchell 1991). Galli and Teubal (1997) argue that this ambivalence toward the knowledge infrastructure is changing at present. Before the Second World War, NSIs (National Systems of Innovation) developed within a relatively well-defined sectoral or sub-system configuration schematically based on three R&D performing sectors (business sector, public sector, and universities), with relatively weak linkages between them, and a fourth basic infrastructural sub-system (bureau of standards, patent office, etc.). Every organisation within a building block fulfilled a specific role or function. For universities, this was higher education and basic research; for government labs, mission-oriented research; for business firms, applied research and technological development. Nowadays, it is necessary to distinguish between function and organisation, as the latter tends to play increasingly multiple roles. The major trends in all three sectors can be summarised by, on the one hand, a growing connectivity within and between the building blocks, and, on the other, a stronger alignment of knowledge generation and knowledge demand. For all actors involved, there seems to be a growing emphasis on linkages, on interaction, and on knowledge exchange and transfer (Galli and Teubal 1997). Although these observations are very appealing, they lack a sound theoretical explanation and an empirical basis. The aim of this chapter is to contribute to a more complete and theoretical understanding of the *probability* of interactive learning in innovator firms and the knowledge infrastructure in the context of innovation. Our research question is: why do firms develop linkages, and interact with actors in the knowledge infrastructure?

Our theoretical effort adds to the growing body of literature on technological collaboration, knowledge transfer, and boundary spanning of organisation, and performs several functions. First, we combine linkages, interaction, and learning into 'interactive learning' (Lundvall 1993) and advance an empirical measure for this concept. Second, we explore empirically the *complementarity* of activity and resource-based explanations of cooperation between innovator firms and actors in the knowledge infrastructure. In this chapter, we develop a theoretical account for interactive learning, synthesising the resource-based organisation theories in economics and sociology (Barney 1991; Håkansson 1987; Pfeffer and Salançik 1978) with elements of the knowledge-based theories on networks and learning (Cohen and Levinthal 1990; Edquist 1997; Grant 1996; Hage and Alter 1997; Jin and Stough 1998; Kogut and Zander 1992; Teece and Pisano 1998). Third, whereas much empirical literature focuses on dyadic relations of innovator firms with one external actor, we analyse the innovator firms' interactions with both a technical university (Eindhoven University of Technology, TU/e) and a public research organisation (Dutch Centre for Applied Research, TNO). This allows a comparison that has never been made before.

The structure of this chapter is as follows. First, we describe the components of our theoretical framework. Second, we describe the research design, including the sample and the analytical procedures. Third, we describe our results. Finally, we discuss these results and derive some theoretical and policy inferences.

Research model

Interactive learning

Theoretically, Lundvall's notion of interactive learning specifies the resource dependence argument in the context of innovation (see Figure 8.1). The basic premise of resource dependence theory is that organisations are open systems. From this, it follows that organisations (1) are not self-sufficient; (2) cannot

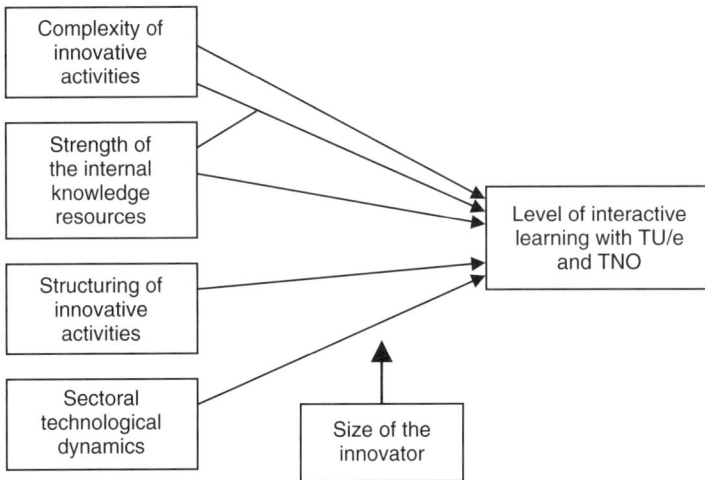

Figure 8.1 A research model of the relationship between interactive learning of innovating firms with divergent actors, the complexity of innovative activities, the strength of the internal knowledge resources, the structuring of innovative activities, effects of sectoral technological dynamics, controlling for size

generate all the necessary resources internally; and (3) must mobilise resources from other organisations in their environments if they want to survive. Acquiring the necessary resources involves interaction with other organisations that control these critical resources (Pfeffer and Salançik 1978: 25–28).

However, given the nature of innovation, the control assumption applied in the context of interactive learning has to be relaxed due to counteracting forces. On the one hand, the non-exclusive and transitory nature of technical knowledge (Cohendet *et al.* 1993) makes the acquisition and protection of information a core competence that enables firms to profit from the innovation, and explains innovator firms' inclination to formalise innovative ties. On the other hand, the complicated nature of technical knowledge (Von Hippel 1987; Lam 1997; Senker and Faulkner 1996; Szulanski 1996), its range, and significance are so difficult to assess that any contractual arrangement pursuing a specification of knowledge transactions would become an unworkable straitjacket. In the context of innovation, the control assumption is also put in perspective by the uncertain outcomes of knowledge exchange and knowledge sharing. Several authors have pointed to the loss of autonomy and increased dependence between collaborating firms (Alter and Hage 1993; Galaskiewicz 1985: 282; Hage and Alter 1997; Saxenian 1994: 148–149). The reluctance to initiate external knowledge acquisition (Huber 1991: 98), and the enhanced imitation risks diminishing innovation rents (Kogut and Zander 1992) also illustrate the limited control possibilities.

If the control of critical resources in innovation – in this case, technical knowledge – is so troublesome, the question arises as to why innovator firms engage in interactive learning. Galli and Teubal's main assumption is that the changing roles of actors in NSIs and the very nature of innovation generate a mutual interest for the producers of innovations and the knowledge infrastructure to interact and to learn.

Lundvall (1985) transformed the notion of user–producer interaction, introduced in the 1970s by Von Hippel (1976), Teubal (1976), and others, into the concept of interactive learning. The level of interactive learning between the innovator firms and external actors indicates the extent to which innovator firms have access to and acquire knowledge from external actors in order to innovate their products and/or processes. Operationally, the level of interactive learning is defined as the frequency with which innovator firms acquire knowledge inputs from external actors and transfer knowledge to external actors in order to effectively innovate products and/or processes. By engaging in interactive learning, firms expect to enhance their innovative and overall economic performance and to create value due to the pooling of complementary knowledge.

Resources

The central tenet of the resource-based approach is that firms select actions that best capitalise on their unique endowments of resources, and that they focus on the production and maintenance of strategic resources in order to remain competitive (Combs and Ketchen Jr. 1999). Performing product or process innovations induces firms to draw on their internal and external environments and forces them to pool all resources conducive to innovation. In the context of innovation, technical knowledge is the primary strategic resource to be acquired and developed (Cohen and Levinthal 1990; Hage and Alter 1997; Kogut and Zander 1992). Without technical knowledge, new technical opportunities would not be recognised, and hence neither product nor process innovations could be achieved. The heterogeneity of the resources – specialised skills, facilities and money – needed in innovation urges firms to actively monitor their resource bases as well as their financial position and to decide how to solve their resource deficits. The strength of internal knowledge resources determines their ability to cope with this heterogeneity. If resources are occupied or not available, a search for complementary resources starts. In that context, the intensification of existing relationships or the formation of new linkages with other firms or, institutional actors like universities are behavioural alternatives enabling innovation strategies. Each external actor can be evaluated with regard to its competencies to complement the resource base of the innovating firm.

Freeman and Soete (1997: 133) contend that knowledge deficits explain the university–industry collaboration. In the chemical sector, the larger firms have tried to develop new specialised products themselves. However, as they did not have the necessary scientific research experience, they were often obliged to collaborate with universities. Monsanto, Hoechst, and ICI all made major agreements with selected university departments and hospitals in the fields of biotechnology.

Therefore, the interaction between innovating firms and a broad variety of firms and institutional actors is, on the one hand, the corollary of their needs for heterogeneous resources. On the other, it is an indication of external actors' capabilities to supplement their partners' resource deficits or shortages (Aiken and Hage 1968: 930; Combs and Ketchen Jr. 1999: 868; Håkansson 1987; Lundvall 1992). Summarising, interactive learning of innovator firms with actors in the knowledge infrastructure permits firms to share resources and thereby overcome resource-based constraints for innovative activities. This yields the following proposition:

Proposition 1   The stronger the innovator firm's internal knowledge resources, the lower the probability of interactive learning with actors in the knowledge infrastructure.

While Proposition 1 suggests a negative monotonic relationship between the level of interactive learning and the innovator firm's internal knowledge base, there are two arguments for alternative propositions. First, Cohen and Levinthal (1990) and Gulati (1995) argue that the ability to evaluate and utilise outside knowledge – firms' absorptive capacity – is largely a function of prior related knowledge. There are few direct tests of the influence of absorptive capacity, but the results of such tests are broadly supportive of this argument (Gambardella 1992; Mowery *et al.* 1996). This yields a competing resource-based hypothesis:

Proposition 2   The stronger the innovator firm's internal knowledge resources, the higher the probability of interactive learning with actors in the knowledge infrastructure.

The second argument pertains to the nature of the empirical relation suggested in Propositions 1 and 2. Both suggest a monotonic relationship between the probability of interactive learning and the strength of the internal knowledge base. However, there are two arguments for a non-monotonic relationship that suggest that a stronger internal knowledge base only leads to a higher probability of interactive learning up to a certain point, after which stronger internal knowledge bases are associated with a lower probability of interactive learning. On the one hand, there is the marginal information value argument (Chung *et al.* 2000; Gulati 1995), which suggests that if knowledge resources are stronger, the probability of diminishing returns of knowledge exchange and knowledge sharing grows, which, in turn, decreases the probability of interactive learning. On the other, there is the monitoring-reassessment argument, which suggests that firms are myopic, and hence have limited capabilities to value their internal knowledge base. As a result of the monitoring of external actors' knowledge bases, innovator firms simultaneously reassess their internal knowledge resources' applicability. Especially for firms with stronger internal knowledge bases, this reassessment reduces the potential complementarity of external knowledge, because of the identification of slack resources. This decreases the probability of interactive learning. Therefore, we propose:

Proposition 3   Innovator firms with knowledge resources of moderate strength have a higher probability of interactive learning with actors in the knowledge infrastructure than innovator firms with weak or strong knowledge resources.

Complexity of innovative activities

The major flaw of the resource-based view of the firm is the fact that resources and activities are conflated (Barney 1991: 101; Wernerfelt 1984: 172), which limits their analytical value. Lundvall's (1988) original account for interactive learning turns out to be more activity-based. In his view, the rate and radicalness of innovations occasion interactive learning. Therefore, it is theoretically useful to extend the resource-based view on interactive learning.

Kogut and Zander (1992: 388) define the complexity of a task as the number of operations required to solve a task. Jones *et al.* (1997: 921) stress another dimension of task complexity by referring to the number of specialised inputs needed to complete a product or service. In accordance with this, we define the complexity of innovative activities in terms of the innovator firm's learning and problem-solving efforts induced by the implemented innovative activities. We discern two complexity dimensions that both significantly enlarge this number of learning and problem-solving operations: first, the heterogeneity and intensity of perceived innovation pressures that compel innovator firms to adapt, and, second, the actual innovation rate. Innovation pressures include, e.g. perceived customer needs, competitor behaviour (Lundvall 1993), proliferation of new technical knowledge, new technical findings (Hage and Alter 1997), legal requirements, emergence of new markets, standardisation (Anderson and Tushman 1990), and cost reduction (Duncan 1972). More heterogeneous innovation pressures imply that more divergent, and probably less compatible, criteria have to be met in the product or process innovation, which requires additional specialised skills and knowledge (Dewar and Hage 1978; Jones *et al.* 1997), or makes existing competencies obsolete (Leonard-Barton and Doyle 1996). The higher the likelihood of incompatible innovation pressures, the higher the required capacity for problem solving, thus the more firms must go beyond the incremental improvement of existing competencies associated with learning by doing and learning by using (Windrum 1999: 1539). If innovation pressures are more heterogeneous, the number of innovation opportunities can grow and this demands more interaction with external actors, primarily buyers and suppliers, but also with the knowledge infrastructure (Freeman and Soete 1997; Mitchell 1991).

The rate of innovation measures the actual innovative behaviour of the innovator firms. The higher the number of implemented product and process innovations, the higher the actual intensity of the problem solving and associated (un-)learning (Dodgson 1993; Henderson and Clark 1990; Rosenbloom and Christensen 1998). High innovation rates erase existing communication codes between users and producers (Lundvall 1992: 58), and raise the likelihood of the innovator firm's needing additional specialised skills of third parties, such as knowledge producers.

In sum, both the heterogeneity of innovation pressures and the rate of innovation demand more coordination and cooperation, the building of external linkages, and the control of many discrete activities, which in tandem generate a higher complexity of innovative activities (Evan 1993: 230; Hage and Alter 1997). The general proposition derived from the complexity argument is as follows:

Proposition 4 Innovator firms performing more complex innovative activities have a higher probability of interactive learning with actors in the knowledge infrastructure.

As was the case with the resource-based propositions, the relation between complexity and interactive learning could be either monotonic or non-monotonic. On the one hand, the argument is that innovative activities with low complexity probably do not require interactive learning, because neither innovation pressures nor innovation rates are high, hence there is no need for complementary knowledge. On the other, innovator firms are more inclined to perform extremely complex innovative activities within organisational boundaries. First, because the innovator firm's reputation might be damaged if external actors find out that the innovator firm cannot solve its own innovation problems (Huber 1991). Second, because the likelihood of finding partners that are able to solve problems associated with highly complex innovative activities decreases after a certain threshold point. Firms initiating innovations with moderate levels of complexity are more likely to detect problems they cannot solve themselves than firms initiating innovations of low complexity, and, simultaneously, the risk of a damaged reputation is lower than when extremely high complexity levels are involved. This increases the chance that a moderate complexity of innovative activities induce a comparatively high probability of interactive learning. This yields the following proposition:

Proposition 5   *Innovator firms performing innovation projects with moderate levels of complexity have a higher probability of interactive learning with actors in the knowledge infrastructure than firms performing innovative activities with low or high levels of complexity.*

The interaction between complexity of innovative activities and the strength of the knowledge resources

An additional reason to combine Lundvall's activity-based and the resource-based explanation of interactive learning is that we expect that their effects are complementary. Actually, a synthesis of the resource-based and the activity-based explanation for interactive learning yields a more comprehensive theoretical account of interactive learning. The complexity of the innovator firms' innovative activities determines whether the strength of the internal knowledge resources is sufficient, and therefore determines the level of interactive learning. More complicated innovative activities draw more heavily on a firm's resource base than routine distribution activities with lower complexity, hence they reveal resource deficits or shortages and affect the probability of interactive learning. This yields the following proposition:

Proposition 6   *The effect of the strength of the internal knowledge resources on the probability of interactive learning with actors in the knowledge infrastructure is moderated by the complexity of the innovative activities.*

A non-monotonic version is also explored for this proposition. We expect that moderate levels of complexity and moderate quality of the resource base are associated with the highest probability of interactive learning. The argument runs parallel with the arguments pertaining to Proposition 3 and Proposition 5.

Proposition 7   *Innovator firms combining moderate levels of complexity of innovative activities with a moderate strength of their knowledge resources are more inclined to interactive learning with actors in the knowledge infrastructure than innovator firms with low or high scores on the interaction term.*

Structure of innovative activities

A final extension of the resource-based perspective on interactive learning concerns the conflation of resources and structures. This conflation of resources with the structuring of organisations contrasts strongly with the newer versions of the resource-based theories, such as the knowledge-based theory of Cohen and Levinthal (1990), Grant (1996), Kogut and Zander (1992) and Teece and Pisano (1998). These authors stress the significance of organisational structuring enhancing relationships between knowledge sharing and knowledge diversity across individuals and departments and plants. The pooling of internal departments' innovative activities becomes more important in the case of a higher complexity of innovative activities (Lawrence and Lorsch 1967). It has become generally accepted that complementary functions or departments within organisations (e.g. R&D, sales and marketing, purchase, production) ought to be tightly interrelated. After all, some amount of redundancy in expertise may be desirable to create what can be called cross-function absorptive capacities (Cohen and Levinthal 1990: 134; Dougherty 1992: 179; Teece and Pisano 1998: 198–200). To the extent that an organisation develops a broad and active network of internal relationships, individual awareness of others' capabilities and knowledge will be strengthened. Inward-looking (production, engineering) and outward-looking (R&D, sales/marketing) departments enable a comparison of the internal and external opportunities for cooperation in innovation projects.

Proposition 8   *A higher level of integration of internal innovative activities increases the probability of interactive learning with actors in the knowledge infrastructure.*

In the systems of innovation literature, a new aspect of the organisational structuring of innovative activities is advanced: the embeddedness of innovating firms in so-called bridging institutions (Edquist 1997; Midgley *et al.* 1992). This may be the central government, but also agents such as technology centres responsible for local knowledge transfer, regional development authorities, trade or industrial associations, chambers of commerce, etc. These organisations are interfacing units that link innovating firms to external actors and facilitate information and technology transfer, as well as technological collaboration (Galli and Teubal 1997: 356–357). Because European and Dutch technology policies are geared toward clustering and networking (Cooke *et al.* 2000), in many EC countries technology subsidies are assigned only if the submitted innovation projects induce (international) collaboration. Many bridging institutions operate in this technology subsidy niche and are rewarded for their 'network' activities, which is conducive to their legitimacy. This yields the final proposition:

Proposition 9   *Stronger links with bridging institutions induce a higher probability of interactive learning with actors in the knowledge infrastructure.*

The generality of our claims

The theoretical model we have developed is probably contingent on several factors one would like to control for, because they limit the generality of our claims. The first contingency we control for is firm size, which is often considered a proxy for resource availability. Empirical research shows that firm size has dual effects. On the one hand, resource availability tends to grow as firms grow. Large firms have qualitatively and quantitatively more comprehensive resource bases and are, therefore, better equipped to innovate successfully and to compete proactively and aggressively. Compared to small and medium-sized firms, large firms are favoured by the availability of internal funds in a world of capital market imperfections. Cash flow, for instance, a measure of internal financial capabilities, is empirically associated with higher levels of R&D intensity (Cohen and Levin 1989: 1072). Simultaneously, slack resources buffer firms from competition and promote insularity, affording economies of scale that capitalise on inertial routines (Miller and Chen 1994). On the other hand, large firms are more bureaucratic than small and medium-sized enterprises. The rigid rules and routines that so profoundly permeate many larger companies may hamper resource utilisation (Miller and Friesen 1982; Tushman and Romanelli 1985).

The second contingency is the enormous difference between sectoral technological dynamics. Pavitt's (1984) research revealed that the technological change between the high-tech and low-tech sectors differs significantly due to higher R&D spending in the former.

Research design

In this research, we combined case study analysis with survey research. We analysed twenty-three innovation projects in eighteen local firms. This helped us to develop a questionnaire allowing for a full treatment of theoretical issues related to innovative behaviour in innovation networks, issues which were left out of the Community Innovation Survey (CIS). This survey was performed in fifteen Member States of the European Union. Although the CIS questionnaire contains 200 questions related to the innovative behaviour of firms, it contains only a limited number of items about innovation networks and learning. Gathering data from a representative sample of firms allows us to generalise our findings.

Sample

A survey was administered to industrial firms with five or more employees in North Brabant (a province in the southern part of the Netherlands). The data gathering took place between December 1992 and January 1993.

The data gathering was performed in a region with typical features. This region is one of the most industrialised regions in the Netherlands. In 1992, the total number of jobs in manufacturing in this region was roughly 210,000, i.e. the manufacturing sector share of employment in the region was 28.8 per cent (the Netherlands, 19.5 per cent). The region of North Brabant has features that differ widely from agricultural regions (Zeeland, Groningen, and Drenthe), and Dutch service-oriented regions like South and North Holland. Brabant's industrialisation started in c. 1850 and was based on traditional industries like dairy, textiles and wool. The North Brabant region has two universities and three innovation centres. A strong group of key players in internationalised industries and its location near important distribution centres like Rotterdam and Antwerp make this region highly attractive for foreign direct investment. In the Dutch context this region is considered a high-tech region, housing multinational enterprises such as Philips, DAF trucks, Royal Dutch Shell, Akzo Chemical, DSM, former Fokker (aircraft) and Fuji. Brabant also accommodates a number of important medium-sized niche international players, like ASM Lithography, OCÉ and Rank Xerox (copiers), ODME (optical disc equipment), Ericsson, EMI (CDs), General Plastics, etc.

The population of firms in the region consists of a mix of small, medium-sized and large enterprises. About 84 per cent of the responding firms have one hundred or less employees. Furthermore, the manufacturing sector has shown a relatively high R&D and export performance (Meeus and Oerlemans 1995).

Our sample is a reliable representation of the population of industrial firms in North Brabant, in which sample strata and population strata deviated within 8 per cent boundaries. The mean deviation between the percentages in the sample and in the response is 6.4 per cent points. The sample of industrial firms is classified according to Pavitt's taxonomy (Oerlemans 1996) (see Table 8.2).

Table 8.2 Population and sample divided into Pavitt sectors

Pavitt sector	Population (%) (N)	Total sample (%) (N)	Sample of innovating respondents (%) (N)
Supplier-dominated	33.5 (1028)	25.7 (149)	22.9 (92)
Scale intensive	41.1 (1261)	36.1 (209)	34.1 (137)
Specialised suppliers	13.6 (478)	21.4 (124)	22.1 (89)
Science-based	11.8 (363)	16.8 (97)	20.9 (84)
Total	100 (3130)	100 (579)	100 (402)

Measurement

Interactive learning is measured as a multidimensional construct, with a learning dimension and an interaction dimension (for the items, see Table 8.3).

The learning dimension of interactive learning was measured in terms of the contents of the transferred knowledge that supplement the innovating firms' knowledge base (Dodgson 1993) and augments the range of their potential behaviour (Huber 1991; Jin and Stough 1998). Our indicators measured the extent to which TNO or TU/e actively contributed to the innovating firms' innovations, either by active participation in or by their contribution of ideas to the innovation process of the innovating firm.

The level of interaction was measured by asking the innovating firms to rate the contact frequency between the innovating firms and the external actors. Social interaction is defined as a sequence of situations in which the behaviours of one actor are consciously reorganised, and influenced by the behaviours of another actor and vice versa (Turner 1988: 14). The measure captures the level of reciprocity between innovator firms and external actors, indicating, on the one hand, the frequency of knowledge transfer initiated by external actors, and, on the other, the frequency of knowledge transfer initiated by the innovator firms.

Table 8.3 Measurement of the dependent variable 'Interactive Learning'

Variable	Indicators
Interactive Learning with Technische Universiteit Eindhoven (Eindhoven University of Technology)	Two items were included in this variable: (1) firms were asked if they acquired information and/or knowledge from Eindhoven University of Technology (TU/e); (2) firms were asked how often Eindhoven University of Technology (TU/e) contributed to their innovation processes by bringing up ideas, or participate actively.
	Item 1 was coded: (1) No, or (2) Yes. For item 2 answers were coded: (1) never; (2) sometimes; (3) regularly; (4) often; (5) always. A sum score was computed. If the resulting sum score equalled 2, this value was coded 0 indicating no interactive learning between the innovating firm and Eindhoven University of Technology (TU/e). A resulting sum score higher than 2 was coded 1 indicating interactive learning between Eindhoven University of Technology (TU/e) and the innovating firm.
Interactive Learning with TNO (Dutch Centre for Applied Research)	Two items were included in this variable: (1) firms were asked if they acquired information and/or knowledge from the Dutch Centre for Applied Research (TNO); (2) firms were asked how often the Dutch Centre for Applied Research (TNO) contributed to their innovation processes by bringing up ideas, or participate actively.
	Item 1 was coded: (1) No, or (2) Yes. For item 2 answers were coded: (1) never; (2) sometimes; (3) regularly; (4) often; (5) always. A sum score was computed. If the resulting sum score equalled 2, this value was coded 0 indicating no interactive learning between the innovating firm and the Dutch Centre for Applied Research (TNO). A resulting sum score higher than 2 was coded 1 indicating interactive learning between the Dutch Centre for Applied Research (TNO) and the innovating firm.

Resources

Scholars have different opinions with regard to the resources involved in innovation. Håkansson (1989) and Smith (1995) defined resources broadly in terms of money enabling investments, a physical and technological infrastructure, a stock of knowledge, information and human skills enabling an organisation to transform inputs into outputs, and decision-making. Hage and Alter (1997) and Cohen and Levinthal (1990) argue that the ability to evaluate and utilise outside knowledge – firms' absorptive capacity – is largely a function of prior related knowledge.

In our research model, we restricted the measurement of the strength of the knowledge resources to three different knowledge-based indicators (see Table 8.4). First, R&D intensity (Baldwin and Scott 1987; Cohen and Levinthal 1990); second, the percentage of higher educated workforce (Jin and Stough 1998; Kleinknecht and Reijnen 1992); third, the number of problems firms had experienced during their innovation projects (Meeus, *et al.* 1996). A large number of innovation problems indicates large resource deficits. In order to align the meaning of this indicator with the other indicators, the raw scores were recoded. High scores on this indicator represent few innovation problems and hence a high problem-solving capability of the innovator firm.

Complexity of innovative activities

We have distinguished two dimensions of complexity of innovative activities, which were combined in one compound independent variable (for separate items, see Table 8.4). The first dimension is the heterogeneity and intensity of perceived innovation pressures, which define the diversity of environmental pressures (Duncan 1972) pushing firms to innovate. The items pertain to customer demands, innovative behaviour of competitors, new market needs, and technical findings, as well as institutional developments. Due to these pressures, existing skills and capabilities can become obsolete and shift the locus of technical expertise from industry incumbents to newly formed ventures and firms from other industries (Pisano 1990; Schumpeter 1975: 83; Tushman and Anderson 1986). The second dimension of complexity of innovative activities is the rate of innovation. It is measured by the percentage of products and processes that were innovated between 1988–93. The rate of innovation measures the extent to which the innovator firm has responded to innovation pressures. Jointly, these indicators represent the degree of difficulty of the innovator firms' learning efforts, which is higher in the case of intense and more heterogeneous innovation pressures and high innovation rates.

Structuring of activities

The structuring of innovative activities is measured using two separate variables: the level of integration of internal innovative activities and the

Table 8.4 Measurement of the independent variables and one control variable

Variable	Indicators	Calculation of scores
Complexity of innovative activities: A sum score was computed using 'the percentage of new processes and products' and 'heterogeneity of innovative pressures'	Percentage of new processes and products in a 5-year period	Firms were asked to indicate to what extent (1) their machines/processes and/or (2) their line of products changed in a 5-year period. Each item was coded: (1) 0–20%; (2) 20–40%; (3) 40–60%; (4) 60–80%; (5) 80–100%. An average score was computed, which was standardised.
	Heterogeneity of innovative pressures	Firms were asked to indicate how often the items mentioned below, were pressures to innovate. Items included were: (1) customers asked for specific new product; (2) customers asked for specific operation method; (3) competitor had comparable new product; (4) competitor had comparable machine/process; (5) improvement of product quality; (6) maintain market share; (7) increase market share; (8) reduction of cost price; (9) improved production time; (10) new market need discovered; (11) technical idea/invention; (12) solve technical product deficiencies; (13) solve technical production problems; (14) improve delivery time; (15) react to regulation; (16) technical standardisation. Items were coded: (1) never; (2) sometimes; (3) regularly; (4) often; (5) always. An average score was computed, which was standardised.
Strength of the internal knowledge resources: A sum score was computed using 'R&D intensity', 'percentage of higher educated employees', and 'resource deficits'	R&D intensity	The percentage of employees working full-time on R&D. The variable was standardised.

Variable	Indicators	Calculation of scores
	Percentage of higher educated employees	The number of higher educated employees as a percentage of the total workforce of the firm. The variable was standardised.
	Resource deficits	Firms were asked to indicate whether or not the following issues hampered their innovative activities: (1) lack of financial resources; (2) lack of time; (3) lack of skilled workers; (4) lack of technical know-how. If an issue hampered innovative activities, it was coded 1, else it was coded 0. A sum score was computed and the resulting variable was recoded and standardised. Low scores indicate high levels of resource deficits, and high scores indicate low levels of resource deficits.
Structuring of innovative activities The separate indicators were used in the estimations	Level of integration of internal innovative activities	The sum of the frequency with which the R&D, marketing and sales, purchase, and production function of the firm contributed to the firm's innovation projects. Answers were coded: (1) never; (2) sometimes; (3) regularly; (4) often; (5) always. After the sum score was computed, the variable was standardised.
	The level of support by bridging institutions	The sum of the frequency with which trade associations, innovation centres, and chambers of commerce contributed to the firm's innovation projects. Answers were coded: (1) never; (2) sometimes; (3) regularly; (4) often; (5) always. After the sum score was computed, the variable was standardised.
Pavitt sector	Pavitt dummy	Firms were coded 0 if they belonged to the supplier dominated or the scale intensive sector (traditional manufacturing, bulk material, assembly); Firms were coded 1 if they belonged to the specialised suppliers or science-based sector (machinery, instruments, electronics, chemicals).
Size control variable	Size dummy	Firms were coded 0 if they had less than 100 employees. Firms were coded 1 if they had 100 employees or more.

level of support of bridging institutions. We measured the integration of internal innovative activities keeping in mind the extent to which internal departments contribute to the firm's innovation process. The external dimension – the level of support from bridging institutions – was measured by the frequency with which chambers of commerce, industrial associations, and innovation centres contributed to the innovating firms' innovation process (for the items, see Table 8.4).

Control variables

The size of the firm (Baldwin and Scott 1987; Cohen and Levin 1989; Vossen and Nooteboom 1996) is a proxy for a firm's ability to invest in innovation (see Table 8.4). We used a dummy variable for the measurement of technological dynamics. We made a distinction between traditional industries (supplier-dominated and scale-intensive industries) and modern industries (specialised suppliers and science-based industries). Empirical research confirmed the differences in participation and R&D spending between Pavitt sectors in the Netherlands. R&D spending in Dutch industries has the following ranking: (4) supplier-dominated; (3) scale-intensive; (2) specialised suppliers; and (1) science-based industries (Vossen and Nooteboom 1996: 165). Earlier research (Oerlemans *et al.* 1998) suggests that patterns of interaction with distinct external actors yield different innovation outcomes in different Pavitt sectors. The impact of sectoral differences requires a control for its effects. Therefore, we distinguish high-tech sectors – the so-called science-based industries (e.g. electronics, chemical industry) and the specialised suppliers (instruments) – and low-tech sectors (the so-called supplier-dominated and scale-intensive industries, e.g. building and construction, textile, and leather), which are dominated by economies of scale.

Analyses

In this chapter, we restrict our analyses to exploratory analyses. After all, no empirical research has tested the same models. For this reason, one must be cautious in generalising the empirical findings. In testing our propositions, we used stepwise logistic regression. Owing to the skewed distribution of the level of interactive learning, and the ordinal dependent and independent variables, ordinary least square regression was not allowed. Six separate models were estimated, exploring the probability of interactive learning with (1) TU/e (Eindhoven University of Technology); (2) TNO (Dutch Centre for Applied Research); (3) TU/e for small and medium-sized innovator firms with less than 100 employees; (4) TU/e for firms with 100 employees or more; (5) TNO for small and medium-sized firms with less than 100 employees; and (6) TNO for firms with 100 employees or more.

The interpretation of our research findings differs for the monotonic and non-monotonic propositions. The variables interactive learning, complexity of innovative activities, the strength of the knowledge resources, the cross-product term 'complexity – strength of the knowledge resources', and the structuring of innovative activities were coded from low to high scores. A significant Exp(b) larger than 1.0 signifies that higher scores on the independent variables are associated with a higher probability of interactive learning. A significant Exp(b) smaller than 1.0 means that higher levels of complexity are associated with a lower probability of interactive learning.

To control for non-monotonic effects, we included squared terms for the strength of the knowledge resources, the complexity of innovative activities, and their cross-product term. For the squared variables, the interpretation is as follows. A significant Exp(b) larger than 1.0 means that the relation between that independent variable and the probability of interactive learning is U-shaped. So, low and high scores on the independent variable are associated with a higher probability of interactive learning, and the moderate scores on that independent variable are associated with a lower probability of interactive learning. A significant Exp(b) smaller than or equal to 1.0 signifies an inverted U-shaped relation between independent variables and the probability of interactive learning. In this case, moderate scores on the independent variable are associated with the highest probability of interactive learning, and low and high scores of the independent variable are associated with low probabilities of interactive learning.

Results

First, we will review the outcomes of our descriptive analyses. Then, the results of Propositions 1–8 will be reviewed.

Table 8.5 reveals that there are only weak correlations between interactive learning and the independent variables. The structuring of innovative activities turns out to be associated positively with interactive learning between innovator firms and both TU/e and TNO. The complexity of innovative activities and the strength of the internal knowledge resources are only correlated with the interactive learning of innovator firms with TU/e. As expected, sectoral technological dynamics impacted on the probability of interactive learning.

Table 8.6 displays the results relevant to our propositions. Proposition 1 and 2 predicted either a positive or a negative effect of the strength of the internal knowledge resources on the probability of interactive learning with external actors. Our findings in Table 8.6 (model 3 Exp(b) = 1.44, $p.$ = 0.05; model 6 Exp (b) = 1.40, $p.$ = 0.10) support Proposition 2 and confirm the absorptive capacity argument. The resource deficit argument rendered in Proposition 1 is rejected by these findings.

Proposition 3 predicted an inverted-U shaped relation between the strength of internal knowledge resources and the probability of interactive learning with external actors. This proposition is supported only for interactive learning of small and medium-sized innovator firms with the TU/e (model 2: Exp(b) 0.85, $p.$ = 0.05). This finding refines the absorptive capacity argument in several

Table 8.5 Descriptive statistics

Variables	Mean scores	SD	Correlation (Spearman's Rho) of independent variables with dependent variables	
			Interactive learning with EUT	Interactive learning with TNO
Interactive learning with Eindhoven University of Technology	0.285	0.452		
Interactive learning with Dutch Centre for Applied Research (TNO)	0.380	0.486		
Complexity of innovative activities	0.004	1.576	0.15[c]	0.06
Complexity of innovative activities [squared]	2.480	3.454	−0.02	−0.07
Strength of internal knowledge resources	0.347	2.175	0.09[a]	0.03
Strength of internal knowledge resources [squared]	4.859	14.202	0.03	0.02
Cross-product term of strength of internal knowledge resources and complexity	0.366	3.501	−0.01	0.01
Cross-product term of strength of internal knowledge resources and complexity [squared]	12.358	52.745	0.01	−0.04
Level of integration of internal innovative activities	0.003	0.999	0.14[b]	0.10[a]
Level of support by bridging institutions	0.003	1.001	0.14[c]	0.19[d]
Pavitt sector	0.432	0.496	0.09[a]	−0.13[b]

Notes
a $p = 0.10$.
b $p = 0.05$.
c $p = 0.01$.
d $p = 0.001$.
Listwise N = 266.

Table 8.6 Stepwise Logistic Regression Analyses with interactive learning with TU/e and TNO as the dependent variable, and complexity of innovative activities, the strength of the internal knowledge resources, the structuring of the innovation process, and Pavitt sectors as the independent variables

Independent variables	Indicators	IL with TU/e			IL with TNO		
		Model 1 All firms Exp(b)	Model 2 Less than 100 Exp(b)	Model 3 100 or more Exp(b)	Model 4 All firms Exp(b)	Model 5 Less than 100 Exp(b)	Model 6 100 or more Exp(b)
Strength of the internal knowledge resources	P1/2 SIKR	1.12	0.94	1.44[b]	1.10	0.96	1.40[a]
	P3 SIKR (Sq.)	0.94	0.85[b]	1.03	0.97	0.95	1.16
Complexity of innovative activities	P4 COMP	1.25[a]	1.15	1.58[a]	0.99	0.92	1.68
	P5 COMP (Sq.)	0.87[a]	0.75[b]	1.17	0.90[a]	0.89	1.02
Interaction effects	P6 COMP*SIKR	0.97	1.04	1.03	1.01	1.04	1.36
	P7 [COMP*SIKR] Sq.	1.03[b]	1.09[c]	0.95	1.03[b]	1.02[b]	0.97
Structuring of innovative activities	P8 LIIA	1.13	0.98	1.14	1.07	0.99	0.87
	P9 LSBI	1.27[a]	1.39[b]	1.45	1.56[c]	1.72[d]	1.79
Pavitt sectors	PAVITT (dummy)	1.46	1.67	1.32	0.57[b]	0.56[a]	0.39
Constant		−1.09[d]	−0.99[d]	−0.57[b]	−0.27	−0.82[d]	0.36
-2LL		279.79	181.10	75.337	329.247	228.064	81.732
Goodness of fit		266.87	194.651	61.747	267.456	205.758	62.106
Significance		0.5605	0.5094	0.1377	0.2742	0.3047	0.1625
Percentage correct		75.9%	61.9%	62.1%	65.4%	73.4%	61.9%
Model Chi Square		13.754	20.394	8.394	20.868	20.117	3.674
Significance		0.0081	0.0004	0.0150	0.0003	0.0002	0.0553
Nagelkerke R Square		7.5%	15.2%	17.0%	10.3%	13.4%	7.6%
N		266	203	63	266	203	63

Notes
a $p = 0.10$.
b $p = 0.05$.
c $p = 0.01$.
d $p = 0.001$.

COMP = Complexity of innovative activities; COMP (Sq.) = Complexity of innovative activities squared; SIKR = Strength of the internal knowledge resources; SIKR (sq.) = Strength of internal knowledge resources squared; COMP*SIKR = Interaction term of complexity of innovative activities and strength of the internal knowledge resources; [COMP*SIKR] Sq. = Interaction term of complexity of innovative activities and strength of the internal knowledge resources squared; LIIA = Level of integration and innovative activities; LSBI = Level of support by bridging institutions; PAVITT = Pavitt sectors.

senses. First, because stronger knowledge resources occasion higher probabilities of interactive learning only up to a threshold, beyond which the presumed absorptive capacity effect is inverted. Second, the effect only holds for small and medium-sized innovator firms' interactive learning with TU/e.

Proposition 4 predicted that a higher complexity of innovative activities would occasion a higher probability of interactive learning with external actors. As Table 8.6 reveals (model 1 (Exp(b) = 1.25, $p.$ = 0.10; model 3 (Exp(b) = 1.58, $p.$ = 0.10), this proposition is supported for the probability of interactive learning with the TU/e. A sample split, controlling for size effects, shows that this complexity effect is significant for innovator firms with more than 100 employees. Proposition 4 was not supported for interactive learning with TNO.

Proposition 5 predicted an inverted U-shaped relation between complexity of innovative activities and the probability of interactive learning. This was confirmed in model 1 (Exp(b) = 0.87, $p.$ = 0.10), model 2 (Exp(b) = 0.75, $p.$ = 0.05) and model 4 (Exp(b) = 0.90, $p.$ = 0.10). This means that innovator firms performing innovative activities with moderate levels of complexity have the highest probability of interactive learning, and innovator firms performing innovative activities with low and high levels of complexity have relatively lower probabilities of interactive learning. However, these findings turned out to be quite sensitive for size effects. In the case of interactive learning with the TU/e, a sample split revealed that Proposition 5 was only valid for innovator firms with more than 100 employees. For the models estimating Proposition 5 for TNO the predicted effects disappeared when the sample was split into two size classes.

Proposition 6 was not supported at all. Proposition 7 predicted an *inverted* U-shaped relation between the cross-product term of 'complexity of innovative activities and strength of knowledge resources' and the probability of interactive learning. This proposition was rejected by our findings, which showed that for both TU/e and TNO there was a U-shaped relation between the interaction effect and the probability of interactive learning. A sample split again showed that this interaction effect occurred especially among small and medium-sized innovator firms.

The results with respect to the effects of the structuring of innovative activities – P8 and P9 – again informed us about the rather specific patterns of interactive learning. Proposition 8 was not supported at all by our findings. The level of support of bridging institutions was found to affect the probability of interactive learning with TU/e and TNO positively (model 1 Exp(b) = 1.27, $p.$ = 0.10; model 2 Exp(b) = 1.39, $p.$ = 0.05; model 4 Exp(b) = 1.56, $p.$ = 0.01; model 5 Exp(b) = 1.72, $p.$ = 0.001). Again, the control for sample size revealed that the effect of embeddedness in bridging institutions was particularly strong among small and medium-sized firms. The effect of sectoral technological dynamics was contrary to our expectations in the sense that the traditional sectors especially (supplier-dominated and scale-intensive) turned out to induce higher probabilities of interactive learning. As was the case with many other tested effects, the technological dynamics appeared to be contingent on the type of actor and size, and were only valid for small and medium-sized innovator firms' interactive learning with TNO.

Conclusion

This study sheds new light on the way in which innovative behaviour affects the link between individual firms and the knowledge infrastructure. Economic theorists have focused on the institutional effects of interactive learning without theorising on its antecedents, whereas network theorists, learning theorists, and resource-base theorists have concentrated either on the governance, structures, outcome effects, or resources shoved around in networks and ignored the specific learning processes going on in networks (Oliver and Ebers 1998). Our theoretical model brings interactive learning into the realm of organisation theory and unites several perspectives by exploring levels of interactive learning with a theoretical model that combines resource dependence, resource-based, and activity-based arguments.

This study provides evidence suggesting that a singular theoretical perspective would yield a very partial explanation of interactive learning between innovator firms and the knowledge infrastructure. Neither a singular resource-based explanation (Cohen and Levinthal 1990), nor a singular activity-based explanation (Lundvall 1992) would explain the probability of interactive learning sufficiently. The significance of the interaction effect between the complexity of innovative activities and strength of the knowledge base of innovator firms convincingly supports our approach of combining theoretical perspectives. Our model of interactive learning suggests that the interactive learning of innovator firms with actors in the knowledge infrastructure can and should be studied by considering the internal knowledge base, the complexity of innovative activities and the external embeddedness of innovator firms in bridging institutions.

The relations we proposed between the complexity of innovative activities, the strength of the internal knowledge resources, the structuring of innovative activities, and the level of interactive learning turned out to be very sensitive for the contingencies we have specified. The significant effects were found either after a sample split (Table 8.6: P1/2, model 3 and 4; P3 model 2), or disappeared after a sample split (Table 8.6: P5, model 4), or remained significant after a sample split for one of the size categories (Table 8.6: P4, model 1 and 3; P5, model 1, and 3; P7, model 1, 2, 4, and 5; P9, model 1, 2, 4, and 5). There were also differences between the science-oriented TU/e and TNO, which performs applied science. The empirical findings suggest that our theoretical model yields more significant results for the interactive learning with TU/e. For the small and medium-sized innovator firms, a proximity effect might explain this phenomenon, as TNO's head office is located in another province. However, such an explanation does not hold for larger firms.

Our approach of testing monotonic effects in combination with non-monotonic effects, interaction effects, and a control for size and type of actor proved to be very fruitful theoretically. It allowed us to specify the main arguments advanced. The significance of non-monotonic effects allowed for a refinement of the absorptive capacity argument (Cohen and Levinthal 1990) and the resource deficits arguments of Aiken and Hage (1968) and Evan (1993). The significance of the non-monotonic effects of the complexity of innovative activities enhances a refinement of the complexity argument (Lundvall 1988; Pfeffer and Salançik 1978), and illustrates that the absorptive capacity effect is conditional on the complexity of innovative activities. Our findings contrast strongly with the general notion of interactive learning in the systems of innovation literature (Edquist 1997; Lundvall 1992, 1993). The results suggest that there is more than one avenue for initiating interactive learning between the enormous variety of actors involved in the innovation process. Practically speaking, it may be possible to facilitate interactive learning by investing in a highly skilled workforce and pooling social and technical disciplines by means of intelligent organisational designs and project management. However, this would probably yield different effects on the level of interactive learning with, e.g. the customers, than on the level of interactive learning with the (public) knowledge infrastructure, and it would work out differently in distinct industrial sectors. For future research, this implies that scholars of interactive learning should include and specify a broad variety of external actors and industrial sectors in their analyses.

Caution is needed in assessing the contribution of our study, as there is no comparable research available that has empirically tested explanations of interactive learning. Caution should also be exercised because an important control variable – regional economic difference – was not included here. As described in our sample section, this region has specific features that, combined with a consensus-driven Dutch regulatory style, might induce very distinct patterns of interaction between industry and knowledge infrastructure. A strategy for dealing with this problem might be a comparison of external linkages of innovating firms within several comparable regions. Furthermore, given the low utilisation of regional resources in this specific region, we recommend research focusing on the comparison of strategies for the acquisition of distinct resources and their relative contributions to innovative performance. This would allow us to support the efficiency of network strategies as well as the efficacy of regional innovation systems more solidly.

References

Aiken, M. and Hage, J. (1968) 'Organizational Interdependence and Intra-organizational Structure', *American Sociological Review* 33: 912–929.
Alter, C. and Hage, J. (1993) *Organizations Working Together*, Newbury Park, CA: Sage Publications.
Anderson, P. and Tushman, M. L. (1990) 'Technological Discontinuities and Dominant Designs: A Cyclical Model of Technological Change', *Administrative Science Quarterly* 35: 604–633.

Baldwin, W. L. and Scott, J. T. (1987) *Market Structure and Technological Change*, London: Harwood Academic Publishers.

Barney, J. (1991) 'Firm Resources and Sustained Competitive Advantage', *Journal of Management Studies* 17: 99–120.

Chung, S., Singh, H. and Lee, K. (2000) 'Complementarity, Status Similarity and Social Capital as Drivers of Alliance Formation', *Strategic Management Journal* 21: 1–22.

Cohen, W. M. and Levin, R. C. (1989) 'Empirical Studies of Innovation and Market Structure', in R. Schmalensee and R. D. Willig (eds) *Handbook of Industrial Organisation*, Amsterdam: Elsevier Science Publishers, pp. 1060–1170.

Cohen, W. M. and Levinthal, D. A. (1990) 'Absorptive Capacity: A New Perspective on Learning and Innovation', *Administrative Science Quarterly* 35: 128–152.

Cohendet, P., Héraud, J. A. A. and Zuscovitch, E. (1993) 'Technological Learning, Economic Networks and Innovation Appropriability', in D. Foray and C. Freeman (eds) *Technology and the Wealth of Nations: The Dynamics of Constructed Advantage*, London: Pinter Publishers, pp. 66–76.

Combs, J. G. and Ketchen Jr., D. J. (1999) 'Explaining Interfirm Cooperation and Performance: Toward a Reconciliation of Predictions from the Resource-based View and Organizational Economics', *Strategic Management Journal* 20: 867–888.

Cooke, P., Boekholt, P. and Tödtling, F. (eds) (2000) *The Governance of Innovation in Europe: Regional Perspectives on Global Competitiveness*, London: Pinter.

Dewar, R. and Hage, J. (1978) 'Size, Technology, Complexity and Structural Differentiation: Toward a Theoretical Synthesis', *Administrative Science Quarterly* 23: 111–136.

Dodgson, M. (1993) 'Organizational Learning: A Review of Some Literatures', *Organization Studies* 14: 375–394.

Dougherty, D. (1992) 'Interpretive Barriers to Succesful Product Innovation in Large Firms', *Organization Science* 3: 179–202.

Duncan, R. B. (1972) 'Characteristics of Organizational Environments and Perceived Environmental Uncertainty', *Administrative Science Quarterly* 17: 313–327.

Edquist, C. (ed.) (1997) *Systems of Innovation: Technologies, Institutions and Organizations*, London: Pinter.

Evan, W. (1993) *Organization Theory: Research and Design*, New York: Maxwell MacMillan Publishing Company.

Freeman, C. and Soete, L. (1997) *The Economics of Innovation*, London: Pinter.

Galaskiewicz, J. (1985) 'Interorganizational Relations', *Annual Review of Sociology* 11: 281–304.

Galli, R. and Teubal, M. (1997) 'Paradigmatic Shifts in National Innovation Systems', in C. Edquist (ed.) *Systems of Innovation: Technologies, Institutions and Organizations*, London: Pinter, pp. 343–370.

Gambardella, A. (1992) 'Competitive Advantages from In-house Scientific Research: The U.S. Pharmaceutical Industry in the 1980's', *Research Policy* 21: 391–407.

Grandori, A. (1997) 'An Organizational Assessment of Interfirm Coordination Modes', *Organization Studies* 18: 897–925.

Grant, R. (1996) 'Prospering in Dynamically-competitive Environments: Organizational Capability as Knowledge Integration', *Organization Science* 7: 375–387.

Gulati, R. (1995) 'Social Structure and Alliance Formation: A Longitudinal Analysis', *Administrative Science Quarterly* 40: 619–652.

Hage, J. and Alter, C. (1997) 'A Typology of Interorganizational Relationships and Networks', in J. R. Hollingsworth and R. Boyer (eds) *Contemporary Capitalism: The Embeddedness of Institutions*, Cambridge: Cambridge University Press, pp. 94–126.

Håkansson, H. (1987) *Industrial Technological Development: A Network Approach*, London: Croom Helm.

Håkansson, H. (1989) *Corporate Technological Behavior: Co-operation and Networks*, London: Routledge.

Henderson, R. M. and Clark, K. B. (1990) 'Architectural Innovation: The Reconfiguration of Existing Products and the Failure of Established Firms', *Administrative Science Quarterly* 35: 9–30.

Huber, G. P. (1991) 'Organizational Learning: The Contributing Process and the Literatures', *Organizational Science* 2: 88–115.

Jin, D. J. and Stough, R. R. (1998) 'Learning and Learning Capability in the Fordist and Post-Fordist Age: An Integrative Framework', *Environment and Planning A* 30: 1255–1278.

Jones, C., Hesterly, W. S. and Borgatti, S. P. (1997) 'A General Theory of Network Governance: Exchange Conditions and Social Mechanisms', *Academy of Management Review* 22: 911–945.

Kleinknecht, A. and Reijen, J. O. N. (1992) 'Why Do Firms Cooperate on R&D? An Empirical Study', *Research Policy* 21: 347–360.

Kogut, B. and Zander, U. (1992) 'Knowledge of the Firm, Combinative Capabilities, and the Replication of Technology', *Organization Science* 3: 383–397.

Lam, A. (1997) 'Embedded Firms, Embedded Knowledge: Problems of Collaboration and Knowledge Transfer in Global Cooperative Ventures', *Organization Studies* 18: 973–996.

Lawrence, P. R. and Lorsch, J. W. (1967) *Organization and Environment: Managing Differentiation and Integration*, Harvard Graduate School of Business Administration, Cambridge, MA: Harvard University Press.

Leonard-Barton, D. and Doyle, J. L. (1996) 'Commercializing Technology: Imaginative Understanding of User Needs', in R. S. Rosenbloom and W. J. Spencer (eds) *Engines of Innovation: U.S. Industrial Research at the End of the Era*, Cambridge, MA: Harvard Business School Press, Boston, pp. 177–208.

Lundvall, B.-Å. (1985) *Product Innovation and User-Producer Interaction*, Aalborg: Aalborg University Press.

Lundvall, B.-Å. (1988) 'Innovation as an Interactive Process', in G. Dosi, C. Freeman, R. Nelson, G. Silverberg and L. Soete (eds) *Technical Change and Economic Theory*, London: Pinter, pp. 349–369.

Lundvall, B.-Å. (1992) 'User-producer Relationships, National Systems of Innovations and Internationalisation', in D. Foray and C. Freeman (eds) *Technology and the Wealth of Nations: The Dynamics of Constructed Advantage*, London: Pinter, pp. 277–300.

Lundvall, B.-Å. (1993) 'User-producer Relationships, National Systems of Innovation and Internationalization', in B.-Å. Lundvall (ed.) *National Systems of Innovation: Towards a Theory of Innovation and Interactive Learning*, London: Pinter, pp. 45–67.

Mansfield, E. (1991) 'Academic Research and Industrial Innovation', *Research Policy* 20: 1–12.

Meeus, M. T. H. and Oerlemans, L. A. G. (1993) 'Economic Network Research: A Methodological State of the Art', in P. Beije, J. Groenwegen and O. Nuys (eds) *Networking in Dutch Industries*, Leuven and Apeldoorn: Garant, pp. 37–68.

Meeus, M. T. H. and Oerlemans, L. A. G. (1995) 'The Competitiveness of Firms in the Region of North-Brabant', in P. Beije and O. Nuys (eds) *The Dutch Diamond: The Usefulness of Porter in Analyzing Small Countries*, Leuven and Apeldoorn: Garant/ Siswo, pp. 223–256.

Meeus, M. T. H., Oerlemans, L. A. G. and Boekema, F. W. M. (1996) 'Knowledge Indicators and Innovative Performance' (in Dutch), in O. Atzema and J. van Dijk (eds) *Technology and the Regional Labour Market*, Assen: Van Gorcum, pp. 144–161.

Meeus, M. T. H., Oerlemans, L. A. G. and Dijck, J. van (2000) 'Interactive Learning within a Regional System of Innovation: A Case Study in a Dutch Region', in F. Boekema, K. Morgan, S. Bakkers and R. Rutten (eds) *Knowledge, Innovation and Economic Growth: The Theory and Practice of Learning Regions*, Cheltenham: Edward Elgar.

Meeus, M. T. H., Oerlemans, L. A. G. and Faber, E. (1997) *IOP Image Processing: Matching Knowledge Demand and Supply by Means of Identification of Knowledge Producers and Users and Network Analysis* (in Dutch), external report commissioned by SENTER for Technology, Energy and Environment, The Hague.

Meeus, M. T. H., Oerlemans, L. A. G. and Hage, J. (1999) *Sectoral Patterns of Interactive Learning: An Empirical Exploration of a Case in a Dutch Region*, ECIS Working Paper Series 99/5, Eindhoven: ECIS.

Midgley, D. F., Morrison, P. D. and Roberts, J. H. (1992) 'The Effects of Networks Structure in Industrial Diffusion Processes', *Research Policy* 21: 533–552.

Miller, D. and Chen, M. J. (1994) 'Sources and Consequences of Competitive Inertia: A Study of the U.S. Airline Industry', *Administrative Science Quarterly* 39: 1–23.

Miller, D. and Friesen, P. H. (1982) 'Innovation in Conservative and Entrepreneurial Firms: Two Models of Strategic Momentum', *Strategic Management Journal* 3: 1–25.

Ministry of Economic Affairs (1995) *Dynamic Knowledge: On Knowledge and Skills in the Dutch Economy* (in Dutch), The Hague: Ministry of Economic Affairs.

Ministry of Economic Affairs (1997) *The Competitiveness Test 1997* (in Dutch), The Hague: Ministry of Economic Affairs.

Mitchell, W. (1991) 'Using Academic Technology: Transfer Methods and Licensing Incidence in the Commercialization of American Diagnostic Imaging Equipment Research, 1945–1988', *Research Policy*, 20: 203–216.

Mowery, D. C., Oxley, J. E. and Silverman, B. S. (1996) 'Strategic Alliances and Interfirm Knowledge Transfer', *Strategic Management Journal* 17: 77–91.

Nelson, R. (1982) 'The Role of Knowledge in R&D Efficiency', *Quarterly Journal of Economics* 97: 453–470.

Nelson, R. (ed.) (1993) *National Innovation Systems: A Comparative Analysis*, New York: Oxford University Press.

Oerlemans, L. (1996) *The Embedded Firm: Innovation in Industrial Networks* (in Dutch), Tilburg: Tilburg University Press.

Oerlemans, L. A. G., Meeus, M. T. H. and Boekema, F. W. M. (1998) 'Do Networks Matter for Innovation', *Journal of Social and Economic Geography* 3: 298–309.

Oerlemans, L. A. G., Meeus, M. T. H. and Kraus, A. (1999) *IOP Human Systems Interaction: Matching Knowledge Demands and Supply by Means of Identification of Knowledge Producers and Users and Network Analysis* (in Dutch), external report commissioned by SENTER for Technology, Energy and Environment, The Hague.

Oliver, A. L. and Ebers, M. (1998) 'Networking Network Studies: An Analysis of Conceptual Configurations in the Study of Inter-organizational Relationships', *Organization Studies* 19: 549–583.

Pavitt, K. (1984) 'Sectoral Patterns of Technical Change: Towards a Taxonomy and a Theory', *Research Policy* 13: 343–373.

Pfeffer, J. and Salançik, G. R. (1978) *The External Control of Organizations: A Resource Dependence Perspective*, New York: Basic Books.

Pisano, G. P. (1990) 'The R&D Boundaries of the Firm: An Empirical Analysis', *Administrative Science Quarterly* 35: 153–176.

Rosenberg, N. and Nelson, R. R. (1996) 'The Role of Universities in the Advance of Industrial Technology', in R. S. Rosenbloom and W. J. Spencer (eds) *Engines of Innovation: U.S. Industrial Research at the End of an Era*, Cambridge, MA: Harvard University Press, pp. 87–110.

Rosenbloom, R. S. and Christensen, C. M. (1998) 'Technological Discontinuities, Organizational Capabilities, and Strategic Commitments', in G. Dosi, D. J. Teece and J. Chytry (eds) *Technology, Organization, and Competitiveness: Perspectives on Industrial and Corporate Change*, Oxford: Oxford University Press, pp. 215–247.

Saxenian, A. (1994) *Regional Advantage: Culture and Competition in Silicon Valley and Route 128*, Cambridge, MA: Harvard University Press.

Schumpeter, J. (1975) *Capitalism, Socialism and Democracy* (third edn), New York: Harper and Row (originally published in 1942 by Harper and Row).

Senker, J. and Faulkner, W. (1996) 'Networks, Tacit Knowledge and Innovation', in R. Coombs, A. Richards, P. P. Saviotti and V. Walsh (eds) *Technological Collaboration: The Dynamics of Cooperation in Industrial Innovation*, Cheltenham: Edward Elgar Publishing Ltd., pp. 76–97.

Smith, K. (1995) 'Interactions in Knowledge Systems: Foundations, Policy Implications and Empirical Methods', *STI Review* 16: 69–102.

Szulanski, G. (1996) 'Exploring Internal Stickiness: Impediments to the Transfer of Best Practice within the Firm', *Strategic Management Journal* 17: 27–43.

Teece, D. and Pisano, G. P. (1998) 'The Dynamic Capabilities of Firms', in G. Dosi, D. J. Teece and J. Chytry (eds) *Technology, Organization, and Competitiveness: Perspectives on Industrial and Corporate Change*, Oxford: Oxford University Press, pp. 193–212.

Teubal, M. (1976) 'On User Needs and Need Determination: Aspects of the Theory of Technological Innovation', *Research Policy* 5: 266–289.

Turner, J. (1988) *A Theory of Social Interaction*, Stanford, CA: Stanford University Press.

Tushman, M. L. and Anderson, P. (1986) 'Technological Discontinuities and Organizational Environments', *Administrative Science Quarterly* 31: 439–465.

Tushman, M. L. and Romanelli, E. (1985) 'Organizational Evolution', in L. L. Cummings and B. S. Staw (eds) *Research in Organizational Behavior: An Annual Series of Analytical Essays and Critical Reviews* 7, Greenwich, CT: JAI Press Inc, pp. 171–222.

Von Hippel, E. (1976) 'The Dominant Role of Users in the Scientific Instrument Innovation Process', *Research Policy* 5: 212–239.

Von Hippel, E. (1987) 'Cooperation between Rivals: Informal Know-how Trading', *Research Policy* 16: 291–302.

Vossen, R. W. and Nooteboom, B. (1996) 'Firm Size and Participation in R&D in A. H. Kleinknecht (ed.) *Determinants of Innovation: The Message from New Indicators*, London: Macmillan Press Ltd, pp. 155–168.

Wernerfelt, B. (1984) 'A Resource-based View of the Firm', *Strategic Management Journal* 5: 171–180.

Windrum, P. (1999) 'Simulation Models of Technological Innovation', *American Behavioral Scientist* 42: 1531–1550.

9 Networking between economy and education

Regional knowledge transfer in Dutch agriculture

Loek Nieuwenhuis, Kees Verhaar and Aimée Hoeve

Introduction

Knowledge infrastructures are changing at a swift pace: driving forces in the global economy and the increasingly rapid development of (information) technology are making it necessary for national governments to reconsider the organisation of national systems of innovation and knowledge production (Edquist 1997). The development of Mode 2 production systems of knowledge, as described by Gibbons (see Chapter 13), is in line with this trend.

Within the Dutch agricultural knowledge system, these changes can be observed at various levels. To begin with, governmental protective policies have been replaced by a market-driven institutional set-up of the knowledge infrastructure. Next, a reversal of production chains can be observed, by which steering from the supply side is replaced by steering from the demand side. This results from the fact that farmers and the food industry have to respond to the needs of consumers and supermarkets, regarding both the quality of products and the quality of production processes (animal welfare and safe food).

Partly as a response, the same reversal can be observed in the knowledge supply chains: supply-led knowledge chains are turning into demand-led chains. For the knowledge-producing and transferring organisations, this reversal implies a major strategic reorientation and organisational adaptation. Universities, research institutes and educational colleges have to reinvent their positions within knowledge networks and technology markets.

In this chapter, we focus on the reconstruction of the agricultural knowledge infrastructure in the Netherlands and the strategic reorientation of agricultural colleges and universities. What are the new challenges in a modern, market-driven agricultural knowledge system for organisations dealing with knowledge production and delivery? Focusing on several research projects in this area, we will look into the changes in the institutional set-up, the innovation processes, and the knowledge demands from agricultural enterprises. We will then present findings from an investigation within educational organisations which shed light on the strategic responses to these developments. In the final section, we will address the question whether or not these answers are adequate, given the fact that these organisations have to develop into respected members of regional innovative networks in this new century.

Institutional reconstruction of the agricultural knowledge system

Links between the educational system and the economic system have existed within Dutch agriculture ever since the emergence of agricultural education during the late nineteenth century and the early years of the twentieth century. During the decades following the Second World War, these links developed into a system, the OVO triangle (*Onderzoek – Voorlichting – Onderwijs*, in English REE: Research – Extension – Education). The logic of the OVO triangle is based on the science orientation of agriculture, the ongoing reorganisation of agricultural practices according to models designed by agrarian sciences (Van der Ploeg 1996). These models were delivered to farmers by an extensive government extension service and a separate education system. The system was legitimised by the modernisation paradigm that dominated Dutch agricultural policy. The central notion of this policy was that small and inefficient farmers should disappear and large promising farms, the so-called vanguard farms, had to be supported (by import protection, export subsidies and guaranteed prices). Entrepreneurs (in agribusiness and farming) derived their parameters largely from agricultural policy supporting generic new technologies to enhance productivity (Van Dijk and Van der Ploeg 1995).

The OVO triangle has proved its worth as it has contributed considerably to the success of Dutch agriculture, making the Netherlands one of the biggest 'agro-powers' in the world. The institutionalisation and the success of the OVO triangle have been described by various authors (De Bruin 1997; Vijverberg 1996).

However, as a result of recent developments, this model is no longer successful. An important development is the recognition that

> the practice of farming is not to be understood as a more or less linear derivation of the 'logic' of the market or as a straightforward application of external technological designs. Markets and technology create a specific room for manoeuvre that allows for differential positions.
>
> (Van der Ploeg and Saccomandi 1995: 15)

Empirical studies by researchers at Wageningen University show a variety of strategies based on rational choice and ensuring a reasonable income. This recognition challenged one of the major principles of the OVO triangle that there is one 'best' farmer practice and, therefore, a need to transform the agricultural knowledge system.

This need for transformation has been strengthened by economic and socio-cultural changes. In the 1990s, Dutch agriculture faced a severe crisis. Because of pressure from the World Trade Organisation, the European Union was forced to reduce economic protection of the agricultural markets, leading to deteriorating incomes in the sector. The crisis was aggravated by a growing public concern about health issues, growing environmental awareness in European society and serious food production scandals (the recent disasters of BSE, swine fever and foot and mouth disease). Moreover, in the 1990s, there was a growing awareness that modernisation had reached its limits as the negative consequences of this strategy became evident:

- overproduction;
- a continuous fall in agricultural employment;
- an increasing social demand to produce without environmental, health, and animal welfare scandals.

Policy-makers, sector representatives and scientists agree that structural changes in the current mode of production are needed, i.e. farmers should produce for a more competitive market and meet growing public demands for quality-oriented and environmentally safe production. To be able to meet these demands, farmers need to re-orientate regarding social and economic incentives. In the latest policy document, entitled *Voedsel en Groen* (Food and Environment) by the Dutch Ministry of Agriculture (2000), the need to stimulate 'modern agro-entrepreneurship' is emphasised. According to the Ministry, the two main conditions of modern entrepreneurship are economic autonomy and socially sound management.

This new policy orientation, thus, no longer legitimises an extensive government-supported OVO triangle. During the 1990s, a large part of the OVO triangle was privatised: knowledge was no longer considered to be a public good that should be provided free of charge by government services.

The need to innovate the knowledge system

The Dutch agricultural sector must undergo fundamental changes in order to meet new demands to develop sustainable ways of production. This calls for an innovative agricultural sector.

This need is mirrored in the main line of thought in evolutionary economics, in which the dynamic aspects of economic development are central (Dosi and Nelson 1994). Schumpeter (Brouwer and Kleinknecht 1994), in the inter-war period, described the process of creative destruction in which enterprises with old-fashioned products are expelled by enterprises with new products (competition on substitution and not on prices, Jacobs 1996). Innovation and technology development are the main tools required to survive this dynamic process.

Protection of 'old' enterprises hinders the process of creative destruction, which should lead to under-investment in innovation. According to Kleinknecht, investments in R&D lead to increasing export and job growth at the enterprise level. Innovative enterprises are more resistant to economic crises.

Innovation leads to company-specific knowledge (tacit knowledge; see Dosi 2000; Nonaka and Takeuchi 1995), which strengthens the 'forward' position of innovative enterprises. Tacit knowledge depends on people: it is important to have long-lasting contracts with the core of the employees. Flexibility should be translated into trainability and not external flexibility. A specific problem for the agricultural sector in this respect is that the traditional view of labour is rather negative. Instead of regarding workers as a strategic asset, many farmers see their employees as mere 'hands' who simply have to meet production targets (Verhaar and Smulders 1999). Competitiveness, innovativeness, and internal craftsmanship are fundamental elements of a healthy company. Maintenance of these requires knowledge management.

Detecting and using external knowledge sources and the organisation of internal learning processes is a central aspect of modern management. Oerlemans (1997) states that innovation is an embedded process (within a knowledge context) in which the exchange of learning and technical sources is elementary, especially for small and medium-sized enterprises (SMEs). Economic networks are basic to the transformation of heterogeneous knowledge sources into useful 'neue Kombinationen'.

The call for socially sound management in agriculture emphasises the need for new knowledge sources. It is clear that agricultural development should no longer be synonymous with technological development. In fact, to overcome the current problems in Dutch agriculture, innovations at the system level are needed, that is, innovations that take account of technological, economical, socio-cultural, ecological, and ethical parameters.

However, regional and national governments have restricted options to facilitate knowledge networks. The establishment of intermediate organisations, which enhance fundamental research, and the maintenance of initial vocational and professional education are aspects which are mentioned in the literature on innovation policies (OECD 1997).

Interactive innovation in micro-enterprises

Company innovation is an embedded process. The innovative process can be characterised as a reforming of existing knowledge into new combinatory knowledge. To organise this combinatory process, companies need to collaborate with other companies and knowledge institutes. This is especially the case for small enterprises as they do not possess large internal knowledge sources and research potential. For effective innovation, small and medium-sized companies have to use external knowledge sources. Non-profit or public agencies and innovation centres at the sectoral and the regional level, technical colleges and universities can play the important role of back-up service for SMEs. In addition, local and regional industrial networks are necessary for the transformation of knowledge into innovative combinations and products.

The entrepreneur, or the employer, with his/her skilled employees, is continuously involved in problem-solving and innovative processes. First, he/she looks for internal solutions. However, soon the use of external sources will become a necessity. Professional journals, financial advisors, suppliers and customers will bring in new knowledge, deliberately or accidentally. As a result, an interactive exchange of knowledge will develop around internal company processes and their external relations. The enterprise is embedded within an expanding knowledge space. The knowledge space surrounding companies is multi-dimensional; at least three dimensions can be discerned: the product chain, the professional sector, and the socio-economic region.

In the chain dimension, learning and innovation take place through the exchange of product requirements and quality information systems. Nieuwenhuis *et al.* (1998) point to the growing complexity of agro (food) chains. As a result of rapidly changing consumer demands, agro (food) chains will transform into networks to organise supply, production, transport and distribution in a flexible way. The agricultural sector will merge more and more with other economic sectors and the agricultural knowledge system will need to link up with other knowledge sources.

In the sectoral dimension, an important aspect is that, at the professional level an exchange of knowledge between professionals within competing companies can be observed. In many cases, common interests exist, pushing competitors into collaborative innovative activities. In Dutch agriculture, the horticultural farmers in particular have a strong history of farmer-to-farmer exchange of information and innovations through so-called study clubs. Some of these study clubs even carry out experimental research, sometimes in close cooperation with a research institute.

In the third dimension, knowledge exchange is seen as a process carried out between companies in the same (sometimes virtual) region. Direct contact via observation, discussion, and mutual shop floor visits is an important feature of knowledge exchange. The supply of skilled labour is also spatially bound.

Depending on the socio-economic preconditions, strategic decisions need to be taken in all three dimensions; the balance between common interests and competitive advantages depends on many variables. In the next two sections, the results of two recent research projects will be described. The central issue within the context of this chapter is how farmers deal with the knowledge space around their enterprises.

Knowledge sources and learning processes of entrepreneurs

We examined the professional learning and search processes of agricultural entrepreneurs (Gielen and Jager 2001). In-depth interviews were conducted with nine farmers regarding the activities they engaged in while searching for company-relevant information. These farmers were not selected for a specific innovative stage: they were just 'ordinary' farmers. However, almost all interviewees have been involved in important innovations during the last few years. Some of them are early innovators; others adopt innovations from elsewhere. The product market is the most important stimulus. Innovations are technical, market-oriented, and socio-organisational. Internal solutions are sought before looking externally. It has been observed that the important learning experiences are not those involving content (technology, new knowledge), but learning processes (new ways of finding innovative information).

In general, farmers are actively looking for new information and knowledge. Most of the interviewees mentioned that they were eager to find out about new developments: they have a 'natural' tendency to learn. With this general orientation, these entrepreneurs keep an eye out for developments in their markets, within their sector, and in society in general. They want (and need) to know what is happening in their economic environment. This helps them define a strategy for the enterprise and provides information on problems within the company which have not been detected yet. All interviewees were aware of the need to be open to external developments.

Specific information is gathered on technological and market aspects. Greenhouse farmers need daily information on auction price developments and specific technological information for the optimisation of processes and products.

For problem solving, specific information sources are used. Journals, networks, and databases are used to look for specific solutions. For technical problems, the knowledge infrastructure offers rather good information; for marketing problems the interviewees have to search using more of their own resources.

The most important sources of new information are specific journals, colleagues, competitors, suppliers and customers. These sources were mentioned as very reliable. Employees are not often seen as an important source of information: there is a knowledge concentration with the entrepreneur. Training, extension, and fairs were also mentioned, but were not regarded as very useful. Research and technological institutes were rarely mentioned: the 'psychological' distance is too large. Information is looked for locally as well as internationally, depending on the problem. Most of the interviewees are not afraid of looking internationally: they have rather professional ways of searching for new information.

Networks of colleagues, based on a sectoral organisation, were mentioned as among the most powerful sources of innovative information. Participation in these networks is seen as a normal activity. Farmers use different networks for different types of knowledge fields: financial, social, technical, and political. Long-lasting network contacts are mostly rather informally organised. The information exchange is based on gentlemen's agreements: one can only participate when one is seen as a source of knowledge. Entrepreneurs are seen as a source of powerful information and knowledge and they are aware of the economic value of that knowledge. In former times, farmers' networks were quite publicly organised because of the government financing of these activities. Recently, some of these networks have become closed organisations: the competitive advantage of the exchanged knowledge is too great for open publicity. This is compatible with the observations of Von Hippel on knowledge exchange between steel mill engineers (1988).

'Mega'-Farms

In a second research project, we studied the entrepreneural behaviour of 'mega-farmers' (Verhaar and Hoeve 1999). The notion of knowledge as an important competitive resource is certainly acknowledged by mega-farmers. Within the context of Dutch agriculture, mega-farms are large firms although, in general terms, they are classified as medium-sized enterprises. The most crucial attribute of mega-farms is the entrepreneurial character of the mega-farmer. We concluded that mega-farmers' entrepreneurship is pro-active, aimed at growth, developing pluri-activity, and taking advantage of socio-economic developments. Contrary to popular belief, this includes the way they deal with 'sustainability' and 'animal welfare'. The main reason for this pro-active behaviour is their desire to gain an advantage on the market – which relates to the development from supply-driven to demand-driven, as discussed above. Mega-farms may consist of a number of formally independent companies ('conglomerate'-like). They may be active in more than one type of agricultural production. They may take part in cooperation networks. Partners in such networks may be equal, although the mega-farmer is the initiator and (informal) group leader, but 'ordinary farmers' may also be subcontracted by the mega-farmer. Mega-farmers may extend their activities to other parts of the production chain or to the distribution of the products. An example of this is the production of pig fodder by a pig breeding farmer, both for his own pigs and to sell to other farmers. Farmers may also diversify into activities that do not relate to primary production. Some of the farmers in our study took part in the service economy by setting up a land and farm agency. Another option is to set up new economic activities abroad. Mega-farmers quite often combine a number of activities.

The mega-farmers make sure that they acquire knowledge themselves: they do not want to rely on the knowledge of others. Even if an employee is a specialist in an area of work, the mega-farmer will still make sure that he or she is well versed in that area. Knowledge sources vary. Farmer organisations are used as a source of knowledge, as are suppliers and clients. Some mega-farmers opt for a strategy of knowledge provision. Providing knowledge may even be one of the commercial activities of the mega-farm. This last observation demonstrates the changing role of knowledge in the Dutch agricultural setting (knowledge as competitive resource and as a commercial product, see Von Hippel 1988).

A second important observation, relating to the notion of knowledge as a competitive resource, is the changing nature of networks, e.g. as a result of chain integration (trans-sectoral, transregional). Many mega-farmers see little use in joining the traditional study clubs (in terms of knowledge resource; for a number of these farmers, the social aspect of these study clubs remains important). These farmers often create their own innovation networks, strictly selecting specific innovation partners. Sometimes, cooperation is sought with colleagues but also with research institutes (universities or private institutes), advisory agencies, and suppliers both within and outside the agricultural sector.

Conclusion

The results of the two research projects show that the knowledge space around Dutch farming enterprises encompasses all three dimensions, that is, the product chain, the professional sector, and the socio-economic region.

Traditionally, knowledge exchange between farmers (the professional dimension) has been very important in Dutch agriculture. Farmers themselves consider networks of colleagues, either informally or formally organised, as one of the most powerful sources of innovation. A few years ago, it was unthinkable not to participate in farmer networks. However, with the decline of the OVO triangle, knowledge is becoming more and more a competitive resource. This is underpinned by research among the mega-farmers as, for some of them, the provision of knowledge is even one of their commercial activities. The commercialisation of knowledge has important consequences for an effective knowledge infrastructure. Knowledge creation in modern enterprises is becoming more like Mode 2 knowledge production (see Gibbons, Chapter 13). One of the challenges of the next decade will be to develop interactive ways of knowledge production within a competitive global economy. At this moment, there is no single solution for this problem.

One important strategy of mega-farms is to search for added value production, e.g. through chain integration. The knowledge dimension of the product chain is, therefore, becoming more important. The interviews with 'ordinary' and mega-farmers make it clear that agricultural development involves more than just technological development. Above, we mentioned the need for innovation at the system level, taking into account socio-cultural, economical, ecological, technological and ethical parameters. Such innovation requires new knowledge sources. As the agricultural knowledge infrastructure has long been focused on technological innovation, non-agricultural sources can contribute greatly to these innovations. The socio-economic region will play an important role in this respect.

Networking strategies by agricultural colleges

Vocational education and training in the network economy

Vocational and professional education and training occur, at present, mainly in the regional dimension. Producing a highly skilled labour force is the main task of technical and agricultural colleges. As mobility of the labour force is regionally bound, the impact of education and training is likewise regional. In the building of competitive regional economies, colleges are major players, as is shown by Rosenfeld (1998). In addition to supplying and maintaining a skilled labour force, a new task area is indicated for technical colleges: the brokering of (new) knowledge to the local economy. This implies regional strategies for economic development, of which education and training should be an integral part.

Vocational education and training are also important in the sectoral dimension. Occupational identity is an important instrument in hedging the economic activities of professional groups. Vocational courses and qualifications play an important role in this hedging process (De Bruyn and Nieuwenhuis 1994). Also, the development of technical and vocational courses is often based on skill definitions from the professional group. Trade unions and employer organisations play their roles in defining vocational courses in German and Dutch apprenticeship systems and in the formulation of national vocational qualification standards in the UK system. Vocational education and training deliver and develop occupational standards, interacting with the professional sectors. Employers and skilled workers use their professional institutions to maintain and upgrade their skills. Innovative shifts in occupational require-ments often stem from developments within the educational system. So, also, in the sectoral dimension, vocational education has the potential to facilitate innovation within small and medium-sized enterprises. This also goes for the agricultural sector, as agricultural education has been a part of and, in fact, still is a remnant of the OVO triangle.

The production chain is a rather new perspective on analysing innovative processes and related skill developments. Joint innovative activities are often based on chain-linked relations between enterprises, but skill developments are not yet related to chain developments. However, as production chains have a large potential for new economic and innovative perspectives, this is an interesting new area for developing vocational education and training strategies.

To enhance knowledge transfer processes, vocational education, training, and extension should play four important roles (Nieuwenhuis and Figueira forthcoming, Rosenfeld 1998):

- the education and training of new employees and employers, which scaffold the knowledge base in companies; the delivery of initial vocational education and training, based on new instructional designs as cognitive apprenticeships; this cluster also includes attention to disadvantaged youth and on adequate recruitment for technical vacancies;
- the supply of information and training facilities to update the knowledge and skills of the workforce; adaptation of the workforce to new technology by upgrading skills and retraining. This includes the formation of training networks and reskilling of displaced workers;
- the facilitation of technology adaptation; acceleration of the deployment of new technologies through the establishment of an intermediate role in several forms;
- the organisation of active networks of enterprises to facilitate interactive learning processes; establishment of networks of learning companies and learning communities.

Training institutes should take up the challenge of the knowledge transfer process by ensuring a high degree of responsiveness to the results of science and technology development. Regional training colleges, supported by sectoral innovation centres, have the opportunity to become pivotal in the learning networks of small and medium-sized enterprises, by using innovative knowledge from the R&D infrastructure in their courses. Intermediate structures established by industrial sectors to enhance communication between R&D and educational systems are central to this model. These intermediate structures depend on sectoral features (economic cohesion, cooperation between companies, relevance of human capital), innovative processes (interactive vs. linear; market or science-oriented), and features of the sectoral training and innovation system (school-/company-based; job or domain-oriented; based on collective agreements).

Vocational education and training stand at the crossroads of regional and sectoral policy perspectives: labour markets are regionally defined; the supply and demand of employment are spatially bound because of mobility limits. Yet, craftsmanship is highly sectorally bound because of the intertwining between occupational domains and economic activities. Educational policies are more or less connected to sectoral policies, depending on national educational systems and socio-economic constraints. Colleges have to build both sectoral and regional networks in order to efficiently supply a well-qualified labour force, prepared for life-long learning and innovative employment.

Agricultural colleges in regional innovative networks

Based on the models and ideas presented, the managers of all Dutch agricultural colleges were interviewed in 1998, and were questioned on their strategies and policies with regard to their role in the regional knowledge infrastructure. Most colleges are aware of the urgency to develop new strategies for the development of a spider role in regional innovative networks, but, at the same time, most colleges do not possess the necessary instruments and tools to reach that goal. They do not belong to regional networks and are not seen as interesting network partners in the eyes of regional entrepreneurs.

The agricultural colleges' aim is to become transfer points for new technology and knowledge through courses, adaptation processes, and brokering. They do not see an active role in knowledge development for themselves: they see regional networks as the sources of new knowledge, but they are not able to play a collaborative role. Within the new institutional set-up, this is not considered adequate: they are not accepted as recognised members of these innovative networks. Thus, their ties with the innovative practices within enterprises are loosening or even disappearing and the colleges are ending up on the margins of the knowledge system. As a result of this process, the prerequisites for a responsive vocational education and training supply have been lost and the quality of the preparation of youngsters for the labour market has been endangered.

The colleges' networks deal with other knowledge organisations for extension, practical research, and knowledge transfer. Public and governmental organisations are also part of their networks. Most of their networks are restricted to agricultural organisations: innovative impulses from other economic fields are rare. This is endangering the adequacy of labour market preparation because of the merging of several economic and societal fields (e.g. the field of rural development, in which agricultural, urban and environmental issues are mixed up in new activities concerning tourism and leisure).

In summary, from the interviews, it can be concluded that internal constraints form a major obstacle to the development of innovative and interactive colleges, achieving the goals described by Rosenfeld (1998). The educational staff, in particular, is not capable of industrial innovation because of the lack of (recent) practical experience and the lack of economic pressure to compete. The latter can be seen as a relic of the supply-driven past of the OVO triangle. Moreover, innovative entrepreneurs are more competent all-round than specialised teachers, and do not see teachers as partners in problem-solving situations.

To be considered innovation-facilitating organisations, colleges have to develop targeted knowledge management systems and exchange programmes for their staff. Many colleges have started with these forms of staff development programmes, but they still have to overcome major problems before they can reach the goal of being a responsive education and innovation-oriented knowledge organisation.

Conclusion

The interviews show that industrial innovation is an economically driven process in which the role of agricultural education and training is marginal. This observation is also true for other educational sectors and other European educational systems (Nieuwenhuis and Figueira forthcoming). Although the traditional delivery of vocational courses is still the prime target of technical and vocational colleges, it is no longer an adequate response to the increasingly changing skill demands. Most colleges stick to the first goal stated by Rosenfeld (1998): education as a gateway to the workplace. The other three areas of innovative training and skilling (upgrading skills, technology adaptation, and forming networks) are only observed in some specific cases: they are not common for colleges.

To be able to operate in such a strategic way, colleges should have clear goals and a strategic vision embedded in their strategic management. Rosenfeld (1998) argues that the most entrepreneurial and innovative colleges are characterised, at least, by (1) an economic development mission statement; (2) a focus on their region, including cluster specialisation; (3) being a repository of know-how for SMEs, which is easy to access for individual entrepreneurs; (4) being capable of relating technology adaptation to skill requirements and offering suitable training courses when companies are involved in technology investments; (5) exhibition of flexibility and adaptability (responsiveness) in their training supply; and (6) facilitating interaction and common learning activities among people in different organisations.

Colleges should become learning organisations in order to develop these organisational skills. National and regional governments should encourage and facilitate colleges in that direction. Colleges should become spiders in regional learning networks, with open information connections with the local economic community, on the one hand, and with sectoral knowledge sources, on the other hand. Within this network strategy, colleges should be aware of their own core competences and form alliances with complementary knowledge institutes. Specialisation in regional industrial clusters can strengthen the pivotal position of the colleges. By expanding their role from initial vocational education and training to the facilitation of regional and sectoral innovation and technology adaptation, vocational education and training (VET) colleges have the potential to be among the most important knowledge institutes for local and regional economic development.

Perspectives on regional knowledge transfer in agriculture

The knowledge context of agricultural enterprises in the Netherlands is changing dramatically: from the stable OVO triangle with its linear knowledge transfer principles, towards an unstable, interactive innovation arena, where competitive knowledge is developed in changing networks of collaborative enterprises. These networks are built in a sectoral dimension, but chain relations and regional contacts are becoming increasingly important. Competitive enterprises, like the mega-farms, regard innovative knowledge as a competitive input. Sharing this input is restricted to hedged networks, where partners give and take, based on gentlemen's agreements. Keeping in mind that in agriculture, we are dealing with small and medium-sized enterprises, most of these networks are established at a local or regional level. Agricultural colleges have the potential to become important knowledge institutes for the development of farms and rural areas, but should be accepted as valued partners in the new innovative networks. This is not to deny the contribution that can be made by an agricultural university. However, in most cases, a university is too far away, both in a literal and a metaphorical sense. A university, however, can be an important player in the network of the colleges, providing them with the latest insights (e.g. *Agrarisch Onderwijs* 1999) and knowledge. The universities' regional role should be understood as a national one as well. An agricultural university is an important knowledge source in the sectoral dimension.

To be effective at a regional level, regional players should be aware of the chain dimension and the local dimension of the knowledge context: agricultural colleges should not focus only on agricultural knowledge institutes. As regional players, they should serve local firms and networks by being open to both sectoral and chain-related knowledge sources, and by scanning opportunities to make 'neue Kombinationen' with local firms from other economic clusters. Some mega-farmers have attempted to undertake these opportunities, e.g. by developing combinations of farming and psychological health care in farming and the leisure industry. New initiatives to expand farming in the direction of related activities in the food chain can also be seen as new combinations of economic activities. Such innovative initiatives need local support in the area of networking, opening of knowledge channels and training for skills shifts, which should be offered by technical and agricultural colleges. If colleges do not accept this challenge, other players will do so and banish colleges to the margins of the regional economy.

Obviously, it is not easy for colleges to take up this new task. The facilitation of lifelong learning implies a fundamental change of role for the colleges. The learning enterprise in the traditional vocational education, developed within the industrial economy of the twentieth century, is completely different from the innovative learning processes within knowledge-intensive companies. These differences in learning processes create different professional profiles for teachers and educators, on the one hand, and for professionals in companies, on the other. The design of agricultural education for the knowledge economy involves not only a reorganisation of the course supply, but also redesigning the fundamental processes and the culture inside the colleges.

Traditionally, vocational education is designed within a context of certainty: the knowledge is judged to be true and objective, and the instructional techniques are authoritarian, receptive, and non-participative. Vocational education is trapped in the decontextualisation and meaningless broadening of skills, and has to search for new forms of participatory didactics and assessment in the context of experientally rich communities of practice (Wenger 1998). The college as a place of practice for teachers is a sterile reality in which codified knowledge and skills are central: methods, books, and curricula form an intermediary between learners and practice. According to Wenger (1998), codification has its costs and rewards: it facilitates the acquisition of new knowledge, but it hinders the giving of meaning to that knowledge through participation. In the practice of industrially designed vocational education, the equilibrium between codification and participation disappears. Teachers have little chance to develop their expertise and identity as participants in innovative processes and are no longer strong role models for their students, because they are no longer representatives of the future communities of practice the students are heading for. Teachers are no longer seen by professionals and entrepreneurs as recognised partners in innovative networks. In the developing agriculture in the Netherlands, teachers no longer play a pivotal role in regional development and they cannot support the entrance of their students into the world of work.

The participation of teachers in regional and sectoral knowledge networks requires a new vision of the role of vocational colleges in the local economy. The traditional role as a gateway to the regional labour market is becoming increasingly less important: colleges should make every effort to develop an attractive supply of labour-oriented courses for the regional market. This supply should be embedded in, and fostered by, a flexible supply of courses and services for the maintenance of skills in the labour force and for technology adaptation trajectories. This requires a coherent vision at the level of college management, a human resource development (HRD) strategy inside the colleges and the development of exciting and attractive teaching–learning arrangements and assessments. Agricultural colleges should develop into innovative, learning organisations if they wish to be recognised and welcomed by the local rural communities as partners in technology development and innovation.

References

Agrarisch Onderwijs (1999) 'Wageningen ondersteunt AOC's en IPC's bij Onderwijs Plattelandsvernieuwing' (Wageningen [University] Supports Agricultural Colleges with Training for Rural Renewal), 19, 8 December: 25–27.

Brouwer N. and Kleinknecht, A. (1994) *Technologie, werkgelegenheid, winsten en lonen in Nederlandse bedrijven*, The Hague: OSA (Werkdocument W114).

Bruin, R. de (1997) *Dynamiek en Duurzaamheid: Beschouwingen over Bedrijfsstijlen, Bestuur en Beleid* (proefschrift Wageningen), Wageningen: LUW.

Bruyn, E. de and Nieuwenhuis, A. F. M. (1994) 'The Development of Vocational Education: Industry and Service Compared', in W. J. Nijhof and J. N. Streumer (eds) *Flexibility in Training and Vocational Education*, Utrecht: Lemma B.V., pp. 109–131.

Dijk, G. van and Ploeg, J. D. van der (1995) 'Is There Anything Beyond Modernization?', in J. D. van der Ploeg and G. van Dijk (eds) *Beyond Modernization: The Impact of Endogenous Rural Development*, Assen: Van Gorcum.

Dosi, G. (2000) *Innovation, Organization and Economic Dynamics: Selected Essays*, Cheltenham: Edward Elgar.

Dosi, G. and Nelson, R. R. (1994) 'An Introduction to Evolutionary Theories in Economics', *Journal of Evolutionary Economics* 4, pp. 153–172.

Edquist, C. (1997) *Systems of Innovation: Technologies, Institutions and Organisations*, London: Pinter.

Gielen, P. and Jager, A. (2001) *Zoektochten van Agrarisch Ondernemers* (Quests of Agricultural Entrepreneurs), Wageningen: Stoas Research.

Jacobs, D. (1996) *Het Kennisoffensief: Slim concurreren in de Kenniseconomie* (The Knowledge Attack: Smart Competition in the Knowledge Economy), Alphen: Samson.

Kleinknecht, A. (1994) 'Heeft Nederland een loongolf nodig?', *Tijdschrift voor politieke economie*, 17–22.

Ministry of Agriculture, Nature Management and Fisheries (2000) *Voedsel en Groen* (Policy Programme for 2000–2004), The Hague: Ministry of Agriculture, Nature Management and Fisheries.

Nieuwenhuis, A. F. M., le Rütte, R. J. M., Verkaik, A. P. and Dijkveld Stol, N. A. (1998) *Landbouwonderwijs in Toekomstperspectief: Agenda voor Strategische Discussie* (Report 98/24), Den Haag: NRLO.

Nieuwenhuis, L. F. M. and Figueira a.o, E. (forthcoming) *Knowledge Spiders in Europe: Vocational and Technical Colleges within Regional and Sectoral Innovation Networks* (EU-Report, Leonardo da Vinci), Wageningen: Stoas Research.

Nonaka, I. and Takeuchi, H. (1995) *The Knowledge-Creating Company: How Japanese Companies Create the Dynamics of Innovation*, Oxford: Oxford University Press.

OECD (1997) *Creativity, Innovation and Job Creation*, Paris: OECD.

Oerlemans, L. (1997) *De Ingebedde Onderneming: Innoveren in Industriële Netwerken*, Tilburg: Tilburg University Press.

Ploeg, J. D. van der (1996) 'Going Beyond Modernization', in C. H. A. Verhaar *et al.* (eds) *On the Challenges of Unemployment in a Regional Europe*, Aldershot: Avebury, pp. 303–329.

Ploeg, J. D. van der and Saccomandi, V. (1995) 'On the Impact of Endogenous Development in European Agriculture', in J. D. van der Ploeg and G. van Dijk (eds) *Beyond Modernization: The Impact of Endogenous Rural Development*, Assen: Van Gorcum, pp. 10–28.

Rosenfeld, S. (1998) 'Technical Colleges, Technology Development, and Regional Development', Regional Technology Strategies, Inc., Chapel Hill, North Carolina, paper presented at the international conference on Building Competitive Regional Economies: Up-grading Knowledge and Diffusing Technology to Small Firms, Modena, Italy, 28–29 May.

Verhaar, C. H. A. and Hoeve, A. (1999) *Megabedrijven in Agrarisch Nederland* (Mega-Firms in Dutch Agriculture), Wageningen: Stoas Research.

Verhaar, C. H. A. and Smulders, H. S. M. (1999) 'Employability in Practice', *Journal of European Industrial Training* 23, 6–7: 268–274.

Vijverberg, A. J. (1996) *Glastuinbouw in Ontwikkeling* (Horticulture in Development), Delft: Eburon.

von Hippel, E. (1988) *Sources of Innovation*, Oxford: Oxford University Press.

Wenger, E. (1998) *Communities of Practice: Learning Meaning and Identity*, Cambridge: Cambridge University Press.

Part III
Policy response

10 The national approach concerning the learning regions paradigm

Paul Huijts[1]

Introduction

At the present time we are living in a shrinking world. Developments in the field of technology are blurring or even obliterating traditional national boundaries. Globalisation is the trend in our knowledge economy. Modern communication techniques have turned the remote into the proximate. This certainly applies in the field of knowledge development and knowledge transfer. It is, therefore, justifiable to ask whether we should speak of learning regions in terms of a paradigm or a paradox. What is the purpose of a learning region if knowledge is no longer location-dependent, but available anywhere in the world? For businesses to survive in such a global economy, they must apply international benchmarks to wage costs, productivity, innovation and all other factors of competition.

There is an apparent paradox in that – despite this globalisation – a number of regions are still performing better than others. In other words, it seems as though the region does serve some purpose. Perhaps the globalisation process is, in fact, a source of opportunities for regions to flourish. If that is so, we may speak of a paradigm instead of a paradox.

Trends indicate globalisation

Globalisation is most in evidence at the economic level. In recent years, the pace of economic internationalisation has accelerated enormously. Driving forces behind that acceleration are above all economic factors such as the integration of financial markets, the world-wide liberalisation of trade and investment and the integration of nations into large trading blocs (EU, NAFTA). By increasing the ease and reducing the cost of world-wide communications and transport, technological development also contributes to this acceleration. The economic internationalisation process is reflected, among other things, in growing flows of capital, goods and information between countries.

Knowledge and science have also globalised. Developments in the field of communications have played an important role here. This is exemplified by the development of the Internet, which originated as a tool to improve communication between scientists. Since then, the Internet has branched out on its own, but the small distance between scientists remains. These days, it is hardly possible to identify an internationally challenging theme that is not open to debate by scientists or research groups on the Internet.

Modern daily life, as we know it, has become unimaginable without globalisation. It is equally difficult to conceive of any remaining unexplored areas of culture, music, film, food, drink, vacations, etc. Well into the twentieth century, newspapers were still sending out correspondents simply to satisfy their readers' curiosity about far-away countries, the entire world is now on sale on the shelves of the supermarket just around the corner or directly on view on our television screens.

People are perfectly capable of expanding their own personal horizons by means of a wide range of communication media. Fax, e-mail and mobile telephony have developed enormously in recent years. Telecommunication charges are falling spectacularly. New applications are coming ever closer within our reach.

The death of distance?

The tremendous scope of IT applications is capable of leading to a geographic revolution. The location of any given activity is far less dependent on the location of any other activity.

Does it therefore still make sense to speak of national or even regional entities if the world has become a single large market in which the free movement of goods, knowledge and people has primacy? Does this mean that we have seen 'the death of distance'? To answer these questions, it is a good idea to look at the factors that give meaning to the terms 'national' and 'regional'.

There are a number of factors defining the specific form and content of the term 'national'. These factors have nothing to do with the trend towards globalisation, particularly in the realms of economics and communication. Here, a given country's tax system can be taken into consideration, which distinguishes it from all other countries. Socio-economic structure as well as political stability vary greatly from country to country. The same applies to the structure and quality of a country's educational system, the way in which its labour relations are regulated, its environmental legislation, spatial planning, etc.

The term 'regional' is given expression by the degree in which certain characteristics leave their mark on a region's individuality. These characteristics are manifest at the administrative level (the role of local and provincial governments, European funds, etc.), in the business location policy (office space, industrial estates, possibilities for future expansion), with regard to infrastructure (freight and people as well as telecommunications), in the nature of the economic activities (varied or specialised economic structure), and in the regional labour market (work ethic, presence of skilled personnel).

The terms national and regional thus appear to offer sufficient grounds to term the region a relevant economic entity. But what role does knowledge then play to warrant the term 'learning region'?

Knowledge economy and networks

Globalisation, knowledge intensification, and technological advances have led to the development of a world-wide network economy. Economic development, knowledge development, and innovation are processes that are increasingly taking place in clusters of industrial, service and logistical activities, and 'public knowledge centres'. Factors such as the quality of the environment, the labour market, the presence of knowledge and innovation networks, and the electronic infrastructure have become decisive competitive-factors.

Knowledge should not, however, be equated with Research and Development. Economically relevant knowledge is broader in nature, and comprises that knowledge which is utilised to ensure that economic activities take place at a lower cost, more efficiently, more sustainably, and more effectively. It includes technological knowledge, knowledge of logistics and organisation, cultural achievements, and social processes.

Knowledge-intensive sectors occupy an important position in the economy. These sectors already account for 35 per cent of the value added by the private sector in OECD countries (Ministry of Economic Affairs 1999: 35). Knowledge-intensive sectors are also important growth sectors for job creation purposes.

Increasing competition and high costs of knowledge development spur businesses to seek partnerships with other businesses and with research and educational institutes. This need to cooperate is one of the reasons for the development of international and national networks in the realms of business, education, and research. In the Netherlands, approximately 25 per cent of businesses undertaking innovative activities are part of an innovation network (Central Bureau of Statistics 1998: 82–87).

The development of the network economy has created a new economic landscape in which the competitiveness of businesses, regions, and nations is increasingly dependent on the ability to develop, update, disseminate, and apply knowledge.

In a network economy, cooperation and competition go hand in hand. Competition forces businesses to push themselves to the limit: they have to maintain a constant search for the most efficient and newest production processes and procedures in order to innovate. However, they can best accomplish this if they are able to make use of the advanced knowledge which is available elsewhere, with their partners in business.

Distance (still) matters

Empiricism has demonstrated the importance of networks and cooperation. Businesses with many network partners innovate more than businesses with fewer network partners. Businesses in network partnerships obtain knowledge from suppliers, are stimulated by customers, and through their contacts with knowledge centres they gain access to the most advanced techniques and technologies.

Modern communication techniques have relieved businesses from their traditional dependence on the availability of services or knowledge in their physical proximity. Digitally exchangeable information is available everywhere.

However, a great deal of knowledge and information is not digitally exchangeable. In practice, many businesses still depend on face-to-face contacts. Thus, on the regional scale, business requirements in terms of knowledge are services and information not digitally available or accessible. One of the most important of these information sources is tacit knowledge.

Tacit knowledge can only be shared through personal contact. Tacit knowledge is developed in practice, and it is context-dependent. Something may work, but you cannot explain why and how it works. Codified, or documented, knowledge can be specified in a formula, rule or product specification. The transfer of tacit knowledge requires close cooperation. To transfer it from a remote source is difficult or costly or both. Activities that are based on tacit knowledge are not suitable for globalisation. Codified knowledge lends itself to dissemination over large distances, and at ever-faster speeds.

Tacit knowledge can also be understood as referring to the development of new knowledge. New knowledge is more tacit by nature, and only after a certain period of experience does it become codified or documented knowledge that can be put to world-wide use. In the development of new knowledge, elements of products and processes are combined experimentally to produce new combinations. This variation of combinations is best assured in a complex of businesses and research institutes. Innovation requires variation, exchange and selection in cooperation at short geographic distances because of the tacit nature of knowledge at this stage. Once the innovation has been incorporated in a dominant concept, knowledge can become more codifiable and can be disseminated over greater distances. Certain activities of businesses, therefore, require knowledge that is region-dependent.

Glocalisation

Thus, a smoothly performing regional network of suppliers, knowledge providers, and knowledge centres may be a reason for businesses to locate or continue to operate in a given region. In recent years, many firms have decentralised their development activities in the direction of major markets, in order to optimise these activities in terms of market prospects. This combination of global and local developments is sometimes referred to as 'glocalisation'.

In this process of 'glocalisation', the labour market is a decisive factor for locating a given business in a certain region. The labour factor is not by definition mobile, and this is particularly not the case in Europe. Innovative businesses, in particular, demand types of labour which tend to be in short supply. Therefore, it is not surprising that the labour market features bottlenecks which are regional in nature, such as shortages of technicians and ICT personnel.

The situation on the labour market varies from region to region, however. Given that labour is relatively immobile, it is vital for companies to look for regions with a knowledge infrastructure that is flexible enough to meet the demands for specific competencies. In the regions of Twente, Eindhoven and Amsterdam, for instance, a concentration of ICT businesses can be found observed. It is no coincidence that those same regions have university centres that the ICT sector can call on for research, cooperation, training capability and personnel. But what about the relevance of scale? In other words: big or small?

The relevant scale: big or small?

Multinational enterprises can make their knowledge demands on a world-wide scale. They are not dependent on one single country. Nevertheless, the knowledge level of local employees does constitute an important consideration when deciding on a location in a given country. Clustering is essential. International developments are increasingly being governed by knowledge-intensive businesses. This requires research, and, thus, a large knowledge potential.

A good example of the synergy between a region and a multinational is Philips Research. Philips is currently developing its Physics Laboratory into a Technology Campus, a high-tech centre of competence with an impact on the entire region. The underlying philosophy is that combining laboratories and facilitating contacts between their staff will tend to create synergy at a much earlier stage. This synergy will not only be valuable to large-scale businesses but also to small and medium-sized enterprises (SMEs). Such a development is supported not only by the historical ties between the city of Eindhoven and the business, but also by the fact that the region provides Philips with favourable preconditions in training capacity, labour market, and the presence of leading knowledge centres and suppliers.

The Philips' Group Management relocation to Amsterdam is yet a further example of 'glocalisation', illustrating that even within a small country like the Netherlands regional differences matter. There is no such thing as 'a single best region'. It depends on the specific business activities involved. The example of Philips has everything to do with the importance of Amsterdam with respect to its commercial activities and the significance of Eindhoven with regard to its R&D endeavours.

Like large businesses, small and medium-sized enterprises also depend on other institutes for their innovation and research efforts. They have to cooperate or be able to call on a polytechnic, the TNO organisation, a university or another partner. If a large knowledge potential is present in a given region, as it is around Eindhoven, it will attract a broad range of activities. In this fashion, a snowball effect can be generated in a region's development.

The flexibility of SMEs enables them to adapt rapidly to certain market trends. Their diversity means that they can explore new markets. They have lower start-up costs, and they can create new jobs more easily. These factors allow the SME sector to develop swiftly in line with economic trends. The reverse of this adaptability is that the SME sector is far more dependent on regionally or locally available knowledge than large-scale businesses.

Ultimately, the crux of the matter – for both large-scale businesses and SMEs – is the availability and accessibility of knowledge in a given region. Both classes of business have an interest in the other's presence in the region as well as the ample availability of research capacity, venture capital, and human talent.

The role of national authorities

The national government has the duty to encourage and facilitate regional economic policy, and to remove barriers to regional cooperation and economic development. The Ministry of Economic Affairs does this by means of specific policy in a number of areas:

- *Cooperation and spatial economic knowledge*. Solid regional economic policy requires knowledge of the type of industrial estate needed or knowledge of the specific strengths and weaknesses of the regional economy. In cooperation with provincial and municipal governments, the Ministry of Economic Affairs endeavours to develop knowledge products capable of supporting regions in shaping economic policy. Examples of this are the policy covenant on this subject between the Ministry and the provinces, and the international benchmark system for regional business location climates. Here, it is not only the end product that is important but also the creation of a knowledge network between provinces, cities, and the central government.
- *Financial incentives*. Above all, these relate to support for the restructuring and development of industrial estates. At the same time, the government provides support in a more traditional fashion through incentive measures and fiscal arrangements for innovative and cooperative activities by organisations.
- *Organising capability of a region*. Regional network organisations are indispensable to businesses in their search for knowledge and knowledge partners. It is important for regional supply and demand in the field of knowledge and innovation to be effectively matched. The mechanisms for knowledge dissemination and knowledge transfer must be in good working order. The Ministry supports organisations such as Syntens and the Regional Development Agencies. These organisations play a pre-eminent brokering role, bringing together those supplying and those requiring knowledge and technology.
- *Public consultant*. At the national level, the central government can perform the role of public consultant on behalf of the region. This government role

can be observed in the 'Technology Radar' programme recently presented by the Ministry. Players in various fields of technology are brought together in workshops to seek ways and means of improving the arrangements between partners.

In the past, the government's regional economic policy was based primarily on attracting large-scale businesses. The assumption was that these businesses would generate positive external effects in the regions. That policy was successful in itself, although these businesses were not always able to achieve the appropriate embedding within their direct environment.

Subsequently, priority shifted to autonomous regional economic growth. In this approach, the focus is on making use of the maximum number of sector-specific features. The emphasis is automatically on improving the competitiveness of the regional SME sector and assuring space for industrial estates. An improved regional production environment is, in itself, attractive to large enterprises looking to locate in such a well-developed region. In this way, those enterprises will also find the necessary embedding in the local economy.

The role of regional authorities: strengthening the networks

As was previously argued, the sound geographical embedding of clusters also places high demands on the quality of the public knowledge infrastructure and the labour market.

With respect to the knowledge infrastructure, there is still a mismatch between the knowledge supply from public educational and research institutions and the needs of regional business and industry. Communication between the vocational and research establishment and regional business and industry should be in place or initiated. This dialogue must be based on a willingness to adapt to the trends and needs of business.

On the basis of this dialogue, the knowledge infrastructure should provide high quality education, training (lifelong learning), and research facilities. This ensures an effective start for the regional process of knowledge circulation, consisting of knowledge acquisition, application, updating and accumulation. The regional clustering of businesses and knowledge centres then contributes towards the strength of that region in a broader sense, that is, in terms of economic development, innovation and the labour market.

Conclusion

The regional government can facilitate this kind of development by performing a brokering and liaison function and bringing together the various players in the region. This is at the heart of the national approach to the learning region paradigm. In order to strengthen the innovative potential, organisations in a regional network can upgrade their collective learning capability effectively and efficiently. The principle is that this capability should be coordinated to the region-specific characteristics. In this manner, the optimised match can be found in terms of knowledge infrastructure, the labour market, and the physical infrastructure. As a result, participating organisations can develop their core competencies more rapidly and more vigorously.

The learning region thus becomes a network of learning organisations of a varied nature that can and does prove its strength primarily in the field of knowledge circulation and innovation. It is clear that universities in such a learning region can and must perform an important and proactive role.

Note

1 This text is based on the presentation by Paul Huijts at the Seminar on Universities, Knowledge Infrastructure, and the Learning Region.

References

Central Bureau of Statistics (1998) *Kennis en Economie 1998*, Voorburg/Heerlen: 82–87.
Ministry of Economic Affairs (1999) *Nota Ruimtelijk Economisch Beleid*, The Hague: Ministry of Economic Affairs: 35.

11 The national view on knowledge production

Jacqueline Bax[1]

Introduction

In this chapter, the Dutch national view on knowledge production is presented. The actual title of the seminar was 'Universities, Knowledge Infrastructure and the Learning Region'. This means that it is also necessary to zoom in on the region. Initially, however, some facts and figures and an explanation of some of the special features that relate to research and science in the Netherlands are presented before getting to the core issues of this chapter. The contents of this chapter were to a degree inspired by the views of Michael Gibbons concerning the new mode of knowledge production.

Facts and figures

Dutch society is to an increasing degree influenced by the availability and proper use of knowledge. That knowledge is to a large extent the result of the scientific research carried out in the Dutch research sector. About 14 billion Dutch guilders are spent in this sector annually; private enterprise accounts for 45 per cent, the Dutch government for 40 per cent. The share of research and development in our gross domestic product is 2.12 per cent. Internationally, the Netherlands holds a middle position alongside other developed West European nations. While the Minister of Education, Culture and Science coordinates science policy and sets out the main strategic parameters, the other ministers are responsible for research and the actual practice of science in their own fields. The Ministry of Education, Culture and Science, which provides a total of 3.5 billion guilders – and this is above the 60 per cent mark – is the largest financier on the government side. Not all government finance goes directly to the executive research institutes; some of the funding is distributed through intermediary organisations such as the Netherlands Organisation for Scientific Research (NWO), the research council, and the Royal Netherlands Academy of Arts and Sciences (KNAW).

Research in the Netherlands is carried out in universities, research institutes, and private enterprises. Some 70 per cent of the research carried out by universities is funded through state contributions. An additional 10 per cent of the funding is contributed by the Netherlands Organisation for Scientific Research and the Royal Netherlands Academy of Arts and Sciences. The remainder is financed through third-party contracts. The bulk of the income of semi-public research institutes is also from contract activities. These institutes are typical suppliers of knowledge for the market place; this can be both to private businesses and the government.

The figures on Dutch research publications, a significant indicator of quality, are in line with the international average. The influence of Dutch publications in international journals, measured on the basis of the number of times they are cited, is above average. In particular, in the field of physics, agriculture, astronomy, earth sciences and materials, the Netherlands has achieved a leading international position.

In association with the Ministry of Economic Affairs, which is responsible for technology policy, the Ministry of Education, Culture and Science endeavours to boost that position even further. Important knowledge projects are consequently being undertaken in the Dutch government's investment policy. Cooperation is being stimulated in a cluster of institutes for civil engineering in Delft. An incentive will be introduced for ICT, other science subjects and the biosciences in Amsterdam/Watergraafsmeer. The scientific appeal of both the Amsterdam and Delft clusters will become even more wide-reaching.

Three issues

With these facts and figures in mind, the main part of the chapter can now be discussed. As a policy-maker on national policy for the development of knowledge, I deal with three issues in this context, issues which at certain points can lead to dilemmas of varying degrees. I can say, however, that my Ministry's vision on the production of knowledge is that it must involve the production of 'knowledge of quality' and 'knowledge of relevance'. Moreover, this knowledge must be properly disseminated to ensure the existence of a truly coherent knowledge infrastructure. This knowledge must also be soundly embedded, both nationally and regionally. Yet it is not as simple as that. On the contrary, knowledge is a heterogeneous good: education, research, implicit knowledge, and codified knowledge all fall within this rubric. Regions are also heterogeneous. To go one step further, I have to ask myself: what exactly is a region? Would that be the Tilburg/Eindhoven region, would it be the Netherlands, the Rhine Delta or the European Union? The answer depends on which field of research we are looking at. This is because each field of research has its own, various levels of regional embeddedness. Additionally, there is often a certain amount of tension between what local administrators would like to see, and what the national government is aiming to achieve; tension between the wishes of the administrators of universities and research organisations and the goals of the Ministry of Education, Culture and Science. In short, there are three issues which require attention:

1   the heterogeneity of knowledge;
2   the heterogeneity of regions;
3   the tension between local optima and the national optimum.

This brings me to the heterogeneity of knowledge. I shall first look at this in terms of research and then education.

A great deal of public research is carried out by the pharmaceutical industry in the Netherlands. Yet if I compare the Netherlands with other countries, our pharmaceutical industry is relatively small. In other words, research and embeddedness in the private sector is not one to one.

Things are quite different with regard to clinical medical research. Researchers in this field have a need for direct contact with patients. Thus, research is carried out both within the walls of teaching hospitals, with their numerous patients from the region, and in the immediate vicinity of these premises. Looked at from a national point of view, the Netherlands is fully covered by a comprehensive network of teaching and other hospitals.

In certain fields of scientific research, a somewhat closer link can be seen between industry and research. Because of Philips' location in Eindhoven, a company that has operated research facilities since the beginning of this century, it was quite obvious that a technical university would be established there as well.

This, in turn, prompts the question of whether, in this day and age with multinationals becoming progressively more footloose, it is wise for a government to invest in research at such close proximity to these firms. Let's take a closer look at two distinctions: that between large firms, on the one hand, and small and medium-sized businesses, on the other, and that between codified knowledge and tacit knowledge.

Clustering

This inevitably leads to the subject of clustering. Large companies are often 'glocalised': they operate globally on local strength. Established in a region with certain economic spearheads, they compete in world markets. It is essential that the home region has a vital knowledge system and a developed small and medium-sized business sector. Conversely, the small and medium-sized business sector has a more limited field of vision. For the small and medium-sized businesses 'their region' is often of a limited size: the Eindhoven region for example, or Twente. The presence of institutes able to carry out high quality research that can be highly commercialised by the business community is of vital importance for small businesses. It can even be the actual core of new, small-scale business activity: science parks, for instance. Although we do have some less successful ones in this country, there are also some thriving science parks in the Netherlands, for example, in Twente, in the eastern part of the Netherlands. Twente previously had a flourishing textile industry which collapsed following the Second World War. A technical *hogeschool*, which later became a technical university, was founded in the 1960s. Thanks to the active policy pursued by the University of Twente, a great deal of small-scale business activity has since developed in the vicinity of the university. This business activity has expanded in the past few years. The Telematics Institute was founded here, and Ericsson, the Swedish multinational, has also invested a great deal in the area.

Whereas the Technical University Eindhoven and the University of Twente have totally different origins – resulting from the reindustrialisation process that took place after the end of the Second World War – they have gradually exhibited several common elements of development as far as their relation with the region is concerned. Several institutes have clustered themselves around the university and the existing spin-offs in Twente: the Telematics Institute, and Ericsson's investments, to name two specific examples. In addition to the Technical University Eindhoven, several other institutes were also founded in Eindhoven, around the core company Philips. Recently, several TNO institutes from various locations in the Netherlands were merged into a single institute: the TNO Institute of Industrial Technology in Eindhoven. This is in the centre of the south-eastern part of the Netherlands, the innovative heart of the Netherlands for the manufacturing industry. It was the wish of the TNO Institute of Industrial Technology to establish itself where the action was, so to speak. The Ministry of Education, Culture and Science, together with the Ministry of Economic Affairs, helped to make TNO's proposal to establish this TNO Institute in Eindhoven possible.

The wish to establish a presence in the industrial hot-spot of the Netherlands also applied to Philips itself. Consequently, Philips expanded its research facilities in Eindhoven. Yet in 1998, Philips' sales activities were relocated to Amsterdam, to be near Schiphol, the head offices of the major banks, and the stock exchange. This location was thought to be better for recruiting marketing and financial personnel. The heterogeneity of regions is obvious given the differences between Eindhoven and Amsterdam.

This can be explained to a large extent by the term tacit knowledge, or 'implicit' knowledge. The other form, codified knowledge, is knowledge that has been put down in print or recorded in other tangible forms. This means that such knowledge is widely available. Codified knowledge can easily be tapped, from the Internet, for example, by making use of information and communication technology. Proximity in this case is not all that relevant. In the case of tacit knowledge – the best example is the process a child goes through while learning how to walk or ride a bicycle – this is quite different.

Actual research

It gives me enormous pleasure to see that a great many individuals have devoted so much time and energy to research on the meaning of knowledge for economic development. In many studies, it has been shown that direct human contact is of great importance for tacit knowledge. Proximity seems to be crucial, for example, in consulting with researchers and entrepreneurs in Twente on how to market a 'Twente' telematics product, or in direct consultation on how the Eindhoven University of Technology and Philips could develop expertise in a completely new field.

These Eindhoven and Twente examples also apply to civil engineering at Delft. We have only one real concentration of civil engineering in our country, and that is in Delft. Some 2,500 people work here in teaching and research in this field of knowledge. In other words, there are no centres in those areas which are traditionally subject to the risk of flooding: Zeeland, and the rivers and regions in the northern part of our country. On the contrary, a civil engineering cluster for the whole of the Netherlands emerged in Delft. The Technical University of Delft was founded in 1842. This university arose out of a need for knowledge among Dutch army engineers. Over the years, the Delft Hydraulics laboratory, TNO Building and Construction Research, Delft Geotechnics, and the International Institute for Infrastructural, Hydraulic and Environmental Engineering have all based themselves here. Last year, the Dutch government gave a major investment incentive to this cluster of Delft institutes. Multidisciplinary research into dikes, bridges, underground construction works, wetlands, must produce results that can be put to good use in society. In other words, this resembles Mode 2 knowledge production (see Gibbons, Chapter 13).

I would now like to answer briefly the question whether it is wise for a government to invest in research at such close proximity to firms. The answer is yes. Yes, with the understanding that the investment is linked to a wider concentration of tacit knowledge. It is unwise to establish a solitary university in an area with a very fragile economic structure, to build a castle in the desert. Is it appropriate for the government to invest in a region with an average, but sound economic structure? Yes, with the understanding that the national government clearly has the intention of creating, in association with trade and industry and other regional partners, a concentration of tacit knowledge, as was the case in Twente. That makes it possible for a learning region to develop. In a region of this type, local partners disseminate existing knowledge on a continuous basis. They also develop new knowledge, and subsequently work to the best of their ability to disseminate that knowledge. In short, the dissemination of knowledge is the work of man.

Regional diversity

I would like to go somewhat deeper into the second issue, that of the heterogeneity of regions. Another example in connection with the question 'What exactly is a region?' is that the region could also be the Rhine Delta, which includes Belgium and Luxembourg. Cooperation in the field of nuclear fusion comes to mind here. The tension between national specialisation and the efficiency benefits of international collaboration has been resolved in the case of nuclear fusion. Both Belgium and the Netherlands scaled down their nuclear fusion research effort in their own countries and now work together with

Germany in the Kernforschungsanlage in Jülich near Aachen. Agreements have made it possible for Belgian and Dutch researchers to work together productively. This is an example of the embedding of scientific research.

But matters are often quite different where research in the arts is concerned. In the Netherlands, Sanskrit is taught in Leiden, the location where research in this field is also carried out. But why was Leiden chosen as the location for this field of study? It could have been Amsterdam, for instance, or Nijmegen. The region for this type of arts research is, therefore, the whole of the Netherlands.

This brings me to the third issue. In the field of research in the arts, and teaching in these subjects for that matter, there is often some tension between the local optima and what is best from a national point of view. Universities are at liberty to decide to abolish a chair. Yet in the case of unique expertise, this can lead to a situation arising in which there is not a single chair in that particular field in the entire country. As a ministry, we have resolved this problem by agreeing on an Arts Covenant with the universities concerned. Universities are also given extra funding for what is referred to as the '*kleine letteren*': 'minor subjects within the field of the humanities'. In exchange, they must decide among themselves how to reach a national core portfolio of some 250 chairs. Universities must, therefore, choose their specialisation from that portfolio. Sanskrit at four universities would be somewhat overdone. This covenant resolves the dilemma between 'the local' and 'the national'.

The dilemma of local optima versus what is best in the national dimension can also be observed in higher education. For the sake of competitiveness, it is essential for regions to have a solid knowledge infrastructure. This must be executed across the board, from primary level up to and including higher professional education, and for certain core regions, up to and including university and research institutes. The Ministry of Education, Culture and Science draws up national conditions in this respect. Yet some regional administrators still wish to establish educational institutions across the gamut of the knowledge infrastructure in their municipality or region very literally indeed. In recent years, we have seen the establishment of large numbers of ancillary university departments. Propaedeutic-level students of the University of Amsterdam can now follow their studies in Almere. The University of Twente is spreading its wings in Leeuwarden, and Leiden is doing the same in The Hague. Maastricht and Eindhoven have an eye on Venlo. From the perspective of the administrators of Almere, Venlo and Leeuwarden, it is understandable why they would want to have an ancillary department established in their municipality. They want to be able to offer optimal facilities as this gives the students, the future highly educated workforce, a sense of belonging in the municipality. It is easy to visualise the advantage of that.

Conclusion

I have gradually reached my concluding remarks now that we have looked at three specific issues. Knowledge comes in many shapes and forms. Regions also have many different qualities. And, finally, there is tension between local wishes and national interests. Thus there is no single blueprint available for the development of knowledge in the regions. Nor will my ministry provide any such blueprint. I have discussed successful examples of regions, namely the learning regions Twente and Eindhoven. Nor will I forget Tilburg with its *hogeschool* and its university. Let us take a discriminating look at what we can learn from these regions, what we can learn from one another. Let's sit down in the garden of one of our magnificent Brabant farms, places of tranquillity, and contemplate. To learn for the learning region.

Note

1 This chapter is an adapted version of the speech delivered by Ms Bax at the seminar on 'Universities, Knowledge Infrastructure, and the Learning Region'. The aim of this chapter is to demonstrate how governments, in this case the Dutch Ministry of Education, Culture, and Science, are trying to come to terms with the learning region as a new concept for policy.

12 Associational dilemmas in regional innovation strategy development

Regional innovation support organisations and the RIS/RITTS programmes

Arnoud Lagendijk and Roel Rutten

Introduction

A practical outcome of the recent shift towards a regional-associative approach to learning has been the launching of RIS/RITTS programmes (Regional Innovation Strategy and Regional Innovative and Technology Transfer Strategies) by the European Commission. The aim of this chapter is to discuss the role of regional innovation support organisations in regional innovation strategy development against the background of the assumed associative harmony of the RIS and RITTS programmes. This reflection is built on a number of ambiguities and dilemmas that, in our view, surround the theme of regional innovation strategies. In particular, organisational and strategic aspects of innovation strategies will be discussed. By developing a critical perspective, we aim not only at reflecting upon the RIS/RITTS process, but also at discussing the value of the associative approaches. In doing so, we do not wish to deny the significance of regional innovation strategies and the merits of associative approaches underpinning the concept of 'Learning Regions'. Nevertheless, we hope that a critical approach may contribute to the shaping of regional strategies in the future.

This chapter is structured as follows. We start by addressing the core background and characteristics of the associative approach to regional innovation strategy development in Europe and the way this has informed current strategic policy initiatives. Then, a theoretical-critical perspective is presented with the identification of four dilemmas of associative strategy development. This is followed by a discussion of the organisational dimension of innovation support. We will reflect upon the role of innovation support organisations, i.e. university and higher education transfer agencies and intermediary organisations. Emphasis then is put on particular RIS/RITTS projects, adding some empirical flesh to our theoretical bones. The final section draws lessons from the RIS/RITTS cases and indicates future directions for associative strategy development.

The conceptual background for associative regional innovation strategy development in Europe

In the past decade, regional policy has shifted from placing an emphasis on (inward) investments and promotion of high-tech sectors to focusing on indigenous competitiveness (i.e. competitiveness based on region-specific qualities), hence on taking the *existing* business stock (and support infrastructure) as a starting point. This has been combined with a new governance perspective, which is based on interaction between different regional actors and on the shaping of a collective capacity for communication and joint strategy-making. Much has been written about what is now called the associative approach to regional development (Amin 1999; Cooke and Morgan 1998; Lagendijk 1999). We will not present a summary of this discussion here, but focus rather on the translation of the debate into the practice of regional innovation policy.

What is most relevant for regional policy-making is that the concept of associative approaches may help to overcome what are perceived as current shortcomings in regional economic policy. While the indigenous turn in regional policy has created a strong focus on the innovative performance of SMEs, actual results have been disappointing (Landabaso 2000). This is partly due to the contents and nature of business support. Traditionally, there has been too much focus on technology, and it was difficult to define and reach its specific target group. In particular, traditional forms of technology support to SMEs tended to fail because they were not embedded in strategic frameworks; therefore they lacked focus and coherence and they did not respond to real business needs but tended to be primarily oriented towards promoting existing services. Support tended to go to the same groups of firms, even making them support-dependent. One of the core suggestions for change at present is to encourage a shift from technology development carried out by public research centres *for* firms to support innovation *within and among* firms.

Another, also fundamental, problem is found at the governance level. Especially in more peripheral regions, policy tends to be pervaded by the interests of 'old boys' networks and dominant actors and lobbies, thus prone to the influence of parochial aims and attitudes. Also, at a more basic level, such regions lack the conceptual and organisational competencies to shape and implement more complex forms of policy-making. This blocks the development of more sophisticated, more demanding attitudes to policy-making, which constitutes a prerequisite for effective innovation policy.

Associative approaches focus, in particular, on this softer side of policy intervention. On the one hand, this aims at provoking change in business attitudes, to make businesses more attuned to innovation and, for that purpose, to collaboration with other firms and support providers. On the other, softer measures are geared to changing the attitudes and capacities, cognitive and social, in the regional governance structure. The impact of this conceptual turn in the past decade can be observed in the EU Structural Funds, which has shown a shift from financing 'bricks and mortar' to measures with 'softer' goals, including human and social capital development and innovation.

More fundamentally, the arguments underpinning the rise of associative regional innovation approaches can be traced back to three core arguments found in the literature on innovation, business competitiveness, and regional development (Cooke and Morgan 1998; Dupuy and Gilly 1994; Malmberg, *et al.* 1996; Storper 1997). These are:

1 Our economy has become increasingly knowledge-intensive, making technological development (in a broad sense) and innovation major pillars of competitiveness.
2 Interactions between firms and other organisations are a major component of technological development and innovation, resulting in an interactionist perspective of structural economic development (like cluster approaches).
3 This interaction is established easily and effectively at the regional level, through an associational approach.

Together, these arguments have fostered another tendency in regional policy-making, namely the drive for integral approaches. Three types of policy in particular, technology, structural, and regional policy have become increasingly intertwined (Jacobs 1996; Maskell *et al.* 1998).

How have these notions affected the formulation of regional innovation strategies facilitated by the EU? In an attempt to put new insights into practice, Directorate General (DG) XIII (technology policy) and DG XVI (regional policy) of the European Commission joined hands. This resulted in the launch of the RTP (Regional Technology Plan) pilot project in 1994 (Boekholt 1999). The RTP was an attempt to develop technology policy on a regional level, based on regional strengths and weaknesses in order to further regional economic development. Though the attempt proved to be successful, it was quickly discovered that technology was not the main issue. Most firms do not have a technology problem but, rather, an innovation problem. Technology is usually available, either within the region or somewhere else, and most firms know where to find it. Usually, contacts with other firms are most helpful in this respect. The problem, however, is how to use technology in such a way that product and process innovations can be achieved, and how the other functions of a firm, i.e. management, marketing, logistics, human resources, etc., have to change in order to support technological change. This latter, too, became recognised as a part of 'innovation' (Landabaso 2000). What is at stake is not how to get firms to use technology but how to make them innovative. In practice, this means that support must not be focused on technology support and technology supply but, rather, on the support of innovation in a broad sense. This was emphasised by a change of name from RTP to RIS and RITTS. RIS and RITTS are principally identical programmes, though the former is coordinated through DG XVI and the latter through DG XIII, indicating some differences in emphases and working methods between the two programmes and, indeed, the two DGs (European Commission 1996b).

The translation of new insights into innovation, business competitiveness, and regional development into the specific RTP, RIS, and RITTS programmes took place in a number of steps, in which a number of documents played a dominant role. This includes the White Paper on competitiveness, the Green Paper on innovation, and the reformulation of the Structural Funds in *Agenda 2000* (European Commission 1994a, 1996a, 1997). The latter text depicts a perspective of supporting LFRs (Less Favoured Regions) by promoting diversification, restoring economic dynamism, and promoting an active business culture. Specific attention is drawn to knowledge policies that should bridge the gap between scientific and technological excellence, on the one hand, and industrial/commercial success, on the other, and hence promote innovation among SMEs. The result is a fascinating combination of general aims (innovation, networking, cooperation, strategy formulation), recognising the need to take account of the specific institutional, socio-economic, and cultural characteristics of each region. The European Commission sees its role in creating the organisational framework for 'bottom-up' integral approaches in which general principles and shared policy learning processes are accommodated, in customised ways, to specific regional contexts. In fact, the European Commission distinguishes different roles for the various policy levels. Local and regional authorities should develop and implement action plans that address specific regional needs and potentials. Member States and the European Union, on the other hand, should focus on the creation of national and European conditions – such as the distribution of technological installations, innovation schemes, etc. – to assist regional innovation and to develop policy instruments aligned towards compatible goals (European Commission 1998: 9–10).

In practice, the translation of these ideas and ambitions into practice has produced an innovation approach resting on six pillars (Corvers 1999):

1 A strong emphasis on communicative–cultural–institutional change within regions: awareness of the benefits of a strategic approach, of innovation, and of networking and cooperation among businesses and other organisations.

2 The promotion of a bottom-up approach that takes into account and exploits the specificities of the region.

3 A policy trajectory from reflection to consensual action, in which 'reflection' encompasses an in-depth analysis of the various needs of the business sector and the quality of the innovation support infrastructure. Consensual action, in this context, refers to a learning process creating the capacity to agree, as well as design, put forward, and direct resources to a range of innovation projects, within an essential process of changing the planning culture (Boekholt 1999).

4 A system view, in which competitiveness is seen as being supported by the interaction between a whole range of actors (business especially, but not

exclusively SMEs, business associations, chambers of commerce, development agencies, research centres, HEI, training centres, financial centres,
etc.), and in which the link between SMEs and their working environment is
stressed. Research needs to be embedded in a broader concept of innovation.

5 In sum, support for a bottom-up process of strategy formulation at the
regional level, with the aim of integrating various policy fields, and of
embedding regional action in inter-regional networks in which policy
information and experiences are exchanged and compared.

> There is thus a clear need to formulate integrated RTD (Research and
> Technology Development) and innovation strategies which connect to
> the economic development process in the regions and which, via the
> national system of RTD and innovation support, is integrated into a
> wider European perspective.
>
> (European Commission 1999: 144)

6 The search for new policy approaches also responds to a perceived need to
increase the effectiveness of structural support measures by the EU as well
as Member States. For the EU, RIS/RITTS initiatives are linked to the
ambition to improve the performance of the Structural Funds (Landabaso
2000). At the national level, the initiatives can also be seen to be in line
with the European Commission's ambition to help to 'rationalise the
excessive supply of business support services in the Member States to ensure
a higher degree of specialisation and targeting of the services offered'.
(European Commission 1999: 151)

Associational dilemmas: behind the consensus, ambiguities, and potential conflicts of interests

More than one hundred regional innovation projects (RTP, RIS, RITTS) have
(almost) run their course. This milestone prompts us to reflect upon the new-
style regional innovation programmes and their conceptual background. In this
section, we present various ambiguities and dilemmas that, in our view, require
further attention. As will be shown below, these ambiguities and dilemmas are
basically derived from the ideas and tensions presented in the previous section.
They stem, in particular, from the combination of the six aims. Ambiguities can
be found in four areas: (1) the role of the region; (2) the role of firms and the
articulation of their 'needs'; (3) the role and nature of business support; and (4)
the innovation concept itself. These will be discussed below.

The role of the region: laboratory for innovation or strategic site for balanced economic development?

The first ambiguity concerns the role of the region with regard to the various aims
of the RIS/RITTS programmes and their promoters. Tensions, already mentioned

by observers in previous phases (Nauwelaers 1999), may be traced back to the different positions and interests of the two DGs involved. Essentially, the role allocated to the region may be seen as being dependent on whose interests are at stake. For an organisation interested primarily in enhancing the innovative potential of the Community, like DG XIII, the region presents an effective level of intervention. The region is seen, more precisely, as the localised interaction environment in which firm and other organisations operate (supply chain, cluster). The region, thus, offers an *appropriate setting* to foster innovation and to improve the effectiveness of business support. The starting points for this approach are the system nature of innovation (see pillar 4 on p. 207) and the rationalisation of business support (pillar 6 on p. 208), as well as the notion that observed cases of success and best practices are revealed and exchanged across Europe through a process of mainstreaming (pillar 5 on p. 208). Regions, in this view, are the *laboratories* for innovation and improved business support: they play an *instrumental role* in achieving business excellence across the EU.

On the other hand, for those interested in the fate of Europe's regions, such as DG XVI, the position of the region is more profound. Helping regions, especially lagging regions, to improve indigenous competitiveness is seen as an important contribution to cohesion and to spatially balanced economic development across Europe. The relationship between competitiveness and cohesion is strengthened, moreover, by the notion that the region, as a result of the localised, system nature of innovation, has become a *strategic* site of economic development (Cooke 1999; Storper 1997). This approach represents, in particular, a change in the valuation of regional specificities. Instead of representing hurdles that need to be taken into account while implementing modernisation strategies, regional specificities have turned into assets that, supported by their relatively immobile nature, underpin regional competitiveness (pillar 2 on p. 207). In the words of Cooke:

> From being a *tabula rasa* on which are inscribed the results of past resource-based business decisions, decentralisation effects of central government decisions, and the decisions of both indigenous smaller firms and indigenous or large FDI (Foreign Direct Investment) firms, the regions now become a proactive space in which all assets are mobilised to try to secure regional economic competitiveness.
>
> (1999: 15)

Such assets can stem from the specific ways in which related firms and organisations in certain sectors interact, shaping and nurturing regional 'club goods' in areas such as the labour market, stocks of tacit knowledge, access to intelligence, and technology sources, etc. (Lagendijk 2000; Temple 1998). Such assets can also be of a more symbolic nature, through the association of products and services with aspects of regional identity. Nevertheless, especially for laggard regions, to grasp such opportunities requires fundamental changes in the business culture (pillar 1 on p. 207) and the planning culture (pillar 3 on p. 207).

While, as shown by the RIS/RITTS programme, the instrumental and the strategic interpretations of the role of the region can co-exist comfortably, at a certain point conflicts may emerge. A fundamental issue concerns the object of mainstreaming (1) good practices on business cooperation and innovation emerging from the regional 'laboratories' serving other businesses across Europe; and (2) the methods and instruments that serve regions, by nurturing the localised process of business cooperation and innovation, in order to nurture those assets that underpin regional competitiveness. The danger of the first objective is that it is too much oriented to 'business excellence', ignoring the cohesion aspects of innovation. By focusing on the second objective, on the other hand, one may run the risk of the regional level, and thereby specific regional interests, becoming too predominant in the promotion of innovation and competitiveness. What is at stake is the validity of the basic premise of regional competitiveness. Will laggard regions indeed be able to graft their economic success on becoming specialists in a market niche based on creating their own 'proactive space'? Another issue is the impact of inter-regional competition. Emphasis on regional competitiveness may involve taking the risk that European support will be geared ultimately to regional projects with little benefits for other regions, and sub-optimal consequences for the EU as a whole. While the potential negative impacts of inter-regional competition are much less in the case of indigenous development than with inward investments, attention needs to be paid to keeping the right balance between specific regional interests and wider Community interests. More fundamentally, more attention needs to be devoted to the question of 'how to reconcile the perspectives, on the one hand, of DG XII, based on favouring excellence, and, on the other, of DG XVI, targeting cohesion' (Nauwelaers 1999: 3).

The position of the business sector and the articulation of 'business needs': 'regional' versus 'business' interest

Whereas the position of the 'region' in the context of wider European ambitions may be seen as ambiguous, the same applies to the position of 'business' in the context of regional development. A core element of the demand-driven RTD/ innovation policies is that they respond to business needs (see pillar 3 on p. 207). The issue, thus, is how to define and reveal these needs. It is commonly accepted that needs do not correspond with business 'wants', that is, what businesses *say* they need (Brusco 1992). The latter should be the outcome of 'getting to know' firms rather than polling them (Rosenfeld 1995). Instead, in the context of innovation, many business needs are of a 'hidden' and 'latent' nature (Landabaso 2000). Innovation policy needs to find ways to reveal these latent needs and to make firms aware of their needs. Essentially, an effective way of doing so is to make firms aware of the fact that they can make more money and strengthen their market position through innovation, while also serving broader regional interests. These 'latent needs', thus, raise some intricate questions about the representation of business interests, and how these match with the interests of other regional actors, such as regional policy-makers, universities, HEIs, and intermediary organisations.

The example of the RTP in the Dutch province of Limburg may serve as an illustration here. One of the initial results of the research carried out among firms in Limburg was that most firms said they needed more money to carry out innovation. Since the survey aimed at revealing direct wants as expressed by businesses, such an outcome is hardly surprising. More in-depth research, however, provided more insight into the 'true' business needs. Business analysis indicated that the priorities for business development in Limburg were training and education, the implementation of new production technologies, access to the appropriate sources of support, and information to address shortcomings (Province of Limburg 1996). The lesson here is that policy-makers, intermediary organisations, knowledge providers, etc. must spend sufficient time in finding out the real, often hidden, needs of firms. This even turned out to be the case for larger firms, albeit to a lesser degree, as larger firms usually have a better understanding of their true needs. In-depth analysis, however, also serves another purpose. It signals that the regional policy-makers take the firms seriously, which contributes to regional consensus building. In other words, in-depth analysis is an important element of the associative approach.

As in the case of the previous dilemma, two basic kinds of interests can now be distinguished. First, regional actors, especially policy-makers, have a keen interest in enhancing and sustaining levels of regional wealth and employment. This translates into a specific projection of business needs. The policy-makers' views of business needs in the context of RTD/innovation policy correspond to a role of local business as a modernising, growth-oriented, and hence employment-creating enterprise. This corresponds with the broader policy view in which innovation policies serve cohesion purposes through their contribution to regional growth. In the original RTP document this was stated as follows:

> [R]esearch and technology development (RTD) is not an objective in itself, but a means to attain the objective of cohesion. It is an excellent way to promote economic development, to increase productivity and competitiveness and thus reduce inequalities among regions.
>
> (European Commission 1994b: 11)

Firms, especially SMEs, are essentially regarded by policy-makers as *instruments*, and innovation and growth-orientation are vehicles for SMEs to serve the community goals of employment creation and income generation. This leads to a particular view of business support. Providers of business support are expected to play a 'therapeutic' role for SMEs, to encourage them to implement wider policy goals and to make them accept these community goals and the major route towards them: innovation.

The other point of view is that of the business entrepreneur. For many entrepreneurs, their business primarily represents a means to generate a stable flow of family income and to fulfil specific professional ambitions. For an entrepreneur, therefore, the individual benefits of 'growth-orientation' and 'innovation' may be less obvious. Evidently, some level of innovation may be required for business survival and income generation. The single most important motivation for firms to innovate is to make money. In the associational view of regional innovation strategy development, this is sometimes overshadowed. It is essential to emphasise successful commercialisation of product and process development as an integrated part of innovation. However, innovation and growth strategies may also imply unnecessary risk taking and an unwanted obligation to modify the basic structure and culture of the firms. Indeed, evidence seems to prove the cautious entrepreneur right. According to Churchill and Lewis (1983, see also Sexton et al. 1997), growing small firms especially incur risks of failure, which leads to bankruptcy or take-over. This is due to the fact that growing firms face fundamental changes in organisation and management. Whereas micro-firms can be run by one person, i.e. the entrepreneur, firms with more than 30–50 employees need a more articulated management and support system, in which tasks such as finance, personnel, marketing, logistics, etc., are devolved to dedicated staff. It is often the neglect of, or even resistance to, such changes that causes firms that are highly successful to run into trouble.

Two conclusions can be drawn from this separation of 'regional' and 'business' needs. First, the articulation of business needs cannot be the subject of a simple 'needs analysis', even when the latter aims at detecting 'hidden' or 'latent' needs. What first needs to be established is a common view of what role various firms are expected to play in regional economic development. Such a role should be based on business engagement with matters of regional development. It is not just its own benefit that should inform the entrepreneurial articulation of business needs, but 'enlightened business self-interest' informed by regional interests. Nurturing such 'enlightened self-interest', in which entrepreneurial and regional interests become intertwined, is essentially what an associative approach to regional innovation should be about.

The second conclusion concerns the suggested association between innovation and employment. Essentially, innovation policy must not be confused with labour market or employment policy. Essentially, what RIS/RITTS programmes are focusing on is the impact on the economic structure and business competitiveness. Although there is a relation between the competitiveness of firms and job creation, especially in the long term, other issues also come into play. It should be realised that, in the short term, innovation may even work against employment goals, especially when it results in labour-saving capital investments. The complexities of the innovation–employment relationships are not always adequately accounted for. Indeed, the theoretical foundation of the RIS/RITTS programmes, the learning region paradigm, has been criticised for this. The learning region concept lacks proper attention for social issues (cf. Morgan 1997) such as employment, working conditions, social economic development of a region, etc. The learning region argument, which is also used by the European Commission, that innovation will contribute to solving social issues is too simple. The relations are far more complex.

Ambiguity in the level of support: business firms or populations?

The third ambiguity follows closely from the previous one. Not only should a distinction be made between 'regional' and 'business' needs and perspectives, but there is also the question of the level at which firms should be targeted as 'clients' of innovation support. There are two basic views here. The first sees firms as *individual* clients, emphasising the survival and growth of single firms. The second view focuses on the *collective* performance of firms, that is, on business development at target group level. The crucial difference between these two views stems from the perception of business failure. In an individual orientation, the failure of a supported firm is generally seen as a loss, and something which should be avoided. It may even be interpreted as a sign of insufficient quality of support. In a collective perspective, business failure, however lamentable for the individual entrepreneur, may be interpreted as potentially contributing to the improvement of overall business performance by a process of selection. This corresponds to a population perspective of business development and innovation, in which a strong role is played by competition. Obviously, such a perspective does not exclude the possibility of gearing support to the prevention of business failure, for instance, by providing courses in business growth management. Nevertheless, failure may be seen as *serving*, rather than thwarting, the dynamics of the system.

The argument put forward here is that the associative approach, because of its emphasis on cooperation and communication, tends to ignore the significance of the selection mechanisms at the business population level. In principle, one could argue, it is not the individual firm that should benefit, but the regional economy and living population through the *aggregate* effects of innovation support on the regional business population. In other words, it is not the fate of individual firms that should count, but the overall performance of the targeted group of business firms. Such a 'harsher' view of business development does not correspond to the harmonious perspective of regional development depicted in associational approaches (Cooke and Morgan 1998). While in economic theory some attention is given to the balance between competition and cooperation, more detailed accounts of associative approaches and empirical studies merely focus on the latter aspect.

Also in practice, there seems to be a tendency to focus on the individual level. This can be attributed, to some extent, to the recent developments in the provision of business support. Disappointing results from business support in the past have been attributed, among other factors, to the lack of real engagement between providers and their clients (North *et al.* 1997; Rosenfeld 1995). In response, to become more successful, providers have sought to establish longer-term 'cosy' relationships with clients. Undoubtedly, longer-term relationships may have benefits in terms of the customisation of support, follow-up support, and after-care, and have thus been presented as a way to improve support effectiveness. Indeed, the way agencies are monitored, and sometimes even accounted for, seems to encourage longer-term approaches. Yet, a disadvantage of this approach is that the agencies may start to take too much care of individual business needs, and to become too committed to the survival and growth of firms that are more responsive to their support. Client firms, in turn, may develop a lasting dependency on business support. Rather than learning to trace and acquire knowledge on a commercial basis, they become reliant on the search operations and financial support of business service firms. This not only creates an unwanted reliance but also instils the wrong attitudes among firms. The incentive to seek engagement with less responsive firms – often the more backward ones most in need – may even be reduced.

The way firms are targeted is further complicated by the fact that businesses, especially SMEs, differ substantially in their ability to absorb and apply incentives for innovation (Cohen and Levinthal 1990). SMEs are usually categorised into three groups, i.e. leaders, followers, and jobbers (cf. Province of Limburg 1996). Leaders are the most advanced firms. They are capable of finding their own way through the network of innovation support organisations. Because they are advanced, they are, in general, not a target group for innovation support organisations. These organisations usually do not offer enough specific knowledge and services to be of value to leaders. The market for innovation support organisations, instead, is the followers group. Followers have several characteristics which make them an ideal target group. First, they are aware of the importance of innovation, so they do not have to be convinced of that. Second, because followers are not particularly advanced, they are aware of the fact that they need the help of innovation-support organisations. Moreover, innovation support organisations are, in general, able to assist followers on the basis of their own skills and knowledge, or they can find other knowledge providers to answer followers' questions. Third, followers are usually able to pay for the services offered to them. In short, followers are more or less ideal customers: easy to reach, responsive to the services offered, and able to pay for them. Many innovation-support organisations make a good living out of working with followers. In some cases, this has persuaded (regional) authorities to privatise innovation-support organisations or to cut back on government funds for them, such as in the case of the Dutch Syntens organisation.

Jobbers are a more difficult category of firms to reach. Basically, they are the opposite of followers. Innovation-support organisations have to go through a time-consuming process to try to convince jobbers that innovation is beneficial for them; they then have to help jobbers to articulate their needs in terms of knowledge and management support. They have to do this at a low fee because jobbers usually do not have sufficient financial resources to pay for these services. The number of jobbers is substantial in almost every region. However, given the fact that they are difficult customers, innovation-support organisa-tions do relatively little business with them, particularly when they depend on selling their services in the market instead of government aid. In short, the firms that need innovation support the most receive the least. This can, of course, be explained as a result of authorities failing to appreciate the fact that helping jobbers costs a lot of time and money and of impatient politicians wanting easy victories that cannot be won on jobbers. However, on the other hand, a large number of jobbers are quite happy with the position they are in. They have little, if any, intention of changing and, consequently, public money is better spent on other firms.

Differentiation of target groups is a particular concern of support organisations that operate on a commercial basis. They depend on selling their services in the market for their survival and like to maintain relations with their customers. This market pressure constrains their ability to search for backward (jobbers) firms. Government-funded support organisations do not have to worry about their survival and can spend more time finding and helping backward firms.

An ambiguous innovation concept

A final point concerns the concept of innovation itself. Initially associated with the notion of extracting economic benefits from the commercial application of technology, innovation has come to cover a much broader area of business activities and change. Increasingly, innovation appears to refer to packages of activities required to sustain or improve business competitiveness. Landabaso's interpretation of innovation clearly illustrates this:

> The high road to competitiveness for these firms that are exposed to international competition runs through innovation, which enables them to adapt at the right time to the competition posed by globalisation and the fast pace of technological change. Innovation must apply to all aspects of a small firm's activities (new markets, new, different or better products, processes and services). In this sense, the concept of innovation embraces research and development, technology, training, marketing and commercial activity, design and quality policy, finance, logistics and the business management required for these various functions to mesh together efficiently.
>
> (Landabaso 2000: 76)

The question is whether such a perspective is not too broad, from a conceptual as well as a practical point of view. A conceptual issue is to what extent innovation should at least mean doing something new, rather than the mere effective application of an already existing (set of) practice(s). Opinions clearly differ here. For instance, in one of the preparatory meetings of the RIS/RITTS, one can contrast the interpretation of innovation by Corvers (1999: 138) as doing something new or improved, with Cooke's (1999: 4) statement that innovation is largely about imitation (see also Tsipouri 1999). The latter seems to be relevant especially for more peripheral regions, and basically involves a process of modernisation. Indeed, Landabaso even points to the paradoxical situation that, while peripheral regions should spend more on innovation (in a broad sense), they have less capacity to absorb available funding for innovation:

> Such is the regional innovation paradox. Today, in Europe, advanced regions spend more public money (and in a more strategic way) for the promotion of innovation for their firms than less favoured regions do, thus increasing the innovation gap across Europe.
>
> (2000: 80)

Given the conceptual transformation of the innovation concept, however, one may ask, if there really is such a regional innovation paradox. One may argue that innovation seems to refer to different processes for core and peripheral regions. For core regions, it refers to the development and commercial application of new technologies and organisational practices; besides the development of the region, this also serves the aim of supporting *business excellence* in the EU. For peripheral regions, innovation primarily means modernisation and catching-up, by creating access to external sources of knowledge. Indeed, especially for SMEs in peripheral regions, 'innovation' comes down to basic business improvement, contributing to the aim of achieving spatial cohesion across the EU. The question is to what extent such an expanded innovation concept can keep its clarity and focus. How, when innovation means something different in core and periphery regions, should policy address the issue of differentiation, not only in implementation but also conceptually?

This is not to suggest that regional innovation strategies are unimportant. On the contrary, innovation presents an important, and perhaps the only truly durable solution to the challenges placed upon firms under the condition of increased global competition. Survival in the knowledge-based economy depends on innovation. As the horizons of most SMEs essentially remain regional, the setting of innovation policies in a regional strategy context serves a clear purpose. In this sense, its importance can hardly be underestimated.

From policy to practice: ambiguities become manifest

It is not in the phases of strategy and concept development that the ambiguities identified above really become manifest. To a large extent, the broad discourse on regional development, innovation, and SME development allows one to gloss over more specific questions and conceptual dilemmas. Problems become more apparent at the level of policy praxis, particularly in the area of organisational design. With exception of the last dilemma (innovation concept), all dilemmas refer to the positions and roles of specific actors, and their interactions. This applies to regional actors (e.g. the role of support and the business sector), as well as supra- or inter-regional actors (European Commission, knowledge centres). It is when these positions and roles are (re)defined, and vital organisational and financial decisions are made, that more specific issues and dilemmas emerge. In this section, we focus on the organisational dimension of innovation support, paying specific attention to the role of the university.

An important thing to acknowledge is that associative approaches to regional innovation policy have been implemented in a context in which, at least in most regions, a support structure was already in place. The 1980s witnessed a rapid growth in both support providers (knowledge centres) and intermediary organisations (transfer and relay centres), which linked supply and demand in a variety of ways (Cobbenhagen *et al.* 1996; Cooke and Morgan 1998). The 1990s saw a tendency to reduce the role of intermediaries in favour of the providers, by aiming at the establishment of direct links between suppliers and users. The university and other higher education organisations have thus gained a more prominent position in business support, often supported by an in-house transfer and liaison office.

The university occupies a special position in this organisational domain, which, in effect, underscores some of the ambiguities mentioned before. Traditionally, the university represents 'cosmopolitan' actors. Institutionally and organisationally, it is embedded in cosmopolitan networks driven by the search for, the dissemination of and debate of excellence. The locality, in this context, largely plays the role of *laboratory*, as an empirical testing ground. This could include relationships with local businesses, but such relationships should be seen in the light of the specific research and/or financial interests of the university departments. In contrast, within the discourse of associative regional development, the university has acquired a distinct position as a *regional* actor, which takes a dual role. On the one hand, the university is seen as an important source of business knowledge, both technological and, through the rise of business schools, organisational. On the other hand, the university is regarded as a stakeholder in the process of regional strategy making (Goddard 1998; Goddard and Chatterton 1999). In particular, its role lies in making contributions to the process of regional and business analysis, the design and customisation of innovation strategies, the development of particular projects, the facilitation of the decision-making process, and policy monitoring.

While the role of the university thus appears to become more prominent, this also raises a number of problems. For instance, it is increasingly acknowledged that the university is not well equipped to support SMEs. It is often said the university and SMEs 'speak a different language' (Cobbenhagen *et al.* 1996; Shapira *et al.* 1995). Indeed, the knowledge of the university is of a far more theoretical and fundamental nature than the knowledge of SMEs. SMEs are interested in application, not science. Moreover, the timetable of the university differs significantly from that of SMEs. SMEs want quick answers because they operate in a market that changes daily. Scientific research, however, takes much longer. These differences are responsible for the fact that few collaborations between universities and SMEs are truly successful. At the very least, they are not 'natural partners'. This conclusion can be found in many of the RITTS, RIS, and RTP reports of regions throughout Europe in recent years.[1] More essentially, their interests and ways of practice differ substantially. Also, the 'cosmopolitan' role of the university often seems to clash with its role as regional actor, for instance, when choices need to be made between more fundamental and practical forms of research.

Another issue is the position of the university among other regional support agencies (Jones Evans *et al.* 1999). One way in which the university appears to be becoming regionally engaged is through its support of specific business branches or clusters. This can occur through its involvement in branch-specific technology centres or through relationships between dedicated university departments and key firms in a particular branch. Through its dual local–global role, the university seems to be an apt organisation that acts as gatekeeper, i.e. to absorb 'global' knowledge (technological, but also market-related) and then translate it into the local context. The provision of more generic forms of support, on the other hand, depends generally on the presence and role of a business school, and its interaction with business support organisations and business associations. It is at this level that most problems arise. Especially for SMEs, the provision of support seems to be highly complex, often chaotic (Dankbaar and Cobbenhagen 2000), and subject to frequent overhauls. What is generally lacking is a clear idea about the way the support 'market' should function, what its broader aims are in terms of business (population) development, and how it should be supported.

Invoking the notion of a support 'market' introduces another basic question, that is, the organisational theory and model of regional innovation support. In a simple framework, three models may be distinguished (Cobbenhagen 1998; Dankbaar and Cobbenhagen 2000):

1 A *hierarchical* model, dominated by one core organisation (e.g. a Regional Technology Transfer Centre), which coordinates the matching of demand and supply. This has the advantage that the roles of different actors can be clearly defined and exposed, but it limits flexibility.

2 A *market* model, supported, for instance, by a 'voucher' system, which allows support-seekers to select and use their own provider. A problem with this model is that it can only work if businesses are aware of their 'true' needs and prepared to act upon them, while these needs must be in tune with regional development interests. This, as argued above, cannot be assumed to be the case.

3 A *network* model, allowing various providers to specialise and interact in a broader strategic framework. This model, since it may facilitate both strategic orientation and flexibility, is regarded as the most preferable. A good example of a regional technology network, comprised of branch-specific technology centres, is offered by the Basque Country, although this

does not include a strong role for the university. A problem that remains is how such networks are coordinated, or, more specifically, how they relate to the process of regional strategy-making. Not only the university, but also branch-specific technology centres represent special interests, and will lobby for branch-specific support and investments. How to accommodate these interests in the wider context of regional development remains a fundamental question of regional governance.

In the context of the associative approach, it is not surprising that preference goes to the network model. In such a model, business support does not simply cater for business needs, as in the market model, while it may benefit from the associational economies and flexibility stemming from cooperation. As will be shown in the next section, networking and the shaping of associational forms of governance feature within the RIS/RITTS strategies. The discussion of specific RIS/RITTS cases will also serve to illustrate the impact of the conceptual ambiguities discussed so far.

First lessons drawn from RIS/RITTS cases

As explained before, the RIS/RITTS programme, as the successor of the RTP experience, arose out of collaboration between DG XIII and DG XVI. While similar in approach, structure, and financing (175,000 Euros, on the basis of 100 per cent matched funding), the two strands of RIS and RITTS vary in a way that is in line, to a large extent, with the basic differences in objectives and perspectives as pointed out above. On the one hand, the RIS programme, launched by DG XVI, focuses on the embedding of innovation in regional development strategy. RIS projects are restricted to NUTS II, regions where at least 50 per cent of the population is eligible for the European Regional Development Fund (in the case of Objective 1, linked to Community Support Frameworks). These regions can only be proposed by a regional authority (or delegation). Regional analysis has to be carried out primarily by the local authority, while obligatory but limited involvement of consultants is required for process management. On the other hand, RITTS projects, supported by DG XIII, are applicable to any area (i.e. also non-administrative) within the EU. They can be proposed by any reasonable (group of) regional agents. The RITTS strand focuses more specifically on gearing RTD and innovation support to SMEs. DG XIII demands extensive involvement of consultants, who should cover process management and analysis. At least a third of the work involved in the latter should be undertaken by a foreign consultant. The RIS/RITTS programme does not represent a real compromise between the 'cohesion' (assisting the development of Less Favoured Regions) and 'innovation' (regions as laboratories) objectives, but rather a comfortable co-habitation of both objectives.

RIS and RITTS fully correspond in the way the process is structured. The projects run through three phases, from '0' to '2'.

1   Phase 0 is the preparatory phase during which a management structure is established, i.e. a region-wide Steering Committee and a smaller Management Team to run the day-to-day affairs. A working programme is also developed. The working programme specifies the objectives of the project.
2   Phase 1 is the regional analysis phase. During this phase, the strengths and weaknesses of a region's firms and innovation support infrastructure are assessed.
3   The final phase, Phase 2, concerns the actual strategy development. The outcome of this phase is an action plan for further innovation in the region. The actual implementation of this action plan lies outside the scope of a RITTS/RIS project.

The Steering Committee and the Management Team could be considered as the institutionalisation of the associative perspective. The European Commission – both DG XIII and DG XVI – stresses the importance of region-wide support for the innovation strategy. Regional consensus is considered a key aspect of the RIS/RITTS approach. The Steering Committee and the Management Team should reflect this consensus and the consensus should be developed further during the project. Although there is no conclusive evidence as yet, the first indications reveal that this focus on consensus has had the effect that regional stakeholders are attempting to avoid confrontations. Conflicts of interest are avoided and the resulting innovation strategies reflect first of all what everybody agrees on, which is not necessarily the same as the optimal strategy for the region. It is, for example, difficult to propose structural changes to the organisation and functioning of the intermediary organisations in a regional innovation strategy, when these organisations have to approve of that strategy. Because of the focus on consensus in the projects, suggestions for more structural changes are hardly to be found in the RITTS reports. Hence, there is still room for independent researchers to analyse matters such as these more closely.

This dilemma of maintaining the status quo also manifests itself at the level of service provision. The RIS/RITTS strategies focus on finding solutions to innovation-related problems within the region. Regional innovation support organisations are able to answer most needs of the region's firms concerning general product and process development, organisational innovation (including management skills, logistics, etc.), and human resource development. But where more sophisticated knowledge is concerned, no single region can provide for all the needs of its firms. External links must be developed for this purpose. Although the RIS/RITTS programmes do allow such external links, they are only common in regions that have already developed strong links with other regions, such as border regions. This is, basically, because the knowledge and services a region cannot provide are not on the agenda of regional authorities.

A practical example of these dilemmas can be observed in the Flemish RITTS (Cobbenhagen *et al.* 1996; Cobbenhagen 1998). After a period of detailed analysis and consultation with stakeholders, the RITTS team provided a first outline of how innovation support in Flanders could be improved, emphasising, in particular, the need for organisational change. In practice, this message has not been taken up by the Flemish government. One problem is that, at a strategic regional level, there is little ambition to link SME development to regional development aims. Although the significance of a broad innovation concept is acknowledged, in practice, the Flemish government remains oriented towards technological innovation and towards sustaining a support infrastructure that favours larger enterprises. The attitudes of the Flemish government are thus contrary to the conclusion drawn during the RIS/RITTS project. The latter concluded that, instead of focusing on technological innovation, support to SMEs in Flanders requires an approach that goes beyond innovation policy, even when interpreted in a broad sense. Through the consultation of entrepreneurs and representatives of business associations and other stakeholders, the RITTS project showed that SMEs may benefit greatly from changes in policy areas such as secondary education, wages and social security, taxes, and administrative procedures. Moreover, to organise support, a modification, to the existing, rather centralised structure towards a network model, with the support providers as main actors was suggested. The latter are seen as most suitable as 'innovation gatekeepers' because of their dual position in global and local networks. Local intermediaries, on the other hand, should play the role of temporary 'go-between' and 'dating' agents between support suppliers and customers, rather than that of transfer agents. These suggestions, however, have not been welcomed among policy-makers.

A specific issue which surfaced during the Flemish analysis concerned the role of universities. Following the emphasis on knowledge providers as 'innovation gatekeepers', universities, as well as polytechnics, are granted an important role in innovation support. Moreover, as in most countries, the Flemish universities carry a formal responsibility in this respect. They are not only organisations of knowledge production and academic teaching, but are also obliged to undertake valorisation of knowledge to the benefit of the regional economy and society. In terms of actual support to SMEs, however, the Flemish situation confirms the existence of a strong gap between universities and small businesses, although some polytechnics appear to be quite active in the area of SME support. The way most universities seem to play a role is through their links with branch-specific support organisations, the so-called 'Collective Centres'. In the area of innovation support, however, the Collective Centres (through their in-house Technology Advisory Centres), only reach a small proportion of SMEs, most of which belong to the group of technologically active 'leaders'. The business inventory, moreover, revealed that SMEs generally acknowledge the HE sector as a source of knowledge, but not one which they would approach in practice. So, while universities are considered important actors in the support network, it is to be doubted whether they should be considered to be first 'ports of call' for SMEs. Even the creation of dedicated technology transfer within universities may not be sufficient to bridge the university–business gap in this respect. The challenge is, thus, to find other channels of communication and transfer in the broader support network which may bring SMEs and 'innovation gatekeepers' together.

A final issue of interest here concerns the nature of business needs analysis. Like other RIS/RITTS projects, the Flemish project devoted much attention to the articulation of business needs. Using a method to reveal latent business needs (Dankbaar and Cobbenhagen 2000), the importance of linking innovation to the development of other business capabilities such as marketing and management became clear. The needs analysis showed that entrepreneurs do not attach a high priority to innovation as such. They tend to be focused on product-market combinations and short-term survival strategies. This contrasts with the opinion of the support intermediaries, who claimed that SMEs need innovation but are not aware of it. The question was raised as to what extent policy should promote support that does not correspond with the daily working practices of SMEs and their limited strategic ambitions. The interests of providers and their projected clients clearly do not match in this respect. Again, this finding underscores the tension mentioned earlier between 'real' business needs and needs as projected by regional agents.

Conclusion

Through interactions in the academic as well as the policy domains, the dialogue between themes of innovation and regional development have inspired what is now called the associative approach to regional development. In this approach, building associative governance structures at the regional level is seen as providing a 'high road' to improving the collective learning and innovation capabilities of firms and supporting organisations. Associational capacity, in essence, reflects the overall regional capacity to collaborate within ensembles of firms, states, and systems to keep abreast of knowledge-based competition (Cooke and Morgan 1998), that is, to sustain regional competitiveness and wealth in the long term. As well as this relationship between the region and wealth creation, basically a matter of wealth distribution and cohesion, however, there is also a primarily economic argument at stake. The region is considered to be the appropriate spatial-organisational level for nurturing interactive learning and innovation. Thus, regions can also be perceived as suitable *laboratories* for innovation. In practice, as a result, associative approaches have been grafted onto this twin objective of nurturing innovation and supporting regional development. The state and governance structures also play an important role in the associative approach. The state, rather than steering directly, or adopting an entrepreneurial stance itself, should function as an *animateur*, assisting regional stakeholders in shaping a common view, developing a 'learning' culture, and mobilising resources. Knowledge actors – such as intermediary organisations and the universities – are deemed to play a core role in shaping the associative and learning capacities of the region. However, although universities have a huge stock of knowledge, it is interesting to see that they play only a modest role in most RITTS and RIS projects. Apparently, the type of knowledge and services they offer does not match business development needs. It is beyond the scope of this chapter to specify the role of universities in regional innovation policy, but their role seems difficult to match with the RIS/RITTS approach to regional innovation.

In this chapter, we have aimed at contributing to the associative approach in a critical way, by highlighting certain ambiguities and dilemmas. The issues raised here partly originate from a critical evaluation of concepts and assumptions underlying the associative approach. Most observations, however, are based on our reflections on how the associative approach has been put into practice by the European RIS/RITTS programme. Within Europe, the RIS/RITTS programme undoubtedly represents the most extensive attempt to implement ideas derived from a regional-associative approach. While the evaluation of the programme has only just started, initial findings and observations already allow some interesting initial reflections upon the underlying approach and concepts. Due to this combination of evaluation at a conceptual and a practical level, the dilemmas identified range from the fundamental to the practically oriented. A fundamental issue, for instance, stems from the dual objective of cohesion (balanced regional development) and innovation (region as laboratory). Another fundamental issue is the position of the business firm as support target (individual client vs. population perspective). More practical issues can be found in the articulation of needs and the tendency of associative practices to neglect thorny issues and avoid structural organisational change.

Admittedly, in presenting these dilemmas, we have done little to contribute to the finding of possible solutions and improvements in policy design. At present, what seems to be most pertinent is to proceed with the evaluations of the whole of RIS/RITTS programmes and other similar approaches. This may help to present a clearer view of the conceptual and practical issues that surround the regional-associative approach. A major challenge, as indicated by the 'cohesion-innovation' dilemma and the section on 'business' vs. 'regional' interests, lies in understanding the impact of the intertwining of more socio-political and evolutionary economic perspectives. Another issue, as repeated recently by Tsipouri (1999), is the extent to which general ideas, even if they take account of regional specifities, can be considered to be transferable between, and hence applicable to, regions of very different natures. As the discussion on the innovation concept showed, there may be a need for a stronger customisation of concepts, distinguishing, for instance, more clearly between core areas and LFRs.

Note

1 See, for example, the reports of Limburg (NL), Lorraine (F), Noord-Holland (NL), Sachsen (D), and Wales (UK).

References

Amin, A. (1999) 'An Institutionalist Perspective on Regional Development', *International Journal of Urban and Regional Research* 23, 2: 365–378.

Boekholt, P. (1999) 'The Regional Technology Plans: A New Approach to Regional Development Policy', in J. Cobbenhagen (ed.) *Cohesion, Competitiveness and RTDI: Their Impact on Regions*, Maastricht: Province of Limburg, pp. 35–41.

Brusco, S. (1992) 'Small Firms and the Provision of Real Services', in F. Pyke and W. Sengenberger (eds) *Industrial Districts and Local Economic Regeneration*, Geneva: International Institute for Labour Studies, pp. 177–196.

Churchill, N. C. and Lewis, V. L. (1983) 'The Five Stages of Small Business Growth', *Harvard Business Review* 61, 3: 30–50.

Cobbenhagen, J. (ed.) (1998) *Kiezen voor Innovativiteit: Interne Rapportage Fase 2 van het RITTS Project Vlaanderen*, Maastricht: MERIT.

Cobbenhagen, J., Dankbaar, B. and Wolters, A. (1996) *De Vlaamse Technologische Infrastructuur vanuit de KMO-optiek bekeken: Rapportage Fase 1 van het RITTS Project Vlaanderen*, Maastricht: Maastricht University Press.

Cohen, W. and Levinthal, D. (1990) 'Absorptive Capacity: A New Perspective on Learning and Innovation', *Administrative Science Quarterly* 35: 128–152.

Cooke, P. (1999) 'The Role of Innovation in Regional Competitiveness', in J. Cobbenhagen (ed.) *Cohesion, Competitiveness and RTDI: Their Impact on Regions*, Maastricht: Province of Limburg, pp. 15–27.

Cooke, P. and Morgan, K. (1998) *The Associational Economy: Firms, Regions and Innovation*, Oxford: Oxford University Press.

Corvers, F. (1999) 'Competitiveness, Innovation Policy and European Regions', in J. Cobbenhagen (ed.) *Cohesion, Competitiveness and RTDI: Their Impact on Regions*, Maastricht: Province of Limburg, pp. 137–143.

Dankbaar, B. and Cobbenhagen, J. (2000) 'In Search of a Regional Innovation Strategy for Flanders', in F. Boekema, K. Morgan, S. Bakkers and R. Rutten (eds) *Knowledge, Innovation and Economic Growth: Learning Regions, Theory, Policy and Practice*, Cheltenham: Edward-Elgar, pp. 115–134.

Dupuy, C. and Gilly, J.-P. (1994) *Collective Learning and Territorial Dynamics: A New Approach to the Relations between Industrial Groups and Territories*, Toulouse: Institut d'Economie Régionale de Toulouse.

European Commission (1994a) *Growth, Competitiveness, Employment: The Challenges and Ways Forward into the 21st Century*, White Paper, Luxembourg: Office for Official Publications of the European Communities.

European Commission (1994b) *Regional Technology Plan Guide Book*, Brussels: European Commission DG XVI/ DG XIII.

European Commission (1996a) *Green Paper on Innovation*, Luxembourg: Office for Official Publications of the European Communities.

European Commission (1996b) *Practical Guide to Region Innovation Actions: Regional Innovation Strategies (RIS), Regional Innovation and Technology Transfer Strategies (RITTS)*, Luxembourg: Office for Official Publications of the European Communities.

European Commission (1997) *Agenda 2000: For a Stronger and Wider Union*, Luxembourg: Office for Official Publications of the European Communities.

European Commission (1998) *Reinforcing Cohesion and Competitiveness through RTD and Innovation Policy: Communication from the Commission to the European Parliament, the*

Council, the Committee of the Regions and the Economic and Social Committee, Brussels: European Union.

European Commission (1999) 'Reinforcing Cohesion and Competitiveness through Research, Technological Development and Innovation', in J. Cobbenhagen (ed.) *Cohesion, Competitiveness and RTDI: Their Impact on Regions*, Maastricht: Province of Limburg, pp. 144–154.

Goddard, J. B. (1998) *Universities and Regional Development: Report to the Department for Education and Employment*, Newcastle upon Tyne: University of Newcastle/CURDS.

Goddard, J. B. and Chatterton, P. (1999) 'Regional Development Agencies and the Knowledge Economy: Harnessing the Potential of Universities', *Environment and Planning C, Government and Policy* 17, 6: 685–699.

Jacobs, D. (1996) *Het Kennisoffensief: Slim concurreren in de Kenniseconomie*, Alphen aan den Rijn/Diegem: Samson Bedrijfsinformatie.

Jones Evans, D., Klofsten, M., Andersson, E. and Pandya, D. (1999) 'Creating a Bridge between University and Industry in Small European Countries: The Role of the Industrial Liaison Office', *R&D Management* 29, 1: 47–56.

Lagendijk, A. (1999) 'Regional Cluster Policy in a Global Economy: From Market Competition to Institutional Anchoring: The Cases of the North-east of England and Aragón', *European Planning Studies* 7, 6: 775–792.

Lagendijk, A. (2000) 'Learning in Non-core Regions: Towards "Intelligent Clusters" addressing Business and Regional Needs', in F. Boekema, K. Morgan, S. Bakkers and R. Rutten (eds) *Knowledge, Innovation and Economic Growth: Learning Regions, Theory, Policy and Practice*, Cheltenham: Edward Elgar, pp. 165–191.

Landabaso, M. (2000) 'Innovation and Regional Development Policy', in F. Boekema, K. Morgan, S. Bakkers and R. Rutten (eds) *Knowledge, Innovation and Economic Growth: Learning Regions, Theory, Policy and Practice*, Cheltenham: Edward Elgar, pp. 73–94.

Malmberg, A., Sölvell, Ö. and Zander, I. (1996) 'Spatial Clustering, Local Accumulation of Knowledge and Firm Competitiveness', *Geografiska Annaler*, B 78: 85–97.

Maskell, P., Eskelinen, H., Hannibalsson, I., Malmberg, A. and Vatne, E. (1998) *Competitiveness, Localised Learning and Regional Development*, London: Routledge.

Morgan, K. (1997) 'The Learning Region: Institutions of Industrial Renewal', *Regional Studies* 5, 31: 491–503.

Nauwelaers, C. (1999) 'Cohesion, Innovation and Regional Competitiveness', in J. Cobbenhagen (ed.) *Cohesion, Competitiveness and RTDI: Their Impact on Regions*, Maastricht: Province of Limburg, pp. 1–5.

North, J., Curran, J. and Blackburn, R. (1997) 'Quality and Small Firms: A Policy Mismatch and its Impact on Small Enterprise', in D. Deakins, P. Jennings and C. Mason (eds) *Small Firms: Entrepreneurship in the 1990s*, London: Paul Chapman, pp. 112–126.

Province of Limburg (1996) *Regional Technology Plan Limburg*, Maastricht: Province of Limburg.

Rosenfeld, S. A. (1995) *Regional Business Clusters and Public Policy*, Washington, DC: The Aspen Institute, Rural Economic Policy Program.

Sexton, D. L., Upton, N. B., Wacholtz, L. E. and McDougall, P. P. (1997) 'Learning Needs of Growth-oriented Entrepreneurs', *Journal of Business Venturing* 12, 1: 1–8.

Shapira, P., Roessner, J. D. and Barke, R. (1995) 'New Public Infrastructures for Small Industrial Modernization in the USA', *Entrepreneurship and Regional Development* 7: 63–84.

Storper, M. (1997) *The Regional World*, New York: Guildford Press.

Temple, P. (1998) 'Clusters and Competitiveness: A Policy Perspective', in G. M. P. Swann, M. Prevezer and D. Stout *The Dynamics of Industrial Clustering*, Oxford: Oxford University Press, pp. 257–297.

Tsipouri, L. R. (1999) 'Lessons from RTDI Enhancements in Less-favoured Regions', *The IPTS Report*, 40: 23–29.

Part IV

Conclusions

13 A new mode of knowledge production[1]

Michael Gibbons

Introduction

Today, universities are widely regarded as centres of research. However, it is only recently that universities have organised themselves to carry out this task. Although from the nineteenth century onwards, individuals carried out research at universities, it was not before the end of the Second World War that research, and in particular basic research, was taken on by universities to become a part of their core values. During the second half of the twentieth century, universities made systematic efforts to expand their domain from preserving and transmitting knowledge to generating new knowledge. The process of generating new knowledge, however, is undergoing important changes that challenge the traditional disciplinary structure of knowledge production. This chapter discusses the new mode of knowledge production and it considers the implications of this new mode for the knowledge production system, of which universities (and the higher education sector in general) are an important part.

Changing research patterns

In order to ensure that research results are sound, specific research practices have been developed to support the research structures in universities. The research practices are a kind of manual that allows one to discriminate between good and bad contributions to research, and good and bad researchers, and that explains how researchers can be accredited with good work. Together, these practices constitute what has come to be known as the disciplinary structure of science and this disciplinary structure, in turn, has become dominant in the management and organisation of universities today. Probably the most important characteristic of the disciplinary structure is the fact that it is specialistic. Specialism is considered a secure way to advance knowledge in every branch of science, whether in natural sciences, social sciences, or humanities. The organisational imperatives of specialism have accompanied the implementation of the disciplinary structure of knowledge production everywhere.

Teaching in universities is also affected by the disciplinary structure, as this is the framework for curriculum. Moreover, the disciplinary structure provides the link between research and teaching, making discipline the key argument as to why research and teaching belong together. Research is a dynamic enterprise. Not only does it add to the stock of specialist knowledge but it transforms it as well. The disciplinary structure is articulated through its research practices which, over time, modify the ideas, techniques, and methods that are regarded as essential to the discipline.

Some differences between Mode 1 and Mode 2

The disciplinary structure is the basic model of knowledge production in most universities. The disciplinary structure determines the important problems and how they should be dealt with and by whom. It also specifies what should be regarded as a good contribution to the field. The disciplinary structure has a social dimension, too. Accreditation of new researchers, selection of new university faculty, and criteria for their advancement in academic life are subject to this dimension. In brief, the disciplinary structure defines what shall count as 'good science'. For the purpose of the discussion, the disciplinary mode of knowledge production is hereafter labelled Mode 1.

Universities have become the primary legitimators of the disciplinary structure as it has been institutionalised in them. However, increasing evidence points to the emergence of a new mode of knowledge production. The purpose of this chapter is to persuade readers that this new mode of knowledge production – creatively labelled as Mode 2 – will change the future shape of universities. This being an academic work, most readers will be familiar with the characteristics of Mode 1. As the same may not be true for Mode 2, the following will discuss the principal differences between Mode 1 and Mode 2.

> The term 1 refers to a form of knowledge production – a complex of ideas, methods, values, norms – that has grown up to control the diffusion of the structure of specialisation to more and more fields of enquiry and ensure their compliance with what is considered sound scientific practice.
>
> (Gibbons *et al.* 1994: 2)

This phrase summarises the cognitive and social norms that apply to production, legitimation, and diffusion of knowledge under Mode 1. Research that adheres to the above rules is considered 'scientific' by most people while other forms of research are not. Partly for this reason, the more general terms knowledge and practitioners (or researchers) are required when describing Mode 2, as opposed to the conventional terms science and scientists that are used to describe Mode 1. This is, however, not to suggest that practitioners of Mode 2 conduct research using unscientific methods, but merely to highlight the differences between Mode 1 and Mode 2. A growing body of evidence indicates the emergence of a new, distinct set of cognitive and social practices that constitute a different mode of knowledge production than the practices that govern Mode 1. These differences, which are appearing across the whole of the research spectrum, have a number of attributes that, when taken together, are sufficiently coherent to allow us to speak of a newly emerging mode of knowledge production. Analytically, these attributes can be used to specify the differences between Mode 1 and Mode 2 as follows:

- In Mode 1, problems are set and solved in a context governed by the largely academic interests of a specific community. By contrast, in Mode 2, knowledge is produced in a context of application.
- Mode 1 is disciplinary while Mode 2 is transdisciplinary.
- Mode 1 is characterised by relative homogeneity of skills; Mode 2 by relative heterogeneity.
- In organisational terms, Mode 1 is hierarchical and, in academic life at least, has tended to preserve its form, while in Mode 2 the preference is for flatter hierarchies using organisational structures which are transient.
- In comparison with Mode 1, Mode 2 is more socially accountable and reflexive.
- Mode 1 and Mode 2 each employ a different type of quality control. Peer review certainly still exists, but in Mode 2 it includes a wider, more temporary and heterogeneous set of practitioners, collaborating on a problem defined in a specific and localised context. As such, in comparison with Mode 1, Mode 2 involves a much expanded system of quality control (cf. Gibbons *et al.* 1994: 3).

Some attributes of knowledge production in Mode 2

Knowledge production in Mode 2 has five distinct attributes that distinguish it from Mode 1. These are

1 knowledge produced in the context of application;
2 transdisciplinarity;
3 heterogeneity and organisational diversity;
4 enhanced social accountability and reflexivity;
5 a more broadly based system of quality control.

Each of these characteristics is discussed below.

Knowledge produced in the context of application

Whereas problem solving in Mode 1 takes place according to the codes and practices relevant to a particular discipline, problem solving in Mode 2 is organised around a particular application. In Mode 1, context is defined in terms of the cognitive and social norms that underlie basic research and academic science. A practical goal is often not considered in the case of Mode 1 knowledge production. By contrast, a broader range of considerations is accounted for in Mode 2. From the start, knowledge production in Mode 2 is focused on the application of knowledge, whether in industry, government, or society in general. Continuous negotiating characterises Mode 2 knowledge production, i.e. knowledge production will take place only when the interests of the various actors are accounted for. Such is the context of application. This should not be mistaken for simple research on assignment or for the taking of ideas to the market place, such as in the case of research carried out for industry. Such a view would not do justice to the far broader processes or markets that operate to determine what knowledge is produced. Although demand and supply factors do affect knowledge production in Mode 2, they are far more diverse than in the case of mere commercialisation of knowledge. The sources of supply are increasingly diverse and the demand for differentiated forms of specialist knowledge continues to increase. These processes and markets are needed to specify the context of application. Put differently, Mode 2 science is both a part of the market and beyond it. Knowledge production thus becomes diffused throughout society to a far greater extent than in the case of Mode 1 science. Hence, we can also speak of socially distributed knowledge.

A number of disciplines in the applied sciences and engineering, such as chemical engineering, aeronautical engineering, and, more recently, computer engineering are characterised by the fact that they carry out their research in a context of application. Strictly speaking, though, these sciences cannot be called applied sciences, as universities established them because relevant knowledge in these fields was lacking. Because these sciences were established within universities, they quickly became examples of the traditional disciplinary-based knowledge production of Mode 1. The fact that they were genuinely new forms of knowledge did not mean that their mode knowledge production, too, was new. Although the above-mentioned disciplines share with Mode 2 some aspects of the attribute of knowledge production in the context of application, the context in Mode 2 is more complex. In Mode 2, the context is characterised by a more diverse set of intellectual and social demands, whereas, at the same time, it may give rise to genuine basic research (Gibbons *et al.* 1994: 4).

Transdisciplinarity

To suggest that Mode 2 merely refers to a collection of specialists from various backgrounds working together in teams is too simple. Like in any other form of knowledge production, inquiry in Mode 2 is guided by 'specifiable consensus as to appropriate cognitive and social practice' (Gibbons *et al.* 1994: 4). What distinguishes Mode 2 from Mode 1 is that the consensus is conditioned by the context of application and that it evolves with it. Finding a solution to a problem demands that different skills have to be integrated in a framework of action. The degree to which this framework fits the requirements set by the specific context of application, however, determines how long consensus on the framework will be sustained. In general, consensus will be temporary. Moreover, the solution that is produced will normally involve contributions from several disciplines. It will, in other words, be transdisciplinary.

In order to make the case for Mode 2, it is important to discuss the distinct features of transdisciplinarity carefully. There are four. First, transdisciplinarity helps to guide problem-solving efforts by developing a distinct and evolving framework for this purpose. This framework is not developed first by one group of scientists and then applied to a certain context by a different group of practitioners, rather it is created and sustained within the context of application. Furthermore, application of existing knowledge, though certainly indispensable, is not sufficient to find solutions. Instead, a process of genuine creativity must be initiated to attain a theoretical consensus that cannot be easily reduced to disciplinary parts.

Second, although transdisciplinary solutions are undeniably a contribution to knowledge, they need not necessarily be a contribution to disciplinary knowledge just because they have both theoretical and empirical elements. Moreover, transdisciplinary knowledge is certainly capable of developing its own distinct theoretical structures, research methods, and modes of practice even though it is created within a context of application (Gibbons *et al.* 1994: 5). However, the prevalent disciplinary map may not be able to accommodate this transdisciplinary knowledge.

Third, Mode 2 knowledge is initially diffused in the process of its production because practitioners learn of the results of this process while they participate in it. This contrasts with the communication of knowledge through institutional channels in Mode 1. And, whereas Mode 1 relies on reporting results at conferences and in professional journals, further diffusion of knowledge in Mode 2 takes place when the original practitioners start working on new problems in a new context. In Mode 2, communication links are thus maintained partly through formal and partly through informal channels.

Fourth, transdisciplinarity establishes a dynamic problem-solving capability. New advances will be made from a particular solution. However, it is just as difficult to predict how knowledge will move beyond its initial context, i.e. where it will be applied and how it will be developed, as it is to predict which possible applications will arise from discipline-based research. Ever closer interaction between knowledge production and successive problem contexts is an essential feature of Mode 2. The transiency of problem contexts and the high mobility of practitioners do not distort or disrupt communication networks, rather they make the knowledge contained in them available for application in other configurations.

Heterogeneity and organisational diversity

As people's skills and experiences are heterogeneous, so is Mode 2 knowledge production. And, as the skills and experiences required to solve a problem evolve over time, the composition of problem-solving teams changes as well. This process is not subjected to planning and coordination by a central body; it follows from the way in which challenging problems emerge. As with Mode 1, this occurs in ways that are difficult, if at all possible, to anticipate. Accordingly, it is marked by the following:

- an increase in the number of potential sites where knowledge can be created; no longer only universities and colleges, but non-university institutes, research centres, government agencies, industrial laboratories, 'think tanks', consultancies, in their interaction;
- the linking of sites together in a variety of ways – electronically, organisationally, socially, informally – through functioning networks of communication;
- the simultaneous differentiation, at these sites, of fields and areas of study into finer and finer specialities. The recombination and reconfiguration of these sub-fields form the bases for new forms of useful knowledge. Over time, knowledge production moves increasingly away from traditional disciplinary activity into new societal contexts.

(Gibbons *et al.* 1994: 6)

Because of the changing and transitory nature of the problems Mode 2 addresses, organisational flexibility and response time are crucial factors. This has given rise to a variety of new forms of organisation. A key feature of these organisational forms is the fact that they are temporary. Temporary work teams and networks have members from various backgrounds and they dissolve when a problem is redefined or solved. Consequently, Mode 2 research groups are less firmly institutionalised when compared with Mode 1 research groups, and their members reassemble in different groups to work on different problems, with different people, often in different loci. Experience gathered this way can thus be transferred to new contexts where it is highly valued quickly. Communication patterns that are formed this way persist even though the research groups are short-lived and the problems they are working on transient. New groups and networks dedicated to different problems will be formed from these communication patterns. Knowledge creation in Mode 2 thus takes place in a great variety of organisations and institutions, such as multinational firms, network firms, small high-tech firms based on a particular technology, government institutions, research universities, laboratories, and institutes as well as national and international research programmes (ibid.: 1994: 7). The patterns of funding for Mode 2 research reflect a similar diversity, with the funding coming from a diverse range of organisations with different requirements and expectations which, in turn, enter into the context of application.

Social accountability and reflexivity

In recent years, knowledge production in Mode 2 has been stimulated by growing public concern on issues such as privacy and procreation, health, environment, communications, etc. Advances in science can affect public awareness and interest in a variety of ways and this has led to a growing number of groups wishing to influence the outcome of the research process. The varied composition of research groups reflects this trend, as social scientists work alongside lawyers, natural scientists, engineers, and businessmen. The nature of the problems requires them to do so and the whole knowledge production process, from problem definition and the setting of research priorities to interpretation and diffusion of results, is subject to social accountability. The setting of the policy agenda and the subsequent decision-making process is increasingly affected by so-called concerned groups, who have an interest in the problems in question, demanding representation. Characteristically, knowledge production in Mode 2 is sensitive to the impact of research and the context of application in which knowledge production takes place ensures that this is accounted for from the start.

Counter-intuitive perhaps, but working in the context of application actually makes scientists and technologists more aware of the broader implications of their work. Operating in Mode 2, thus, increases participants' sensitivity; it makes them more reflexive. This is because the issues which forward the development of Mode 2 research cannot be specified in scientific and technical terms alone. Traditionally seen as outside of the scientific and technological system, values and preferences of different groups and individuals now have to be incorporated in the research towards the resolution of problems, because they are bound to influence the implementation of the solutions. These groups and individuals increasingly become active agents, not only in the evaluation of performance, but also in the definition and solution of problems. The need for greater social accountability partly expresses this development. More importantly, it means that without reflecting, i.e. trying to operate from the standpoint of all the actors involved, individuals themselves cannot function effectively in Mode 2. What is considered worthwhile doing, then, to a substantial part follows from the deepening of understanding of the standpoints and values of the actors involved which, in turn, affects the structure of the research itself. Traditionally, reflection of the values implied in human aspirations and projects has been the concern of the humanities. With the spreading of reflexivity within the research process, the humanities also are experiencing an increase in the demand for the sorts of knowledge they have to offer.

Quality control

Mode 2 has different criteria to assess the quality of the work and the teams that carry out the research than is customary in more traditional, disciplinary science. In Mode 1, the quality of contributions made by individuals is essentially determined through peer review judgements. In order to control the production of knowledge, those judged competent to act as peers are carefully selected on the basis of their previous contributions to their discipline. Quality and control, thus, are mutually reinforcing in the peer review process. This sheds light on the cognitive and the social dimensions of this process. The cognitive dimension of the peer review process rests in the 'professional control over what problems and techniques are deemed important to work on', whereas the social dimension decides 'who is qualified to pursue in [the] solution [of the problems and techniques]' (Gibbons *et al.* 1994: 8). The peer review process of disciplinary science channels individuals to work on problems that are judged to be central to the advance of that science. The intellectual preoccupations of the discipline and its gatekeepers largely define these problems.

Additional criteria follow from the context of application of Mode 2, which incorporates a diverse range of intellectual interests as well as other social, economic, and political ones. Moreover, further questions are posed to the criterion of intellectual interests and its interaction. For example, 'Will the solution, if found, be competitive in the market? Will it be cost effective? Will it be socially acceptable?' (ibid.: 1994: 8). Furthermore, 'good science' is more difficult to determine in Mode 2, since quality is determined by a wider set of criteria. These criteria reflect the broadening social composition of the review system. Some may argue that control in Mode 2 is weaker, and will result in a lower quality of work, since the assessment of quality is no longer strictly limited to the judgements of disciplinary peers. This is, however, not the case. The quality control process in Mode 2 certainly is more broadly based because a wider range of expertise is necessary to solve a problem. However, this results in a more composite and multidimensional kind of quality rather than in a lower quality.

The coherence of Mode 2

Although not present in every instance of Mode 2, the attributes discussed above have a coherence that gives a recognisable cognitive and organisational stability to this mode of knowledge production when they appear together. New norms are emerging in Mode 2 that are appropriate to transdisciplinary knowledge, just as the cognitive and social norms of Mode 1 are appropriate to disciplinary knowledge. Varying relationships of tension and balance between individual and collective creativity are found in all kinds of knowledge production. The driving force of development and quality control in Mode 1 is individual creativity while the consensual figure of the scientific community hides its collective side and control aspects. On the other hand, creativity in Mode 2 is mainly manifested as a group phenomenon. The many interests that are accommodated in a given application process seemingly subsume the individual's contributions as part of the process, and quality control is exercised as a socially extended process. Whereas, in Mode 1, accumulation of knowledge takes place through the professionalisation of specialisation largely institutionalised in universities, in Mode 2, it is through the repeated configuration of human resources in flexible, essentially transient forms of organisation that knowledge accumulation takes place. The loop from the context of application through transdisciplinarity, heterogeneity, and organisational diversity is closed by new adaptive and contextual forms of quality control. This results in a more socially accountable and reflexive mode of science. Examples of these phenomena can be drawn abundantly from the biomedical and environmental sciences.

Although distinct modes of knowledge production, Mode 1 and Mode 2 interact with one another, for example, when specialists trained in the disciplinary sciences participate in Mode 2 knowledge production. Some of them may choose to follow a trail of complex problem solving through a sequence of application contexts, while others may return to their original disciplinary base. Conversely, some outputs of transdisciplinary knowledge production, particularly new instruments, may find their way into the disciplinary sciences. Such interactions may be an attempt to reduce the new form to a more familiar form, in other words, to collapse Mode 2 into Mode 1. However, that would involve ignoring the significance of the changes outlined in Mode 2. Mode 2 knowledge production may interact with Mode 1, but it is different from it. There are terms in common usage which still carry many of the social preconceptions of the function of disciplinary science, such as pre-competitive research, strategic research, mission-oriented research, applied research, or industrial research. These social preconceptions are also responsible for the deeply held belief that 'if the disciplines do not flourish then fundamental insights will be missed or that foundational theoretical knowledge cannot be produced and sustained outside of disciplinary structures' (ibid.: 1994: 10). Other examples of this attitude are the idea that disciplinary science provides the inexhaustible well for future applications and the persistence of the linear model of innovation in policy debates. Increasingly, however, in computer, materials, biomedical, and environmental sciences theories are developed in the context of application and continue to further intellectual advances outside disciplinary frameworks. 'In Mode 2 things are done differently and when enough things are done differently one is entitled to say that a new form has emerged' (ibid.: 1994: 10).

It is not hard to understand why this new mode of knowledge production is emerging at the present time. The success of Mode 1 has been indisputable. The most effective way to achieve this success is through a process of professionalisation in the social realm, specialisation in the cognitive realm, and institutionalisation in the political realm. Diffusion of science from one field to another has progressed through this pattern and it has shown little indulgence to those who have tried to circumvent its controls. The successful operation of this pattern of social and cognitive control is thus reflected in the disciplinary structure of knowledge creation. However, the capacity of the disciplinary structure is not nearly sufficient to absorb the numbers of graduates that have been grounded in the ethos of research. Instead, some of these students have established their own laboratories, 'think tanks', and consult-ancies, while others have found employment in industry and government laboratories. This, obviously, has led to an increase in the number of sites where competent research can be carried out. In turn, these sites constitute the social underpinnings and the intellectual resources for Mode 2. From another perspective, the creation of many new sites of knowledge production can be seen as an unintended by-product of mass education and research.

These sites are able to interact through the development of information and communication technologies, and rapid transportation systems. The emerging computer and telecommunication technologies are critical for the success of Mode 2 knowledge production and those who can afford them possess an important advantage. 'The interactions amongst these sites of knowledge have set the stage for an explosion in the numbers of interconnections and possible configurations of knowledge and skill. The outcome can be described as a socially distributed production system' (ibid.: 10).

Existing institutional boundaries no longer interfere with communication within this system and, as a result, a web of nodes is now strung out across the globe with the connections between the nodes growing daily. It should come as no surprise that traditional scientists participating in this are perceived to weaken institutional control and disciplinary loyalty. However, working in the context of application provides a very stimulating environment to most of these scientists, as it is the site of challenging intellectual problems, and it promises close collaboration with experts from a wide range of backgrounds. Institutionalisation in a conventional pattern will not take place in Mode 2. This causes concern in the established structure of science regarding quality control in a socially distributed knowledge production system. The latter, however, is now a fact of life and it is a response to the needs of society as well as of science. Mode 2 is irreversible. The challenge, then, is to understand and manage it.

The emergence of a socially distributed knowledge production system

The key change to note is that knowledge production is becoming less and less a self-contained activity. As practised currently, it is neither the science of the 'universities' nor the 'technology' of industry. It is no longer the preserve of a special type of institution, from which knowledge is expected to spill over, or spin off, to the benefit of other sectors. Knowledge production, not only in its theories and models but also in its methods and techniques, has spread from academia to many different types of institutions. It is in this sense that knowledge production has become a socially distributed process. At its base lies the expansion of the many sites which form the sources for a continual combination and recombination of knowledge resources. What we are seeing is the multiplication of the nerve endings of knowledge. The socially distributed knowledge production system has five principal characteristics:

1   There are an increasing number of places where recognisably competent research is being carried out. This can be easily demonstrated by consulting the addresses of the authors of scientific publications, though change is

taking place so rapidly that the full extent of the social distribution of knowledge production is probably no longer fully captured by the printed word.

2   These sites interact with one another and, thereby, broaden the base of effective interaction. Thus, contributions to the stock of knowledge are derived from an increasing number of tributarial flows from various types of institutions that both contribute to, and draw from, the stock of knowledge.

3   The dynamics of socially distributed knowledge production lie in the flows of knowledge and in the shifting patterns of *connectivity* among these flows. The connections may appear to be random but they move with the problem context rather than according to either disciplinary structures or the dictates of national science policy.

4   The number of interconnections is accelerating, so far apparently unchannelled by existing institutional structures, perhaps for the reason that these connections are intended to be functional and to survive only as long as they are useful. The ebb and flow of connections follow the paths of problem interest, and the paths of problem interest are no longer determined by the disciplinary structure of science.

5   The new mode of knowledge production exhibits heterogeneous, rather than homogeneous, growth. New sites of knowledge production are continually emerging which, in their turn, provide intellectual points of departure for further combinations or configurations of researchers. In this sense, the socially distributed knowledge production system exhibits some of the properties that are often associated with self-organising systems in which the communication density increases rapidly.

In summary, the distributed character of knowledge production constitutes a fundamental change, both in terms of the *numbers* of possible sites of expertise and in their degree of *interactivity*. To it are linked other dimensions of change which cannot be explored within the constraints of the present chapter, but which include the increasing contextualisation of knowledge, including its marketability, the blurring of boundaries between disciplines and institutions and across institutional boundaries, the fungibility of scientific careers, the transdisciplinarity of research, and the increasing importance of hybrid fora – groups constituted through the interplay of experts and non-experts as social actors – in the shaping of knowledge. Of course, all of this has implications for the management of the knowledge production process and for the maintenance of quality control within it.

Conclusion

In the new mode of knowledge production, research in many important areas is cutting loose from the disciplinary structure and generating knowledge which, so far at least, does not seem to be drawn to institutionalise itself in university departments and faculties in the conventional way. At times, it often seems that research centres, institutes, and 'think tanks' are multiplying on the periphery of universities, while faculties and departments are becoming the internal locus of teaching provision. What, then, are the implications of Mode 2 for research in universities?

Leading-edge research

Universities are now confronted with the challenge of how to accommodate the emergence of socially distributed knowledge production. The establishment of the research agenda and its funding are increasingly the outcome of a dialogue between researchers and users, regulators, interest groups, etc., and unless that dialogue produces a consensus, no research will be done. Leading-edge research has become a more participative exercise, involving many actors and experts who move less according to the dynamics of their original disciplines and more according to their interest in problems. Important intellectual problems are emerging in a 'context of application' and scientists want to work on them. Pursuing problem interest means that academics are away from the university, working in teams, with experts from a wide range of intellectual backgrounds, in a variety of organisational settings. They contribute solutions that cannot be easily reduced to a recognisable 'disciplinary contribution'. Those individuals who want to carry out research in this mode must adopt a different set of research practices and, quite likely, take a different perspective on their careers. But, if they do so, they will be out of 'synch' with the existing reward structure of universities. It has been argued that the rubric of survival in academic research is changing from 'publish or perish' to 'partnerships or perish' (Gourley, private communication, 1996). The challenge, then, is to modify existing university structures to take account of this fact.

Research and teaching

Universities that wish to participate at the forefront of research will be active in Mode 2. At the very least, they have to become more open, porous institutions *vis-à-vis* the wider community, with fewer gates and more revolving doors. They will have to become much more entrepreneurial in the ways that they utilise their intellectual capital, and this may mean experimenting with a much broader range of contractual employment arrangements. But, to the extent that universities go down this road, they will be helping to establish two parallel structures within universities; one which will carry teaching (Mode 1) and another for research (Mode 2).

In the new, open, more flexible structures for research, knowledge is codified and transmitted in a different way. Information about the state of the art on a particular question is to be found less in conventional paper publications – whether in paper or electronic form – than in the collective memory of the problem-solving teams. But, as we have seen, these teams are transient groupings. They form and dissolve according to the imperative of their problem solving interest and the memory of what has been accomplished moves with the relevant experts. It is doubtful that traditional modes of publication will be sufficient to grasp the knowledge and information that is produced in this way. The question as to how knowledge produced in this way can be translated in curricula and how it can be transmitted if it is not codified in books and/or papers remains unanswered.

How, then, will these structures which support teaching be related to one another? And, if they are to be related, what would the organisation of such universities look like? If research grows and develops in the manner suggested in this chapter – outside disciplinary structures and more in the context of application – how will the results of research be absorbed by the wider academic community and, through them, make their way into the development of new curricula?

Institutional management: cores and peripheries

Universities in which technology interchange has become a core value, which have 'multiplied up' the number of partnerships and alliances that they are involved in, and which share staff and other resources with problem-solving teams distributed around the world need to be organised differently. The existence of Mode 2 must induce changes in current organisational structures and this is perhaps nowhere so evident than in the view that universities will have to take on their intellectual capital.

Heretofore, universities were seen as 'factories' in which intellectual capital was employed. Faculty members were specialists, working according to the research practices which were identified with Mode 1. The unit of organisation was the department and graduate students were the apprentices. Following the dictates of Mode 1, universities elaborated the departmental structure and have recruited the best staff they could afford. Universities often saw themselves as 'owning' this intellectual resource and used it to establish their reputations *vis-à-vis* one another. Permanent faculty working on specialist topics according to the criteria of 'good science' set down by Mode 1 was the arrangement that dominated the university scene, despite the fragmentation that it encouraged and the financial resources it required.

As argued, different rules operate in Mode 2. In the context of application, the research agenda is formed and funds attracted in a different way. Researchers work in teams on problems that are set in a very complex social process and are relatively transient. They move about according to the dictates of problem interest. Participation in these problem contexts is necessary to keep up with developments. As a consequence, some of the best academics are learning their institutions to join problem configurations of various kinds. To some, this is seen as a weakening of loyalty both to their institution and to their discipline. If they intend to operate at the leading edge of research, universities need to change their view of intellectual capital. They need to ensure that they are able to participate in the appropriate problem-solving contexts. Equally, so diverse and volatile are these that no university can afford to keep 'in-house' all the human resources they would need to guarantee a presence everywhere. Universities need to learn to exploit all the advantages of sharing resources. Here lies the fundamental challenge of the socially distributed knowledge production system.

A model exploiting the economies of shared resources would seem to demand a relatively small core of permanent full-time faculty members together with a much larger periphery of other 'experts' who are associated with the university in various ways. To achieve this, universities need to experiment with a much wider range of employment contracts and accept the fact that they cannot own outright all the human resources they need. To an extent, this puts the universities in a Catch 22 situation. On the one hand, the demands on universities in terms of both teaching and research is not only growing but it is also diversifying and will continue to do so. On the other hand, the costs of holding in-house all the resources it needs to accommodate this expansion is not only too expensive but not flexible enough to meet changing demand. Vice Chancellors in the future will be distinguished by their ability to utilise their intellectual capital together with intellectual capital held by others in a way that maximises their institutions' goals. The implication of this is that not every member of staff needs to be a full-time employee. What needs to be sorted out, then, is how these 'others' will fare in the university setting, how their contributions will be recognised, how they will relate to graduate students, and what teaching they will have to do. It seems clear that the nature of these questions is such that they cannot be answered without changing the nature of universities substantially.

The aim of this chapter was to demonstrate that there are now two co-existing modes of knowledge production: Mode 1 and Mode 2. For the future, the key question facing each university has less to do with deciding whether to be a research or a teaching institution than deciding which mode of research and teaching to adopt. However, to the extent that universities choose to move in the direction of Mode 2, they set themselves the difficult internal problem of keeping research and teaching in some sort of relationship; if, that is, it is still thought worthwhile arguing that a close association of teaching and research ought to be a hallmark of a university.

Technology transfer

Research partnerships are increasing and they are important for universities as institutions as well as for academics, professionally. This is well illustrated by current developments in the field of technology transfer. Of late, many universities have become interested in technology transfer and in commercialising the results of their research. Many have invested significant sums in setting up science parks, technology transfer centres, and venture capital funds to assist academics in commercialising their work. This model, however, is not so much wrong as out of tune with the research practices of Mode 2. The model of technology transfer which is operative at the moment is based on the image of the innovative process as a 'relay race'. In this view, some of the discoveries made by scientists within university departments are deemed to be capable of commercialisation, but there is a gap between the university and the market place. In other words, the ideas are there but for some reason the baton is not being successfully passed between universities and industry in the race to commercialisation. The solution to this dilemma has been to create a range of technology transfer organisations to bridge this gap; to reduce the probability that the baton will be dropped and the race lost.

These organisations are meant to mediate between the world of academe and the world of business. However, in Mode 2, research is carried out in the context of application, in which there is an ongoing dialogue between interested parties – including producers and users of knowledge – from the beginning. In Mode 2, universities that want to play a role in the commercialisation of research need to be involved in the discussion from the beginning. It is certainly not a game that can be played by limiting one's role to the discovery end of the process. The relay race model reflects a Mode 1 view of the knowledge production process, with discovery up front and in the hands of universities. Rather than a relay race, the appropriate model for Mode 2 would be a soccer or a basketball game. In these games, the ball (the baton) moves continually between the players and nobody can afford to neglect either their own game plan or that of their competitors. In particular, no one leaves the field until the game is over. In this model, universities who are interested in generating an income stream from their research activities need to have technology transfer among their core values. They need to form appropriate partnerships with business and government and, in all probability, to invest their own resources in the process. In brief, they need to become actively involved in a process which is less technology transfer and more technology interchange.

Note

1 The argument in this chapter is drawn from Gibbons *et al.* (1994).

Reference

Gibbons, M., Limoges, C., Nowotny, H., Schwartzmen, S., Trow, M. and Scott, P. (1994) *The New Production of Knowledge: The Dynamics of Science and Research in Contemporary Societies*, London: Sage.

14 HEIs, regions and the knowledge-based economy

Roel Rutten, Frans Boekema and Elsa Kuijpers

Introduction

In this book, we have discussed the relationship between HEIs, regional development, and the knowledge-based economy from a variety of perspectives. The micro, meso, and macro perspectives are all present, as are the theoretical, empirical, and policy perspectives. These are necessary in order to understand the complexities of the subject. It is more than just a sector of the economy (or society) that is at issue. This book is about the role that HEIs can and should play in the development of the (regional) economy in twenty-first-century capitalism, i.e. the knowledge-based economy. Ultimately, it is also about the future of HEIs themselves. In the Middle Ages and during the Renaissance, there were few universities but all of them were key centres of learning, philosophy, and debate in society. Today, countless HEIs dot the globe but, with the exception of their educational role, many of them have managed to manoeuvre themselves to the margins of society. Nevertheless, HEIs consume a sizeable share of the gross national product in most (Western) nations. One day, society is going to ask whether or not this is necessary and what it receives in return. HEIs have to find a new role and move back to the centre of the economy and society. This book demonstrated the need for HEIs to change and showed some directions in which they can move. In this final chapter, on the basis of the various contributions in the book, we present a vision for a new role for HEIs and we offer a starting point for further debate.

HEIs and regional development

At the centre of the HEI debate is the assumption that HEIs can and should contribute to economic (and social) development. This assumption has few critics. A more controversial argument, perhaps, centres on the contribution that HEIs can make to regional development. Both issues are dealt with below.

HEIs and the (new) production of knowledge

As Chatterton and Goddard (Chapter 2) argued, HEIs traditionally have two roles: teaching and research. Contributing to (regional) economic development has gradually been accepted as the third role of HEIs. There are two models that explain HEIs' contribution to (regional) economic development. Recently, B. Morgan (2002) referred to them as the 'elite model' and the 'diffusion oriented model'. The elite model can be characterised as the traditional 'trickle-down model' of the industrial economy (cf. Best 1990 and Van Dijck and Havekes 1994: 403–404). This model assumes that HEIs perform research and development that is subsequently transferred to the business community through spin-off firms and traditional interface mechanisms such as knowledge transfer organisations. K. Morgan (1997) already observed that the trickle-down practice fails to promote innovation in regional economies. B. Morgan (2002) explains why this is so. He argues that the elite model fails on two grounds. First,

> it underestimates the importance of higher education in social reproduction, and the creation of high-level skills within the workforce. Such development is necessary in order to capture the incremental improvements in technology, products and processes that tend to occur 'downstream' of research.
>
> (Morgan, B. 2002: 67)

Similarly, K. Morgan (1997) argued that the elite model ignores the value of 'pedestrian forms of knowledge'. Second, the elite model

> tended to be translated into a system where the production of knowledge is more highly valued than its application. . . . [The elite model] is one geared towards the most prestigious forms of knowledge application – commercializing high profile, high-tech, blue skies research in a handful of elite centres of excellence. This means that the role of universities in contributing towards wealth creation is defined in a highly limited fashion.
>
> (Morgan, K. 2002: 67)

In practice, the elite model created what is referred to as 'Cathedrals in the Desert' (see Cobbenhagen 1998 and Morgan, B. 2002). That is, centres of excellence which are poorly, if at all, embedded in the (regional) economy. Lagendijk and Rutten (Chapter 12) referred to this as the failure of (regional) policy to create associative learning capacities. The main objection against the elite model, it becomes clear, is that it belongs to the (post-) industrial economy, whereas today's economy is characterised more accurately as a knowledge-based economy (see Chapter 1). In the knowledge-based economy, competitive advantage is not merely derived from high-tech knowledge but from a combination of many kinds of knowledge, e.g. high-tech knowledge, artisan knowledge, technological knowledge, managerial and organisational knowledge, knowledge of markets, etc. (Jacobs 1996; Maskell *et al.* 1998; Rutten 2002). Consequently, HEIs have to reposition themselves as players within a multi-pole network of knowledge producers and users instead of trying to preserve their hierarchical position at the top of the 'knowledge pyramid', which is, after all, no longer in line with the realities of the knowledge-based economy. To understand the new position of HEIs, B. Morgan's (2002) diffusion-oriented model is very helpful. This model has several inter-related themes that also reflect the key arguments of this book.

- The re-appreciation of skills formation and social reproduction in today's high wage, high value added, and highly skilled economy.
- Tying down the global, i.e. 'the ability of a region to ensure that any inward investment act as a catalyst for local growth by "embedding" the inward investor into the local production system' (Morgan, B. 2002: 66).
- Social capital development, the central premise of which is that 'social networks have value because of the trust, reciprocity, information, and cooperation that follow from them'. HEIs can play a key role in the building of social capital when they 'act as catalysts for civic engagement and collective action and networking' (ibid.: 66).
- The vital role that HEIs have to play to encourage social inclusion, that is, 'in widening access to cohorts from lower socio-economic backgrounds' (ibid.: 67).

The role of HEIs in the knowledge-based economy, thus, is one of an institution that is firmly embedded in its socio-economic context. It has to be in order to play its role as a co-producer of knowledge. Clearly, the relevant paradigm to understand the knowledge production and the role of HEIs in this process is Gibbons' (Chapter 13) new mode (Mode 2) of knowledge production. Moreover, in this book, evidence is presented of how effective knowledge production and transfer takes place in Mode 2. Patchell and Eastham (Chapter 3), for example, show that the governance of university–industry relations is crucial to their success. In their case study of the Hong Kong University of Science and Technology, Patchell and Eastham found that the primary method of governance is contractual. Contracts give individual faculty members the opportunity to engage in the co-production of knowledge with industry. In this way, university–industry collaboration goes beyond formal institutional collaboration, which is an important step in the direction of Mode 2. Similarly, Vermeulen (Chapter 4) argues that universities can benefit from the inputs of SMEs – and vice versa – to a much larger extent than is presently the case, if SME–university interaction is structured along the lines of Mode 2. That is, if universities choose to collaborate more intimately, or even merge, with professional colleges. In this way, universities, professional colleges, and SMEs can form the heterogeneous, transdisciplinary teams that Gibbons (Chapter 13) advocates. In another case study, Vaessen and Van der Velde (Chapter 5) show that, to a substantial degree, knowledge exchange between HEIs and society takes place through informal relations. Moreover, these informal relations are often far more durable than are formal relations. Vaessen and Van der Velde argue that HEIs, through their informal relations with society, make a significant contribution to social and cultural life in their home regions. This, too, fits the Mode 2 perspective which, after all, regards HEI employees as individuals who are embedded in a broader (social and professional) context. Maskell and Törnqvist (Chapter 7), too, stress the importance of informal relations when they explain the contributions that HEIs make to the economic development of the Øresund region, which is one of the most prosperous regions in the world. Finally, Nieuwenhuis, Verhaar, and Hoeve (Chapter 9) show that HEIs need to become network players if they do not want to be banished to the margins of the (regional) economy. Their case study of the Dutch agricultural sector presents a strong argument in support of their claim.

In short, the theoretical arguments and the case studies presented in this book lead us to conclude that in order to understand the contribution of HEIs to regional economic development, one must understand how the processes of knowledge creation and knowledge transfer actually happen. In this respect, Gibbons' Mode 2 of knowledge production is far more promising than the traditional Mode 1. First, because it is much more in line with the realities of today's knowledge-based economy and, second, because it is compatible with theories of organisational knowledge creation as developed, for example, by Nonaka and Takeuchi (1995) and Von Krogh *et al.* (2000). They argue that knowledge creation is a process of constant interaction between individuals in small teams. This fits nicely with Gibbons' heterogeneous, transdisciplinary teams. Of course, more research is necessary to support and elaborate these claims – we will come to that shortly. However, we insist that Mode 2 is the only way in which HEIs can make a substantial contribution to (regional) economic development. It is also the only way in which HEIs can return to the centre of the economy and avoid becoming marginalised players in the knowledge-based economy.

HEIs and the regional context

It is often said that HEIs must work on a global scale since they have to compete with other HEIs around the world to attract top researchers and to perform top research. Consequently, the argument goes, HEIs have no business in the region. Working from the perspective of Mode 2, this is simply not true. The contrast between global and top science, on the one hand, and local and lesser science, on the other, is imaginary. Regional economists, notably Storper (1997), have argued that global and local are two sides of the same coin. 'Think global, act local' is an argument that Porter (1998) also subscribes to. From the perspective of Mode 2, HEIs cannot be healthy institutions without being embedded in a regional context. After all, the key to Mode 2 knowledge production is the heterogeneous, transdisciplinary team. Team members come from a variety of backgrounds, e.g. HEIs, professional colleges, the business community, etc. To a large extent, the knowledge that is created in these teams is tacit knowledge (see Gibbons *et al.* 1994). The knowledge is specific to the particular 'context of application' in which it is created and it becomes 'embedded' in the knowledge, skills, and expertise of the team members. The team members can apply this knowledge in other contexts and, thus, disseminate their knowledge (see Vermeulen, Chapter 4 and Vaessen and Van der Velde, Chapter 5). This is also the way knowledge creation takes place in 'ordinary' teams (see Nonaka and Takeuchi 1995; Von Krogh *et al.* 2000). As argued above, Mode 2 knowledge production is much more in line with the realities of the knowledge-based economy than is Mode 1 knowledge production.

Storper (1997) and Rutten (2002) have argued that the creation of tacit knowledge is subject to the 'geography of knowledge'. Because the creation of tacit knowledge depends on face-to-face communication (between team members), it is difficult, though not impossible, to sustain over long distances. As the heterogeneous, transdisciplinary teams work on the solution of specific problems, the team members have to meet regularly over a prolonged period of time. It would be very inefficient to do this with distant partners and it would be virtually impossible to involve distant companies, particularly SMEs, in such teams. This is precisely why an exclusive focus on Mode 1 production of knowledge turns an HEI into a 'Cathedral in the Desert'. Such HEIs are only looking for 'top science' and they will rarely find this in their backyards. They may become good producers of top knowledge but, because of their ivory tower position, this knowledge is not likely to find its way into the economy (cf. the above criticism of the trickle-down model). Consequently, Mode 1 HEIs are in serious danger of becoming marginalised. The road back to the centre of the economy for HEIs, thus, goes through Mode 2 and, therefore, through the region. A substantial input of artisan knowledge can only come from the regional business community – if only because the region is the relevant scope for many companies (see Cobbenhagen 1998). Moreover, it is difficult to see how HEIs can contribute to social and cultural life beyond their home regions, as this is achieved through HEI employees and they tend to live in the region (cf. Vaessen and Van der Velde, Chapter 5).

These arguments, it should be noted, are perfectly compatible with the learning region paradigm. The learning region, in our view (see Chapter 1), is an institutional or associative (see Lagendijk and Rutten, Chapter 12) perspective of collaboration on learning between regional partners. In line with the think-global-act-local argument, learning regions are a mechanism to link regions to the global economy (see Florida 1995). Obviously, HEIs have an important role to play in this respect. Through the heterogeneous, transdisciplinary teams, they can link the regional business community to the global knowledge arsenal. Moreover, HEIs are home to a substantial portion of the world's cultural elite and the home regions of HEIs around the world have a lot to gain from them. It is this ensemble of economic, social, and cultural knowledge that makes HEIs exciting places. As argued above, the full potential of this knowledge can only be reaped when HEIs are firmly embedded in their home regions. It is clear that, where HEIs often associate the region with provincialism, quite the opposite is true. HEIs are usually located in urban, or even metropolitan, areas which are the focal points of economic, cultural, and social life in (Western) societies. From a Mode 2 perspective, this makes them exciting places. The context of application (Gibbons, Chapter 13), so to say, is at the HEI's front door. The proper environment for an HEI, thus, is a cosmopolitan region and HEIs can make an important contribution to shaping this environment.

Research agenda

The above picture, of course, is an ideal situation and the outlined perspective will probably not convince most critics. That can only be achieved through good research and, in this respect, much needs to be done. First and foremost, however, we need to acknowledge that further research along the lines of the perspective sketched in this book can only be transdisciplinary. Conceptualising the economic geography of higher education requires inputs from regional economy, organisation sociology, organisation economy, and theories on learning organisations and learning regions, which themselves are the fruits of transdisciplinary research. This book draws on a variety of theories, perspectives, and levels of analysis, all of which are relevant. The challenging task that lies ahead is to incorporate these perspectives in a coherent conceptual framework.

High on the priority list is the need for more quantitative research. In this book, only Meeus, Oerlemans, and Hage (Chapter 8) present a substantial quantitative analysis. The case studies presented in the other chapters have produced sufficient leads that merit further quantitative analysis. These leads, of course, are the key issues, whether for quantitative or qualitative analysis, as they point out the directions in which research efforts must focus. In this way, the above-mentioned coherent conceptual framework can be achieved. In random order, these leads are as follows

• How does the process of knowledge creation in heterogeneous, transdisciplinary teams, that is, the practice of Mode 2, work? Can such teams be identified and what are their characteristics in terms of composition, organisation structure, and governance structure? How does knowledge creation in such teams actually happen? In general, the theories of Nonaka and Takeuchi (1995) and Von Krogh *et al.* (2000) offer valuable points of departure, but the role of HEIs must be included more specifically. In addition, more needs to be said about the global–local interplay. Are there examples of cases in which HEIs have made global knowledge available to the region and vice versa? What do these cases teach us about the position of HEIs at the intersection of the global and the local?

- How can the contribution of Mode 2 knowledge production to the economy (and to society) be 'measured'? Measuring – whether quantitative or qualitative – the dissemination of Mode 1 knowledge proved difficult enough (see Cobbenhagen 1998). In the case of Mode 2, where knowledge is not created in 'splendid isolation' but as a process of interaction, this poses whole new challenges. It brings the discussion back to the issue of measuring tacit knowledge. By its very nature, tacit knowledge cannot be counted, so how can it be 'measured' (Boekema *et al.* 2000; Rutten 2002)?
- How do HEIs contribute to social and cultural development in their home regions? This is an exciting line of work that can shed light on the social embeddedness of HEIs which, so far, has been poorly understood.
- A further conceptualisation of the role of HEIs in regional learning (the practice) and learning regions (the institutional materialisation) is necessary. What is the position of HEIs *vis-à-vis* other regional actors in the process of learning? Can HEIs play a central role, as we have argued, or is the psychological distance between HEIs (academe) and the other actors (pedestrian forms of knowledge) too wide to bridge? Concepts such as 'social capital' (Morgan, K. 1997) and 'untraded interdependencies' (Storper 1997) should play a central role here. They can help conceptualise the informal relationship between HEIs and 'the region'. This is particularly relevant as this book has demonstrated that informal contacts of HEIs are far more important in relation to the dissemination of knowledge than is currently acknowledged.
- Elaborating on the above learning perspective, we need to ask ourselves whether or not learning always leads to favourable outcomes. In the present hype of learning organisations and learning regions, we may easily overlook that learning, i.e. mutual and interactive knowledge exchange between organisations, may not always be advantageous to organisations. Hence, we need to know when to encourage learning and when not.
- Finally, and perhaps most importantly, what does a Mode 2 HEI look like? What kind of organisation structure should it adopt and what kind of reward structures and incentives should it have? How far removed is the Mode 2 HEI from the current practices in HEIs around the world?

Directions for HEIs

In essence, this book is about the place of HEIs in the knowledge-based economy. Earlier in this chapter, we argued that, with the exception of their educational role, HEIs are at the margins of the knowledge-based economy. HEIs, and universities in particular, are mainly concerned with academic research. 'Publish or perish' is the name of the game and publishing has degenerated to an objective in itself. Whether the economy or society have anything to gain from these publications is irrelevant. Moreover, even asking this question can turn someone into an academic outcast as the university establishment values its autonomy and independence above everything else. If HEIs were autonomous and independent institutions, this attitude would not be a problem. However, the fact is that HEIs are largely dependent on public funding and, for the majority of HEIs, the 'market', e.g. contract research, will never generate sufficient funding to be able to do without public funding. Consequently, HEIs need society – they cannot survive without it.

Given the trend towards deregulation and privatisation, it will only be a matter of time before governments, i.e. society, will start wondering what they get in return for their money. Of course, HEIs could turn their organisations into education factories and maintain a small elite team of researchers on the basis of 'market revenues'. In that case, science would truly retreat in its ivory tower. The problem is, in the knowledge-based economy, society cannot afford this scenario. It needs HEIs' knowledge to survive in the global competition and to meet the needs of its individualised and post-modernised citizens. Mind you, society needs the knowledge, but it does not necessarily need HEIs! When, after the Second World War, the economy became industrial, and later post-industrial, society, through (massive) government funding, created the HEIs and their accompanying institutional framework that we know today. In the present knowledge-based economy, that framework is rapidly becoming obsolete since it does not give society what it needs, Mode 2 knowledge. Relevant knowledge, that is, knowledge that can help the economy and society advance in the knowledge-based economy is Mode 2 knowledge. If HEIs continue to fail to deliver this knowledge, there is no reason to believe that society, i.e. national and regional governments, the business community, interest groups, etc., will not gain this knowledge through alternative channels. In the middle of the twentieth century, society shaped the HEI and its institutional framework. It can reshape it in the early twenty-first century. Society can create new institutions, outside of HEIs, that produce Mode 2 knowledge. All it needs to do is to attract HEI staff – which should not be too much of a problem when HEIs continue down the road of Mode 1 and burden the majority of their staff with teaching and leave knowledge creation to a privileged elite of 'international top researchers'. In this scenario, the HEI, as we know it, may very well disappear.

The choice is up to the HEIs. Will they start working according to Mode 2 and embark on a, no doubt, difficult journey back to the centre of society, or will they persist in an exclusive Mode 1 attitude and run the risk of becoming marginalised beyond the boundaries of social and economic relevance? Of course, Mode 1 will never completely disappear and changes towards Mode 2 are occurring in HEIs around the globe. However, at the present pace, society and the economy may be changing much faster than HEIs.

References

Best, M. (1990) *The New Competition: Institutions of Industrial Restructuring*, Cambridge: Polity Press.

Boekema, F., Morgan, K., Bakkers, S. and Rutten, R. (2000) *Knowledge, Innovation and Economic Growth: The Theory and Practice of Learning Regions*, Cheltenham: Edward Elgar.

Cobbenhagen, J. (1998) *Cohesion, Competitiveness and RTDI: Their Impact on Regions*, Maastricht: Province Limburg.

Dijck, J. van and Havekes, M. (1994) 'Human Capital Development: Changing Institutional Arrangements', in J. van Dijck and J. Groenewegen (eds) *Changing Business Systems in Europe: An Institutional Approach*, Brussels: VUBpress, pp. 403–420.

Florida, R. (1995) 'Toward the Learning Region', *Futures* 27, 5: 527–536.

Gibbons, M., Limoges, C., Nowotny, H., Schwartzmann, S., Scott, P. and Trow, M. (1994) *The New Production of Knowledge: The Dynamics of Science and Research in Contemporary Societies*, London: Sage.

Jacobs, D. (1996) *Het Kennisoffensief: Slim Concurreren in de Kenniseconomie*, Alphen aan den Rijn: Samson Bedrijfsinformatie.

Krogh, G. von, Ichijo, K. and Nonaka, I. (2000) *Enabling Knowledge Creation: How to Unlock the Mystery of Tacit Knowledge and Release the Power of Innovation*, Oxford: Oxford University Press.

Maskell, P., Eskelinen, H., Hannibalsson, I., Malmberg, A. and Vatne, E. (1998) *Competitiveness, Localised Learning and Regional Development: Specialisation and Prosperity in Small Open Economies*, London: Routledge.

Morgan, B. (2002) 'Higher Education and Regional Economic Development in Wales: An Opportunity for Demonstrating the Efficacy of Devolution in Economic Development', *Regional Studies* 36, 1: 65–73.

Morgan, K. (1997) 'The Learning Region: Institutions, Innovation and Regional Renewal', *Regional Studies* 31, 5: 491–503.

Nonaka, I. and Takeuchi, H. (1995) *The Knowledge-creating Company: How Japanese Companies Create the Dynamics of Innovation*, Oxford: Oxford University Press.

Porter, M. (1998) 'Clusters and the New Economics of Competition', *Harvard Business Review* 76, 6: 77–91.

Rutten, R. (2002) *The Entrepreneurial Coalition: Knowledge-based Collaboration in a Regional Manufacturing Network*, Nijmegen: Wolf Legal Productions.

Storper, M. (1997) *The Regional World: Territorial Development in a Global Economy*, New York: The Guildford Press.

Index

Note: page numbers in **bold** type refer to figures. Page numbers followed by 'n' refer to notes.